I0810531

IMAGES
of America

RIVERBANK

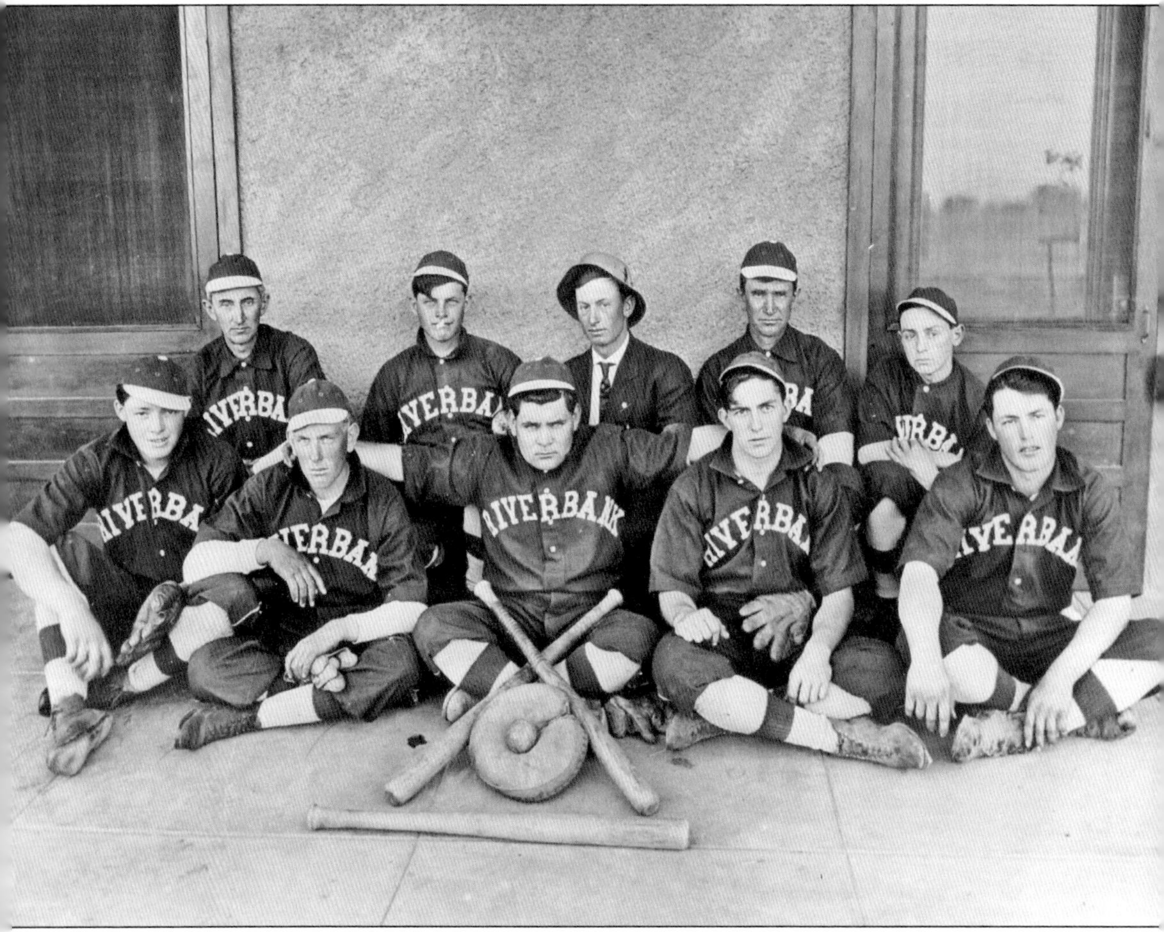

Pictured here is an early Riverbank baseball team. The picture was taken on May 30, 1913, and shows the Riverbank Merchants. Players shown in the picture are, from left to right, (first row) E. Crawford, Ray Crosby, ? Muntz, ? Brown, and A. Crawford; (second row) J.P. Myer, Guy Farrero, Leighton Wells, F.H. Myer, and C. Keeley. (Courtesy of the Riverbank Historical Society.)

On the Cover: The Reichmann brothers, shown here at their tin shop, are famous for starting the Legion Theater in Riverbank. It was first used as a vaudeville theater and community center. Later, in the 1940s, the building became the site of the Riverbank Clubhouse, where country western singers would gather to entertain dancers from miles around. (Courtesy of the Riverbank Historical Society.)

IMAGES
of America

RIVERBANK

Glenn Allen Ditman and
the Riverbank Historical Society

ARCADIA
PUBLISHING

ISBN 978-1-4671-3015-8

Published by Arcadia Publishing
Charleston, South Carolina

Printed in the United States of America

Library of Congress Control Number: 2013934948

For all general information, please contact Arcadia Publishing:
Telephone 843-853-2070
Fax 843-853-0044
E-mail sales@arcadiapublishing.com
For customer service and orders:
Toll-Free 1-888-313-2665

Visit us on the Internet at www.arcadiapublishing.com

This book is dedicated to Dick Landon, Bruce Blakely, and all citizens of Riverbank—past, present, and future—who have worked, are working, and will work to preserve the heritage and culture of the city of Riverbank and continue to make it a wonderful place to live.

Contents

ACKNOWLEDGMENTS

The author would like to acknowledge the help of the Riverbank Historical Society, the Oakdale Heritage Society, and the McHenry Museum in Modesto for making this book possible. Unless otherwise noted, all images are courtesy of the Riverbank Historical Society.

INTRODUCTION

Nestled in between two mountain ranges—in the middle of the San Joaquin Valley and right upon the Stanislaus River—you can find the town of Riverbank, California. The name provides a clue to its location, as it is situated right on the bank of the Stanislaus River. Much of Riverbank's history has to do with the river and the railroad.

Because of the valley and the rich agriculture of the area, the farmers needed a way to get their crops to communities across the river and to bigger markets in Stockton. In the late 1850s or early 1860s, a man named James Burney was enterprising enough to realize that people would want to get to the other side of the river, so he built a ferry, as did others. But Burney's ferry is the one that was the most traveled and, therefore, thrived. A settlement named Burneyville grew because of the ferry.

In 1895, Claus Spreckles and others incorporated the San Francisco & San Joaquin Valley (SF&SJV) Railroad. They continued building in Stockton. In 1895, they finished their trestle across the Stanislaus River at Burneyville. In February 1895, the railroad sent its first train across the trestle. By this time, most of the people once residing in Burneyville had moved from the river into the new area of activity brought on by the railroad. In the spring of 1897, an application for the establishment of a post office was made. The post office department insisted the name of the station be changed, and the name Riverbank was chosen.

The SF&SJV Railroad spent thousands of dollars helping with the establishment of Riverbank. Riverbank adopted the slogan, "The Town with the Big Pay Roll." Riverbank has traded that motto for "The City of Action." There are many stories about how Riverbank came to claim that saying. It could be because of the railroad activity, the farms and the farming activities, or Riverbank's bustling canneries. In 1923, Lorenzo Zerrillo and other businessmen organized the Riverbank Canning Company, which specialized in tomato paste and other tomato products. At one time, it was the largest tomato canning company in the world. Or did Riverbank acquire the "Action" title because of the Riverbank Clubhouse? The clubhouse was well known around the area for its country western music and dancing. Many famous country western personalities showed up and performed there.

In its first 100-plus years, Riverbank has seen many changes. It has a rich and diversified past full of interesting people that brought their culture and heritage to this area. The actual personality remains friendly, enterprising, and happy. We invite you to visit the Riverbank Historical Museum, where many artifacts, photographs, and memorabilia that preserve the town's memories are on display.

One

Early Settlement

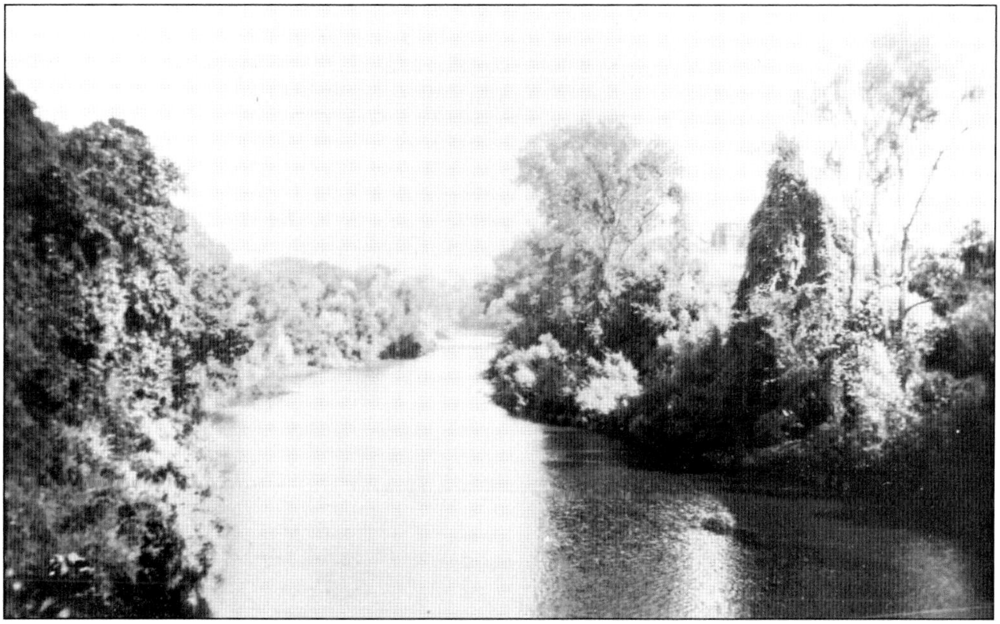

This is the Stanislaus River as it appeared in 1912. The undeveloped and unobstructed view of the river is much like what the Yokut Indians must have seen when they hunted and fished along its shores. The Spanish called the river "Laquismes" for the tule reeds that grew in abundance along it. Later, it was named for an Indian chief, Estanislao, who lead a band of Indians in rebellion against the Spanish missions.

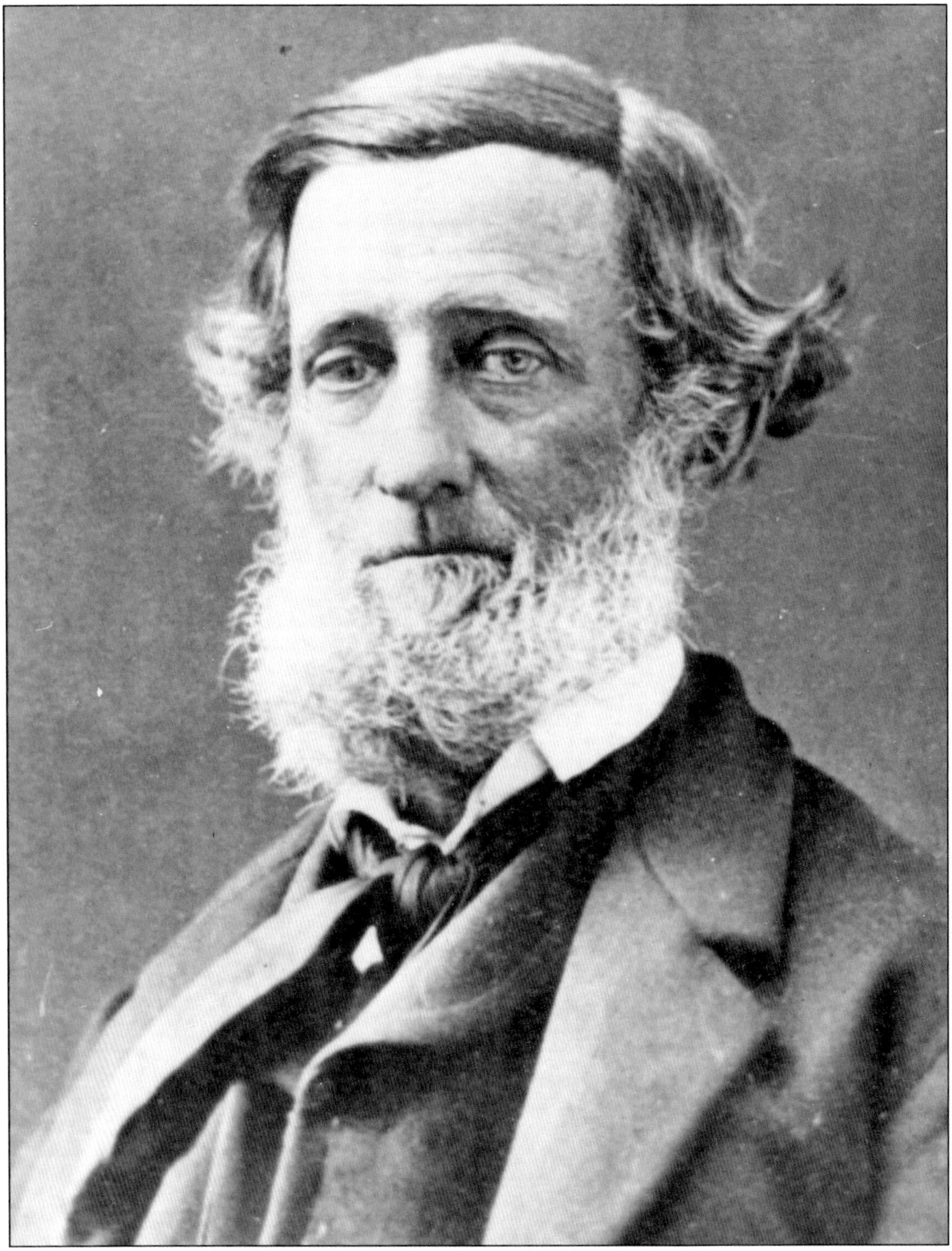

By 1853, there were a number of small ferry boat crossings along the Stanislaus River to help farmers and travelers cross from one side to the other. One of these, known as Islip's Ferry, was constructed a short ways upstream from the present site of Riverbank. The operation was bought out by former Mariposa County sheriff–turned–cattle rancher James Burney, who is pictured here. After 14 years of operating Islip's Ferry, Burney decided upon a new site slightly downstream, and thus began a small ferry operation known as Burney's Ferry. A small settlement grew up by the riverside that became known as Burneyville.

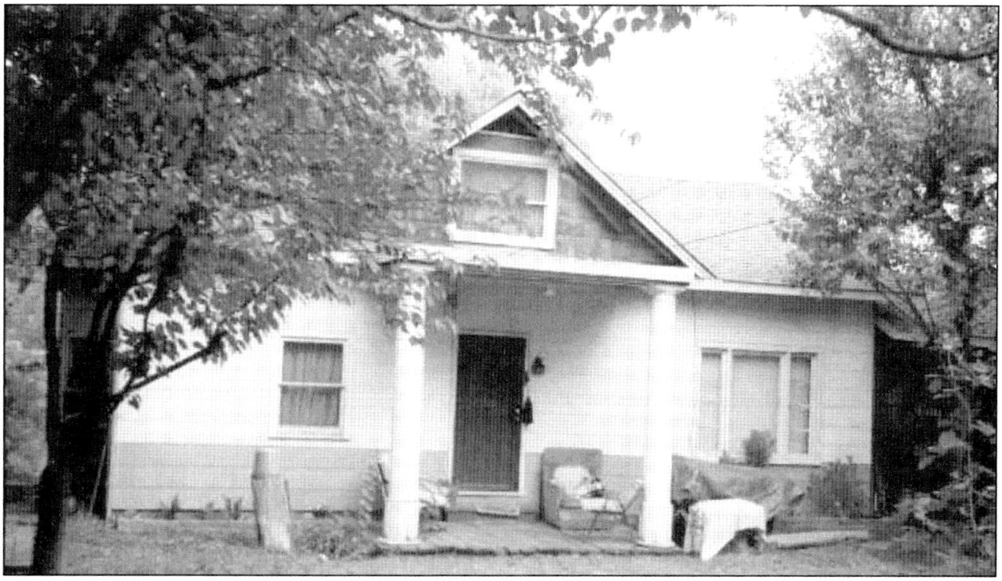

Burney constructed a two-story house just up from the river on the main road in town. The second story of the house caught fire and had to be demolished, making the house into a single-story dwelling. This picture shows that the house has not changed much since its last remodeling.

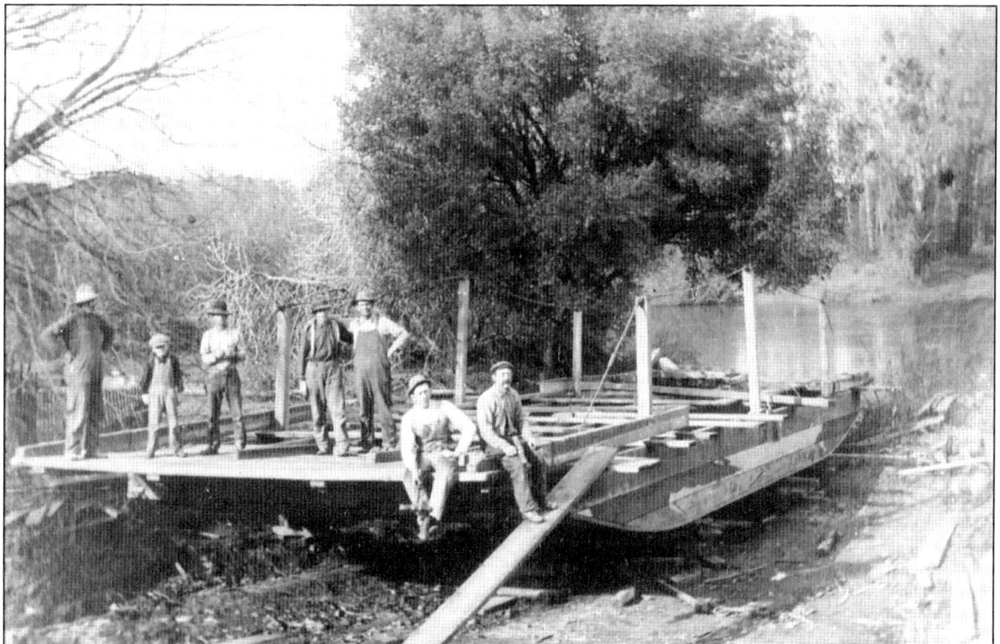

Burney had to buy his own materials in order to construct a ferry, as well as the cables to guide it across the river. Here, the construction of the actual boat is seen long before the town of Burneyville came into existence. The operation of the ferry would not be an easy task due to the finickiness of the river itself. The flow was unreliable because of constantly changing depths and moving sandbars, as well as shifting debris.

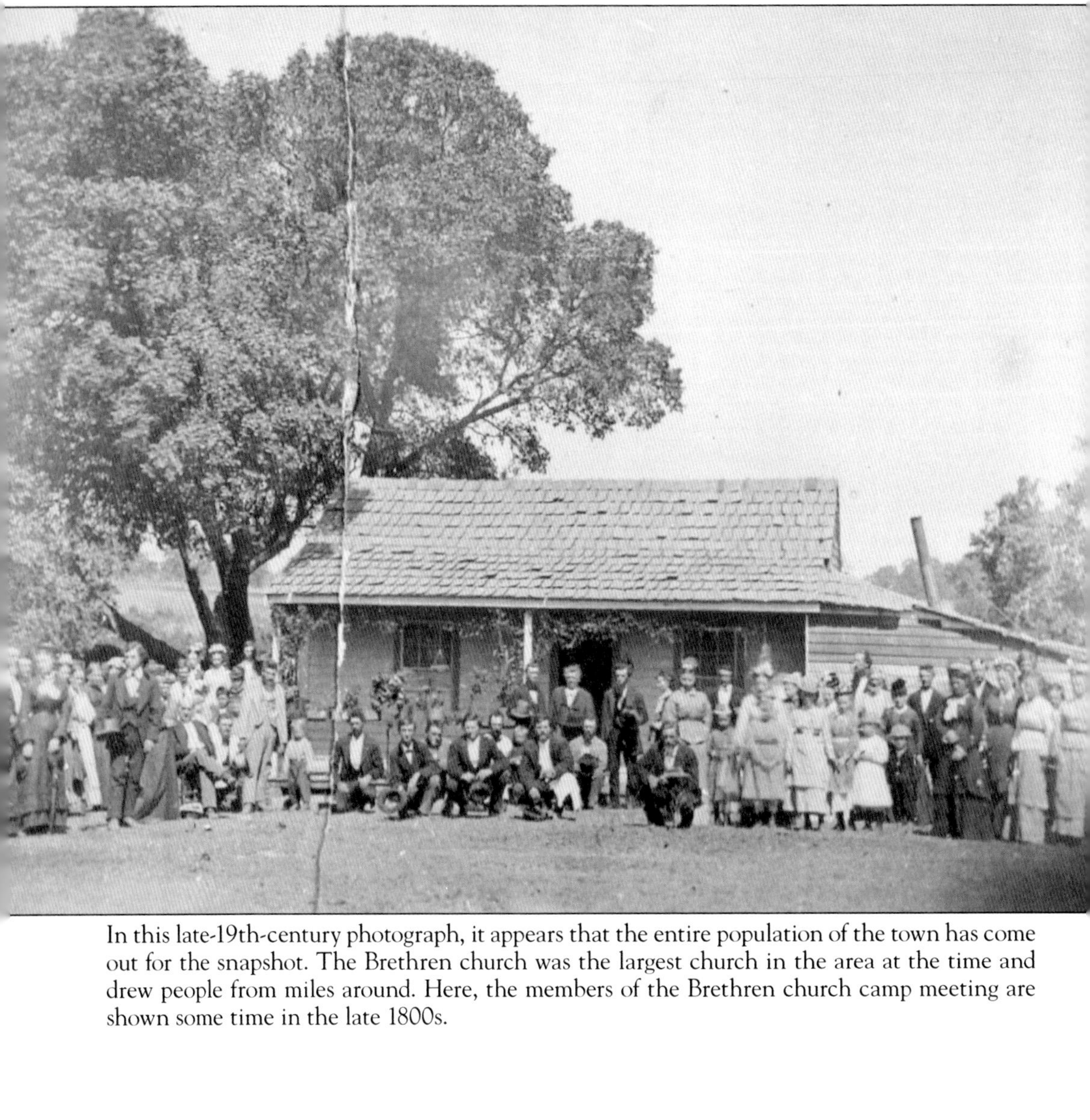

In this late-19th-century photograph, it appears that the entire population of the town has come out for the snapshot. The Brethren church was the largest church in the area at the time and drew people from miles around. Here, the members of the Brethren church camp meeting are shown some time in the late 1800s.

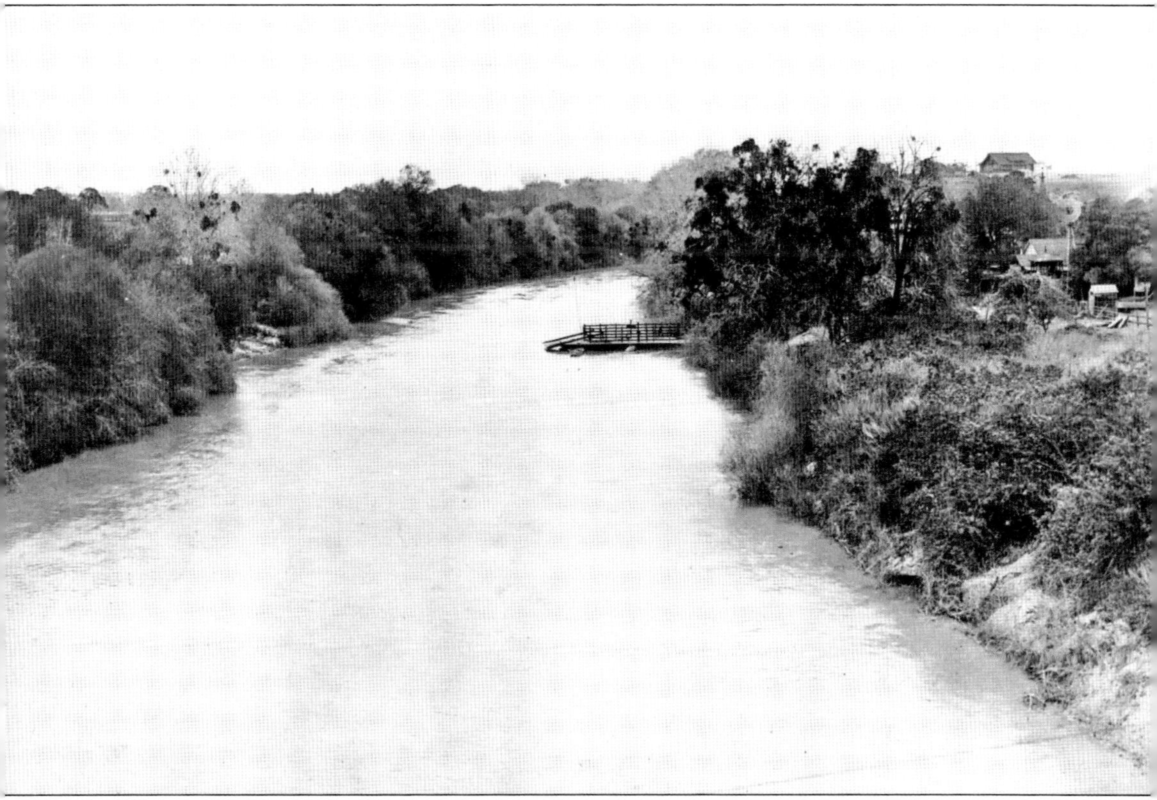

Burneyville was comprised of two roads and mainly sat upon the second bench back from the river. Main Street ran from the ferry to the top of the hill, where it connected to a county road running to Davis Ferry on the Tuolumne River. A second street led off of Main Street and into the town's residential area. Burneyville's entire area was less than 11 acres, with most of it growing in an easterly direction.

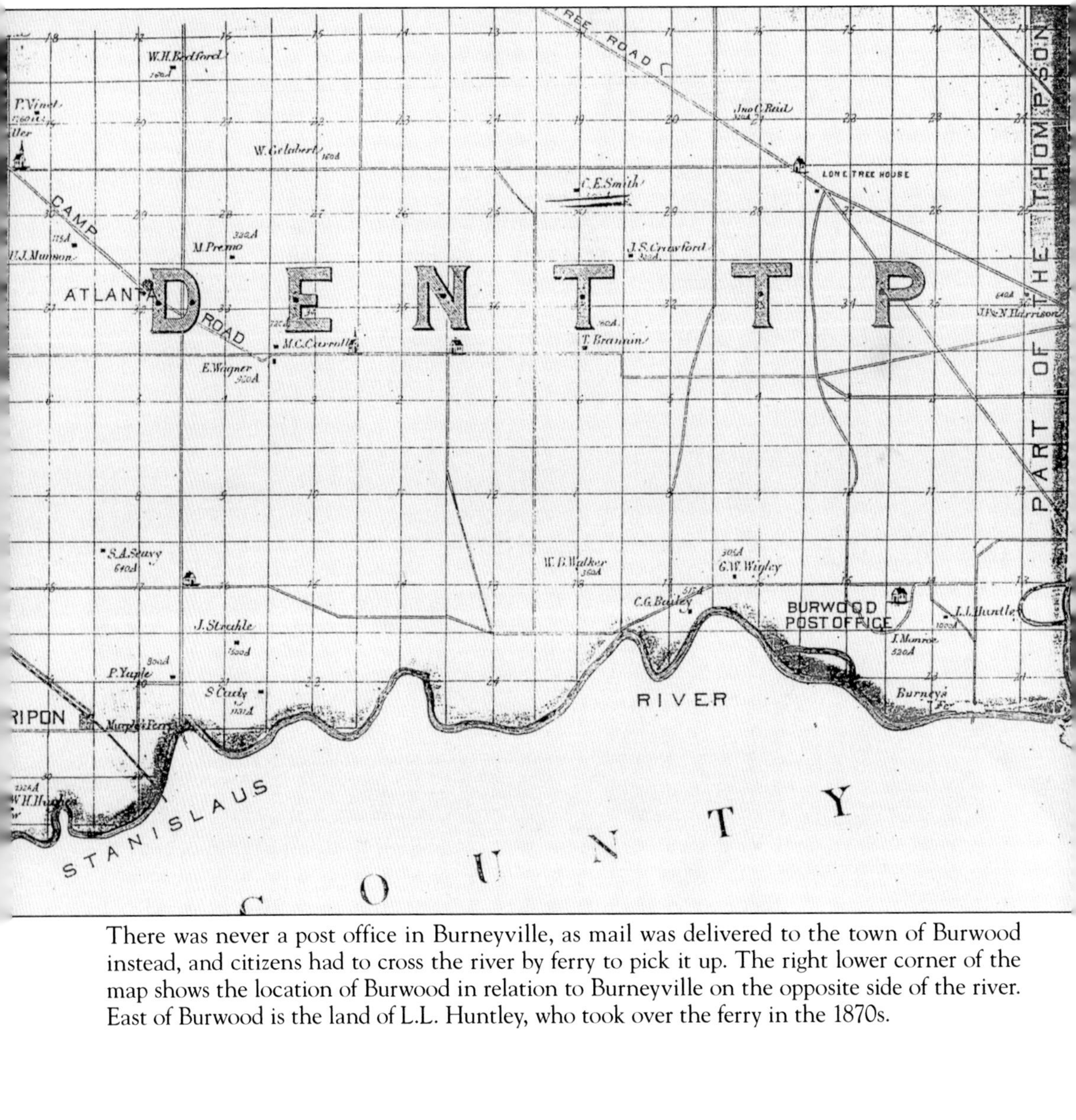

There was never a post office in Burneyville, as mail was delivered to the town of Burwood instead, and citizens had to cross the river by ferry to pick it up. The right lower corner of the map shows the location of Burwood in relation to Burneyville on the opposite side of the river. East of Burwood is the land of L.L. Huntley, who took over the ferry in the 1870s.

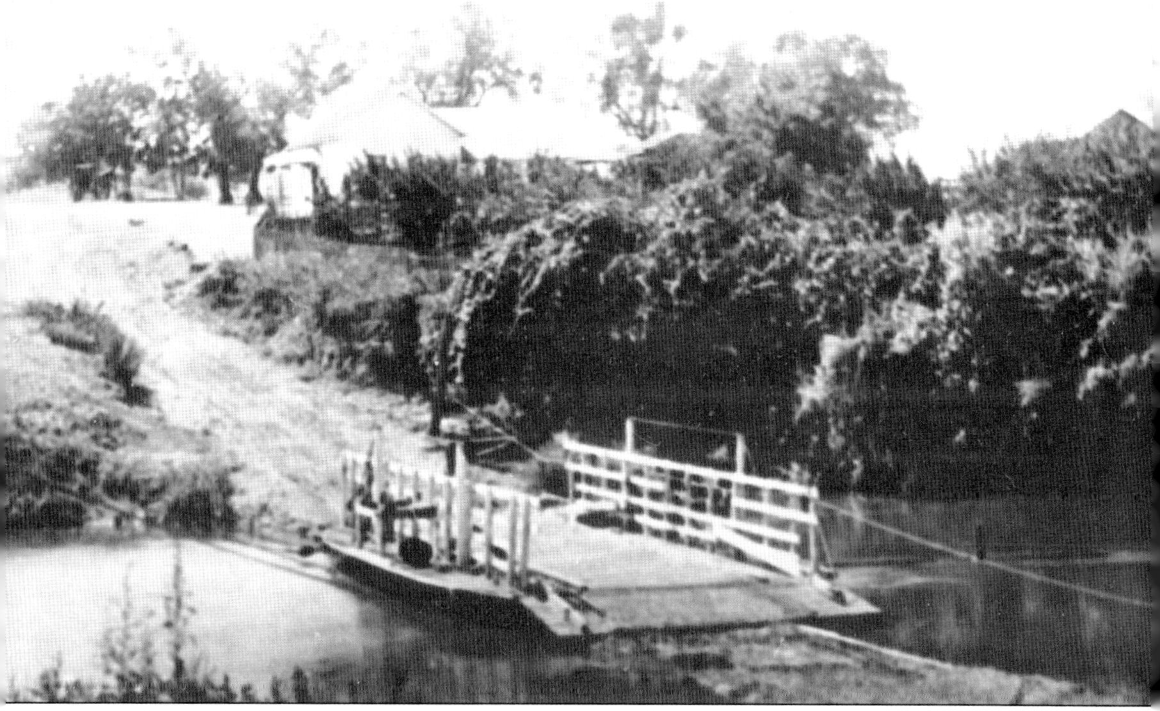

One of the first buildings to be constructed in Burneyville and located on the bank of the river was a warehouse barn owned by Burney that had a very interesting combination of tenants. One side of the warehouse was occupied by a saloon, and the other belonged to the Brethren church. Of course, the saloon did not operate during church hours on Sunday. By the 1870s, Burneyville had several homes, including Burney's own two-story house on Blair Street, along with several other homes, a grocery store, a blacksmith shop, a hotel, two to three saloons, a dry goods store, and a shoe shop.

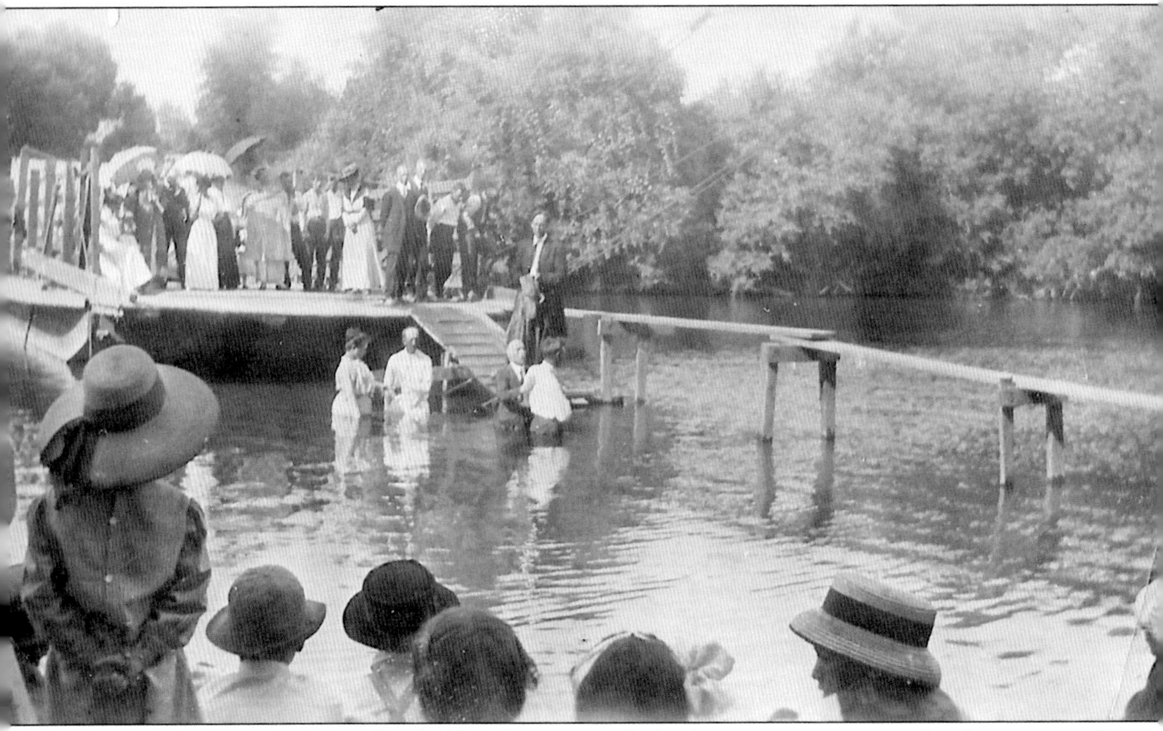

Baptismal services were often held at the river, with the ferry serving as a stage for the pastor and choir. One can see that the citizens of Burneyville were well dressed in fancy gowns, suits, and hats, as well as gloves—their Sunday best.

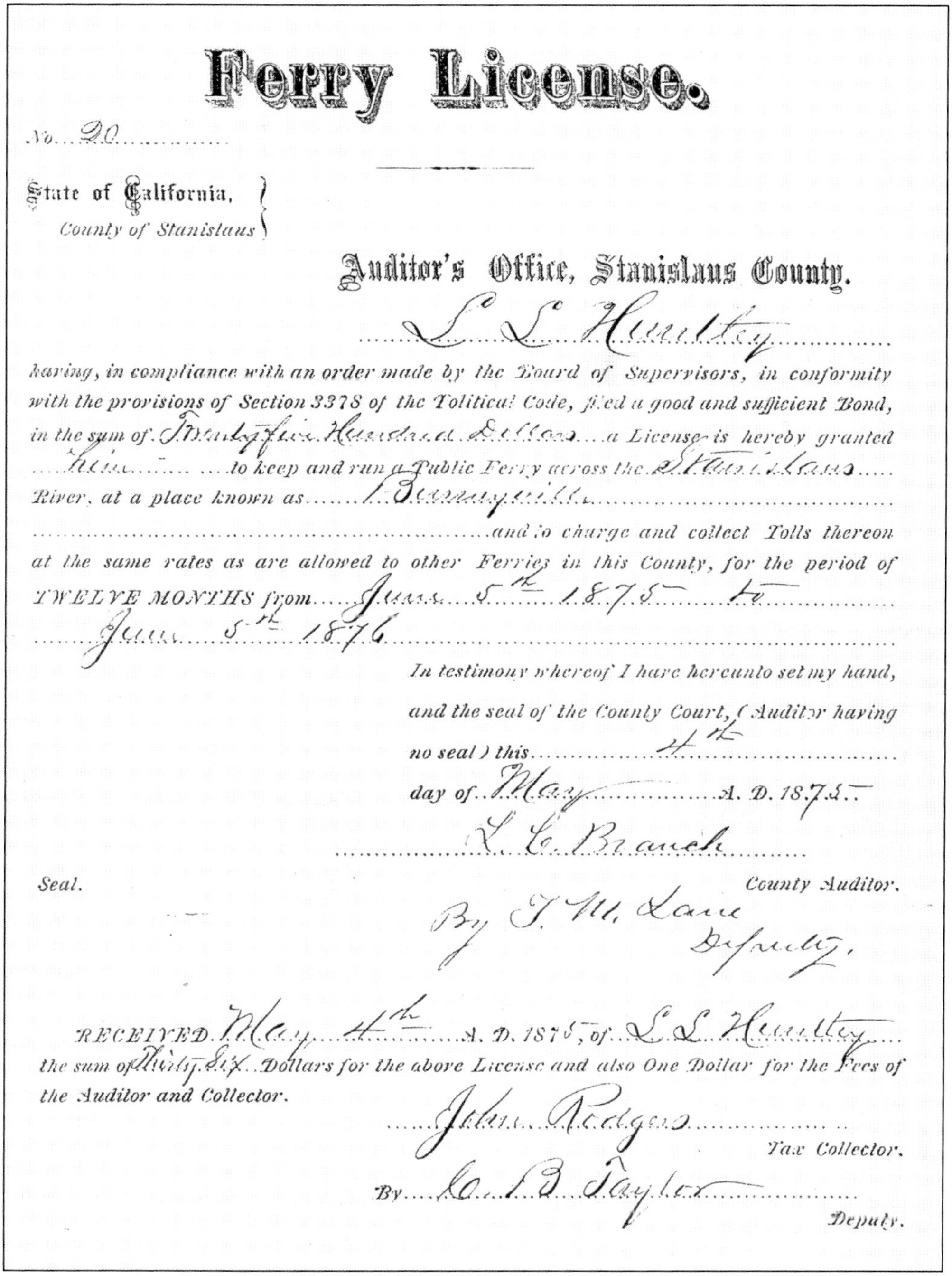

Ferry License.

No. 20

State of California, County of Stanislaus

Auditor's Office, Stanislaus County.

L. L. Huntley

having, in compliance with an order made by the Board of Supervisors, in conformity with the provisions of Section 3378 of the Political Code, filed a good and sufficient Bond, in the sum of Twenty five Hundred Dollars *a License is hereby granted* him *to keep and run a Public Ferry across the* Stanislaus *River, at a place known as* Burneyville *and to charge and collect Tolls thereon at the same rates as are allowed to other Ferries in this County, for the period of TWELVE MONTHS from* June 5th 1875 to June 5th 1876

In testimony whereof I have hereunto set my hand, and the seal of the County Court, (Auditor having no seal) this 4th *day of* May *A. D. 1875.*

L. C. Branch

Seal. *County Auditor.*

By T. M. Lane Deputy.

RECEIVED May 4th *A. D. 1875, of* L L Huntley *the sum of* Thirty Six *Dollars for the above License and also One Dollar for the Fees of the Auditor and Collector.*

John Rodgers

Tax Collector.

By C. B. Taylor

Deputy.

L.L Huntley took over the ferry operation in 1875 for a sum of $2,500. Pictured here is his ferry-operating license.

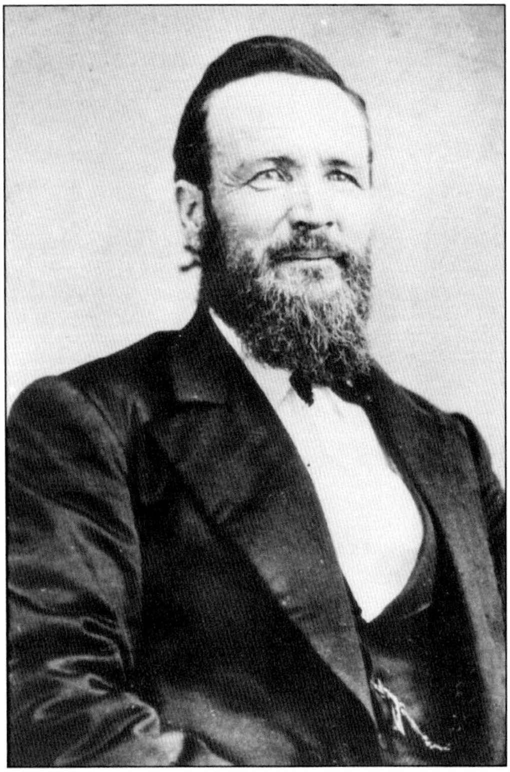

Thomas Ross owned the ferry after Burney decided to move to Modesto to take up a position as the superintendent of Modesto City Schools.

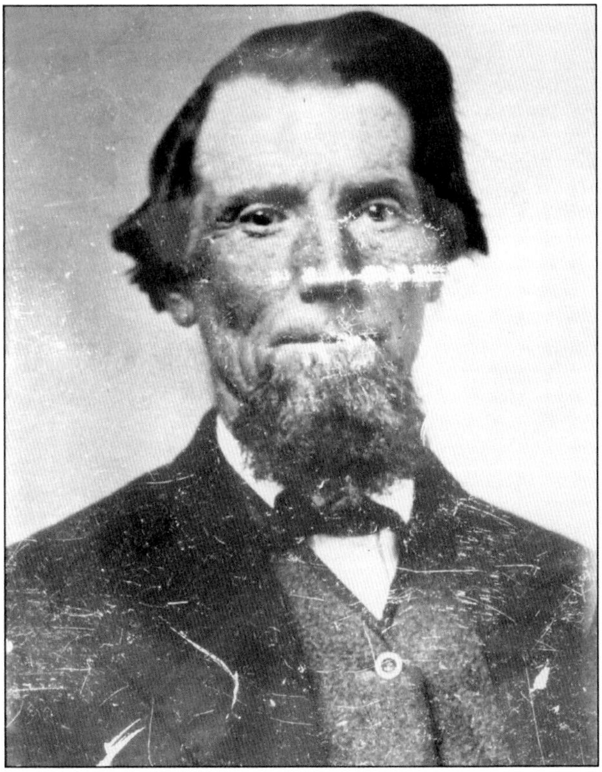

After Huntley, Thomas Ross's son Henry ran the ferry for a short time.

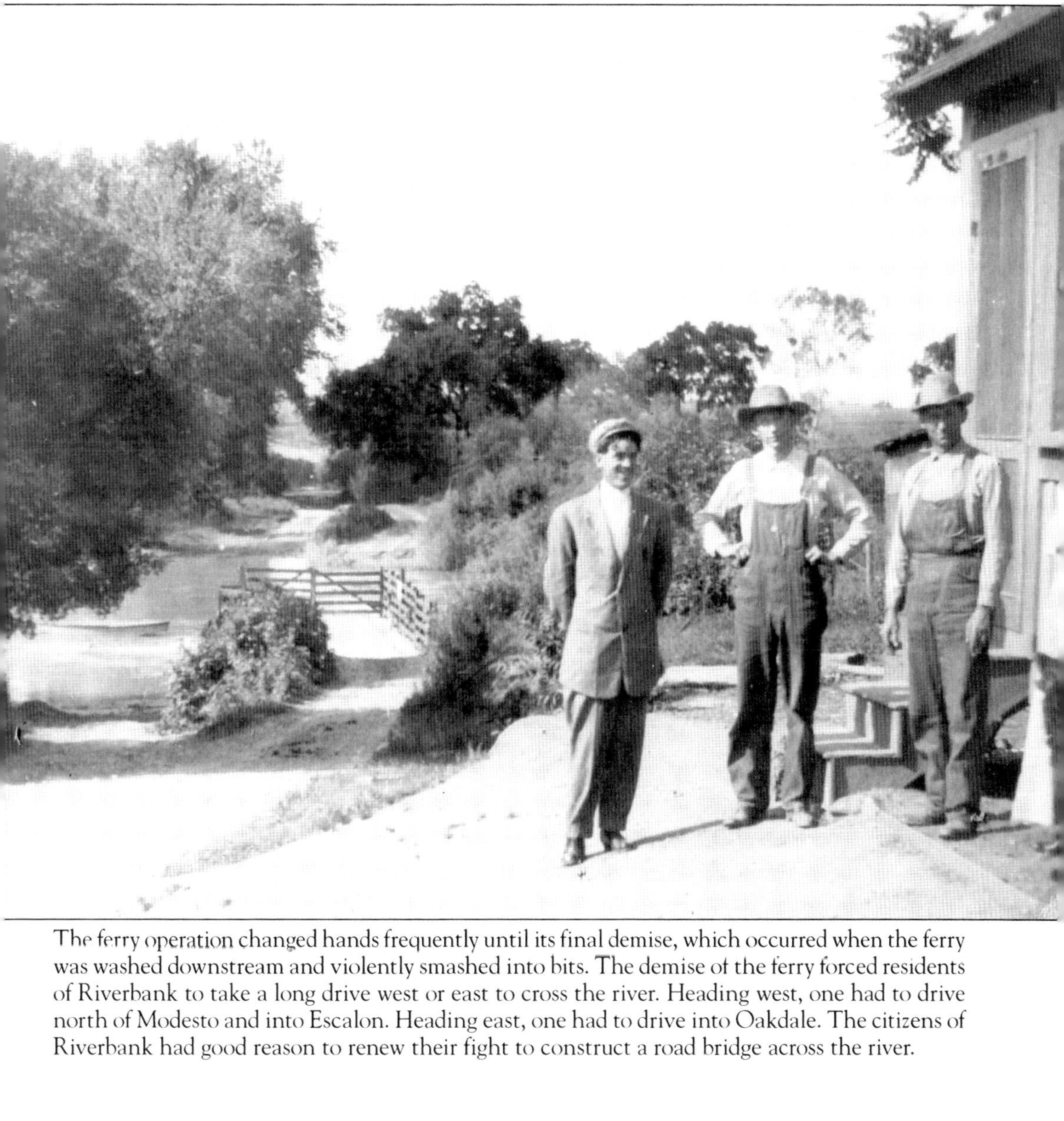

The ferry operation changed hands frequently until its final demise, which occurred when the ferry was washed downstream and violently smashed into bits. The demise of the ferry forced residents of Riverbank to take a long drive west or east to cross the river. Heading west, one had to drive north of Modesto and into Escalon. Heading east, one had to drive into Oakdale. The citizens of Riverbank had good reason to renew their fight to construct a road bridge across the river.

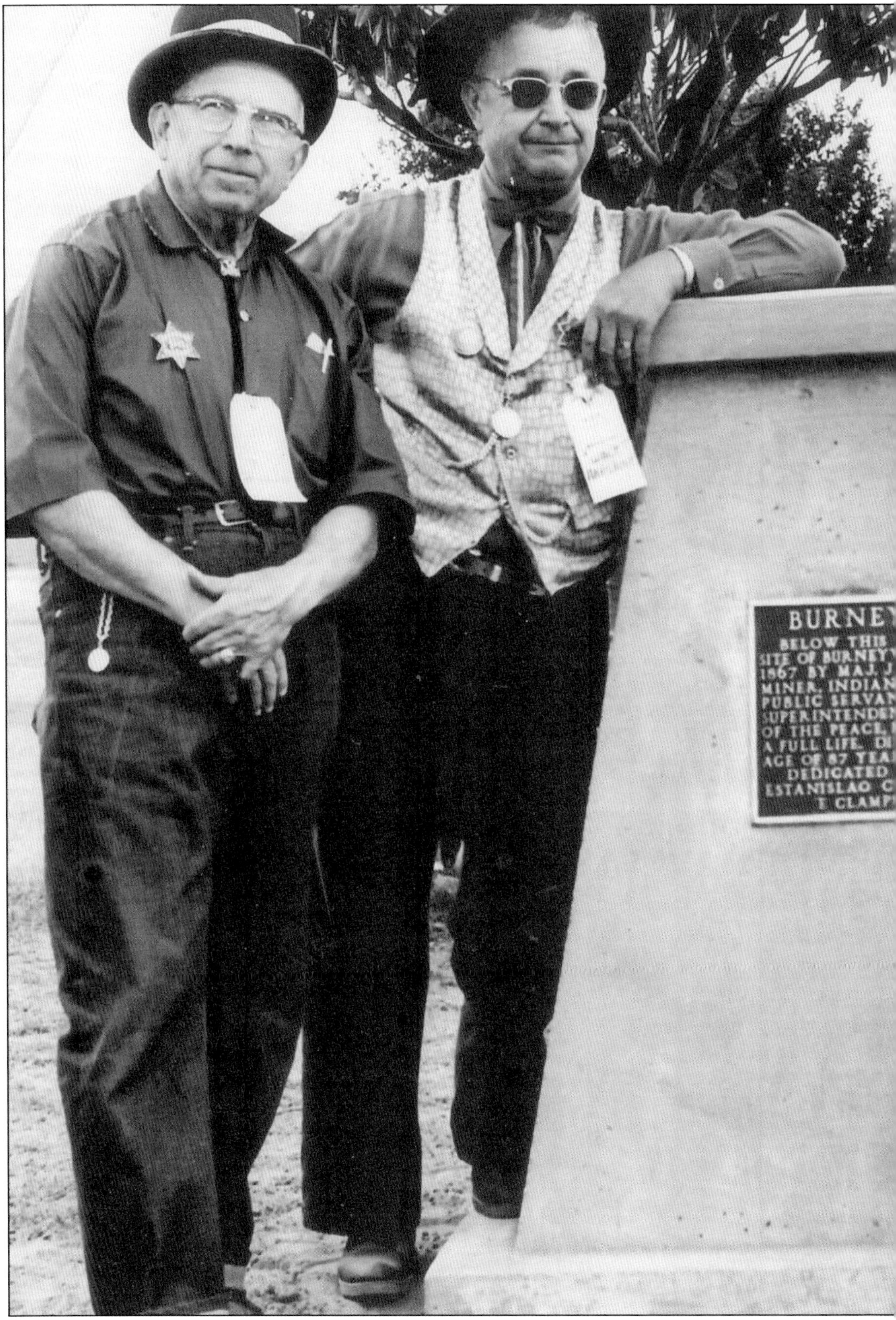
BURNEY
BELOW THIS
SITE OF BURNEY
1867 BY MAJ. J
MINER, INDIAN
PUBLIC SERVAN
SUPERINTENDE
OF THE PEACE,
A FULL LIFE. DI
AGE OF 87 YEA
DEDICATED
ESTANISLAO C
T CLAMP

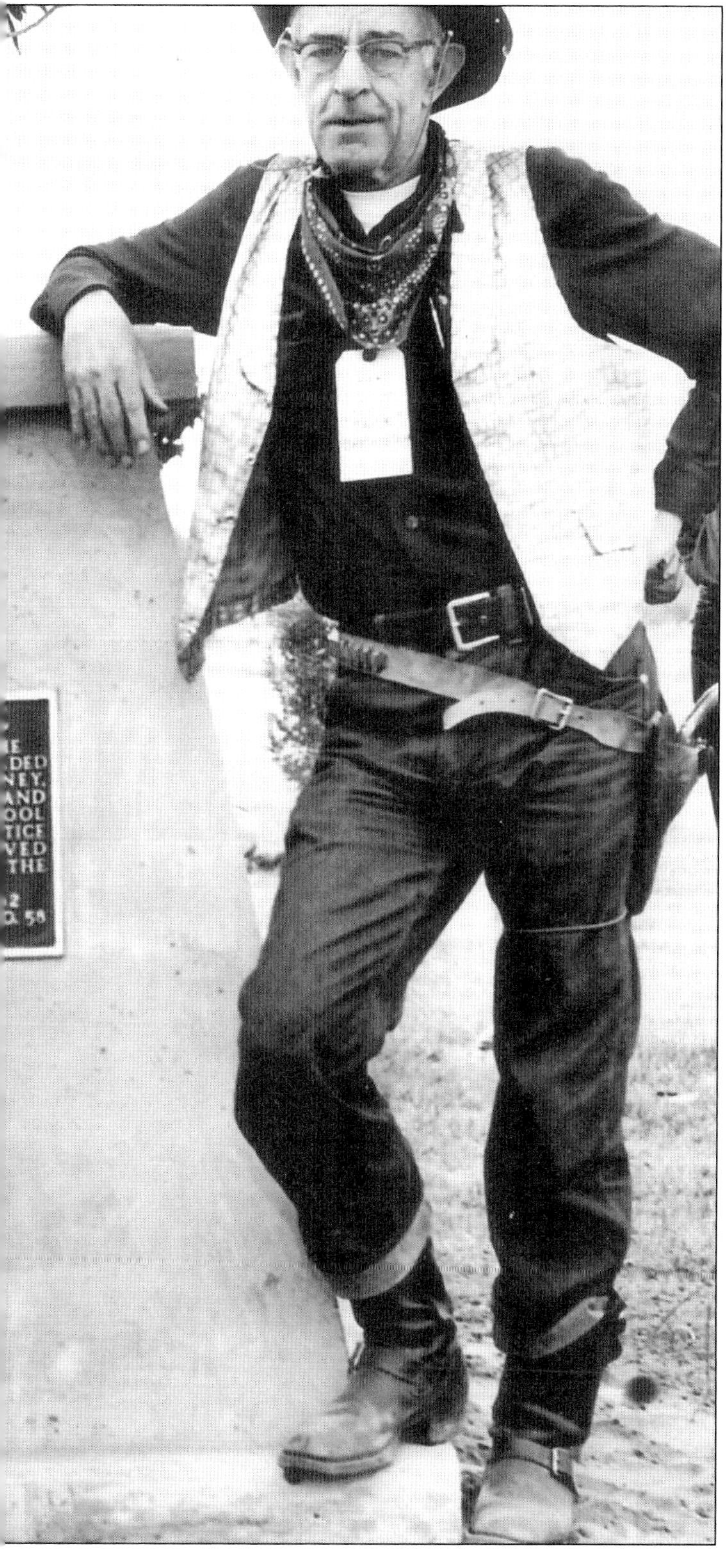

In 1967, a monument was raised in Pioneer Park to mark the location of Burneyville and share the story of founder James Burney.

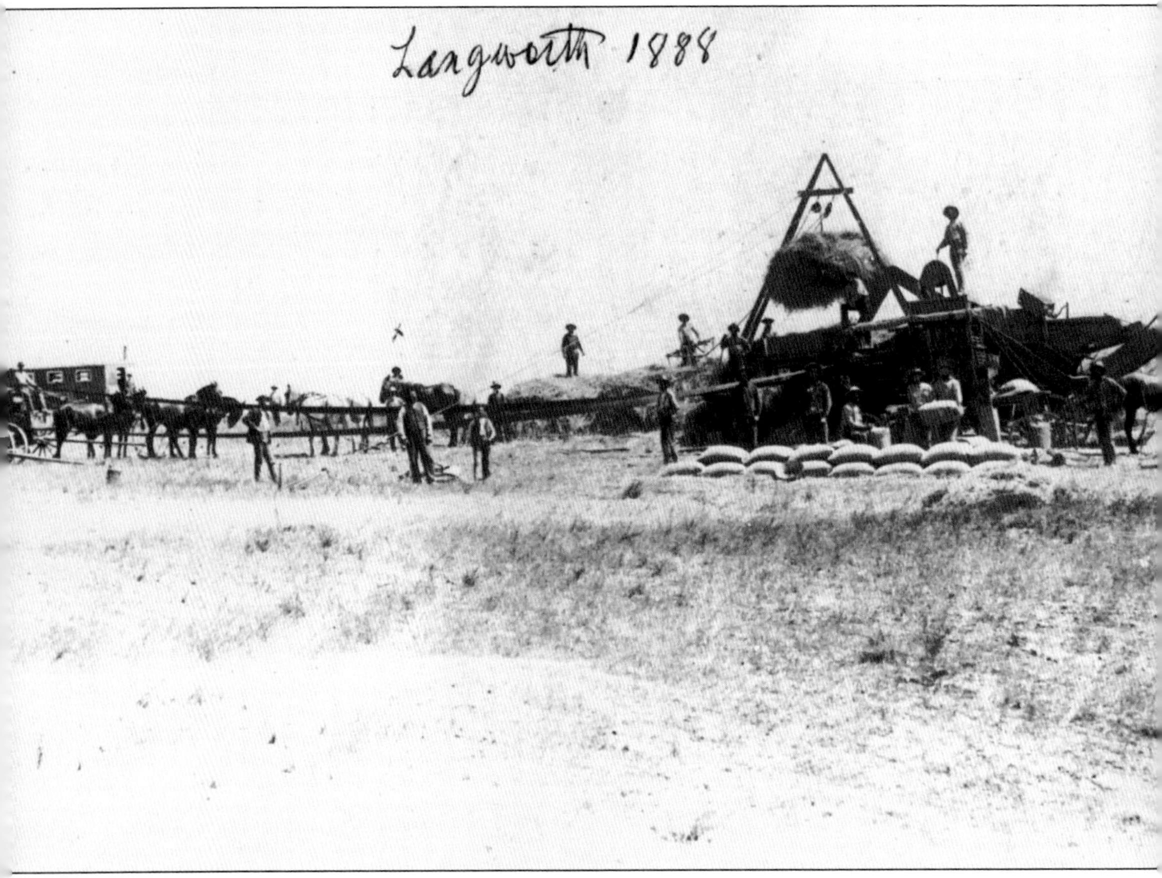

Another town that existed long before the appearance of Riverbank was Langworth, which stood on the county road between Burneyville and Oakdale. In the 1880s, many of the farmers in the area around Langworth harvested wheat crops by using threshing machines, such as the one seen here. The machine was owned by E.H. Gatlin. The two men standing on the stack are George and Elmer Zane, who lived in Glenn Ellen. The wheat was typically taken into warehouses in Oakdale and later ground into flour in Stockton.

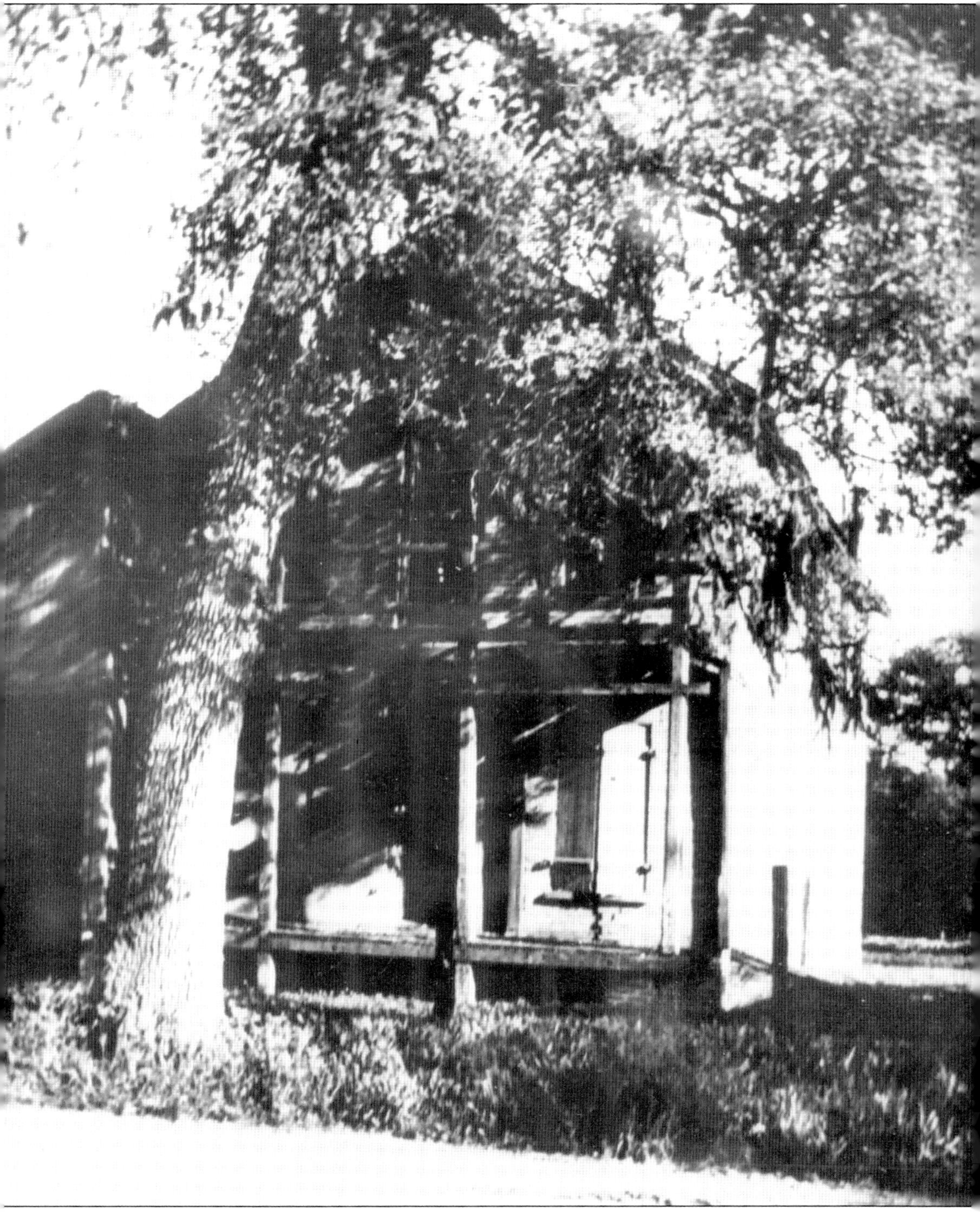

This two-story brick building was occupied by Langworth's post office and a store, while the upper floor was occupied by the Langworth Hotel. The building fell into ruin around the middle part of the 20th century and no longer exists.

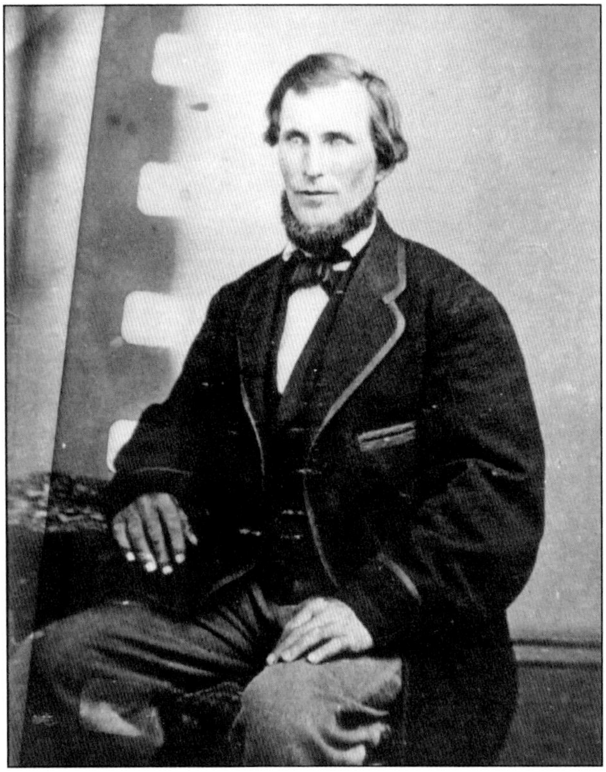

In between the abandonment of Burneyville and the founding of Riverbank, there were several farms in an unincorporated area without a name. One of the more prominent farms was that of Squire Wells, who is pictured to the left.

Squire Wells's farm was located at what is now the southwest corner of Oakdale Road and Highway 108 where Rockland Market and Perko's are today.

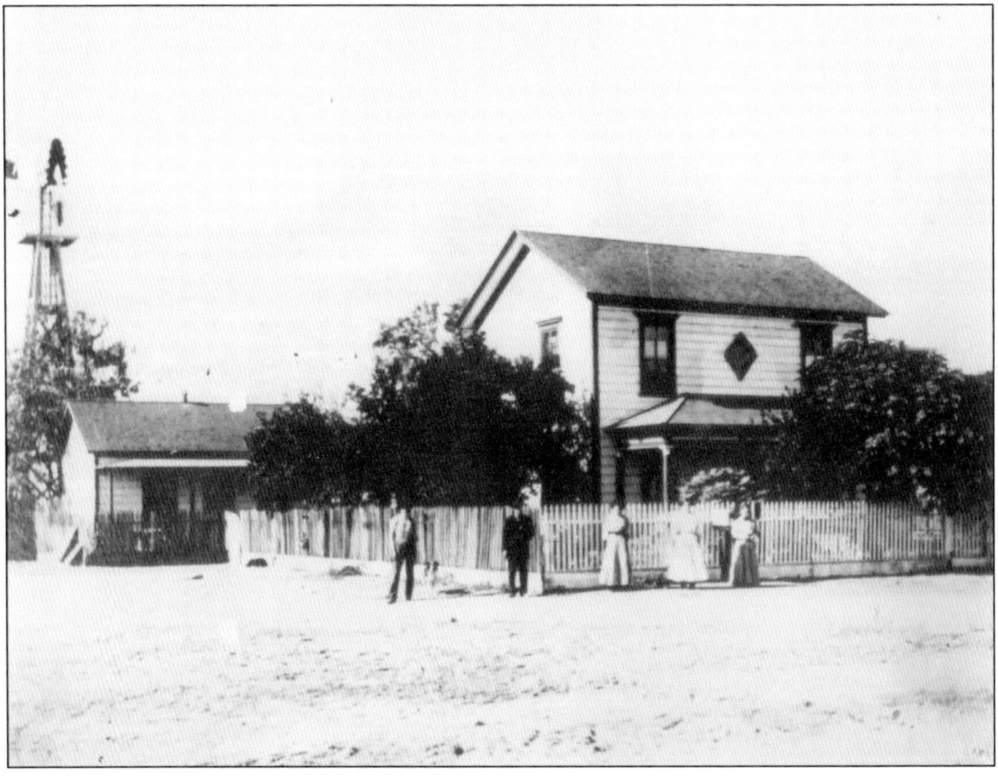

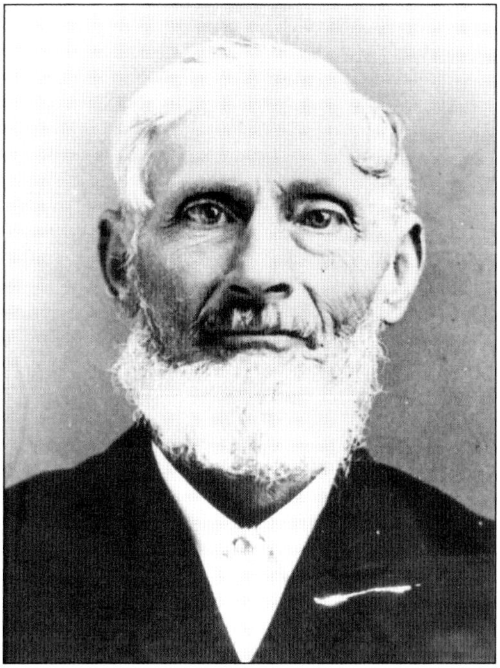
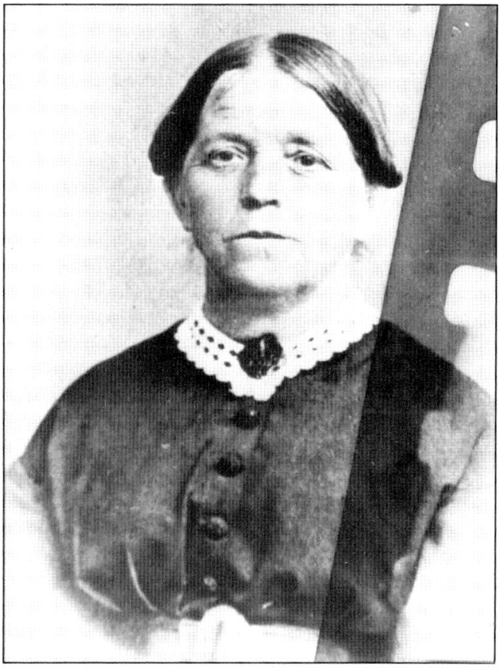

Robert Leighton and his wife, seen in the images above, owned the land on what is now the northeast corner of Oakdale Road and Highway 108 across from Squire Wells's land.

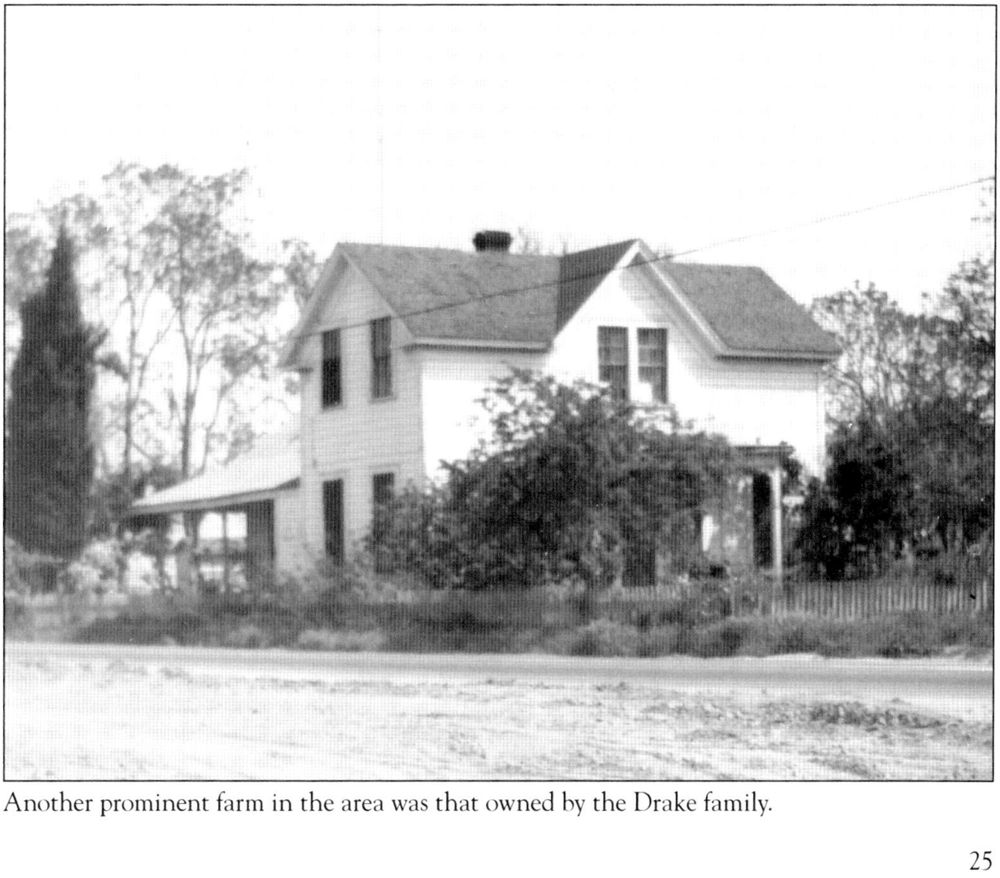

Another prominent farm in the area was that owned by the Drake family.

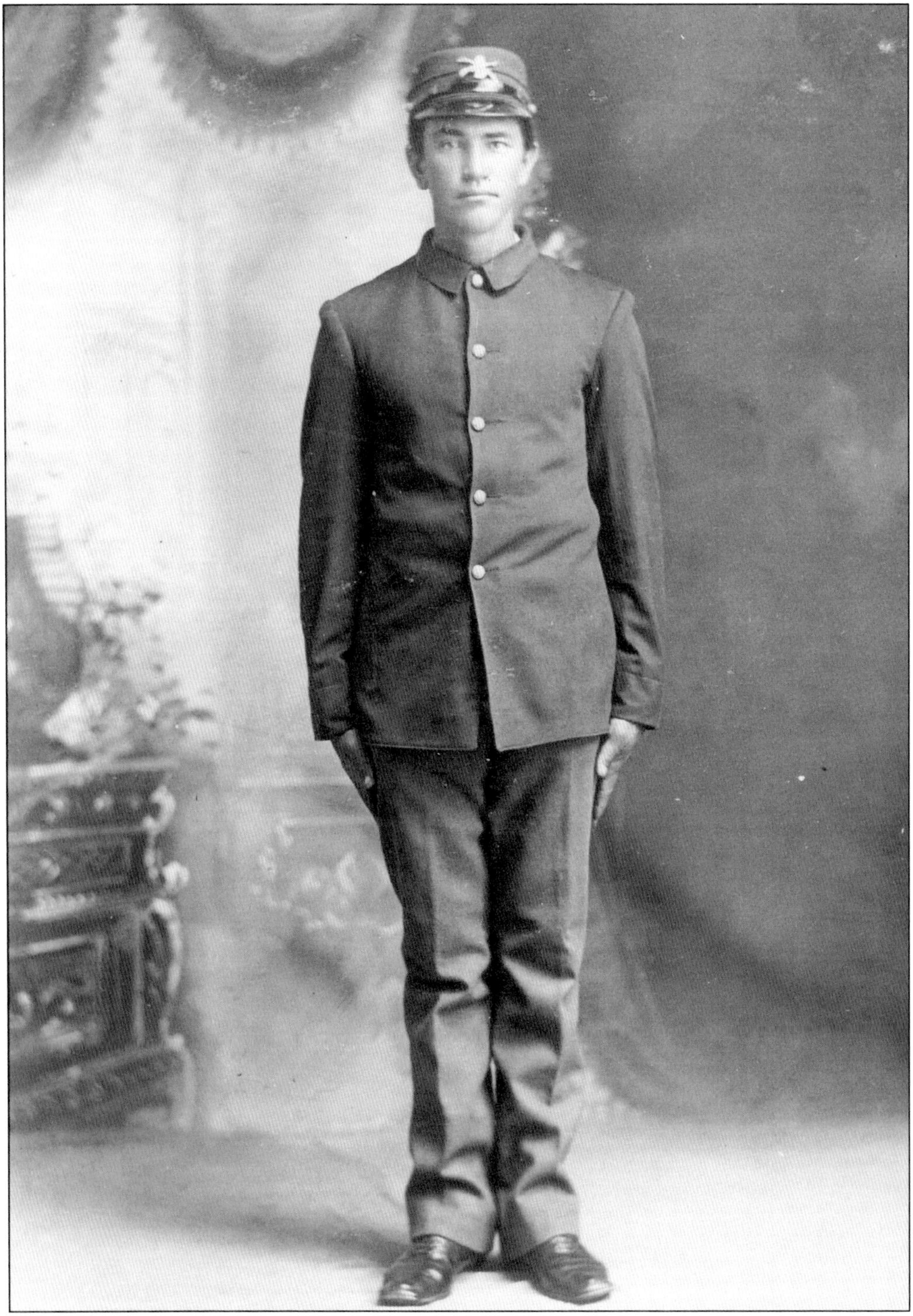

The Myers family owned a large portion of land on the north side of the river. Here, Fred Myers, one of the two brothers who owned the land, is shown in his World War I uniform.

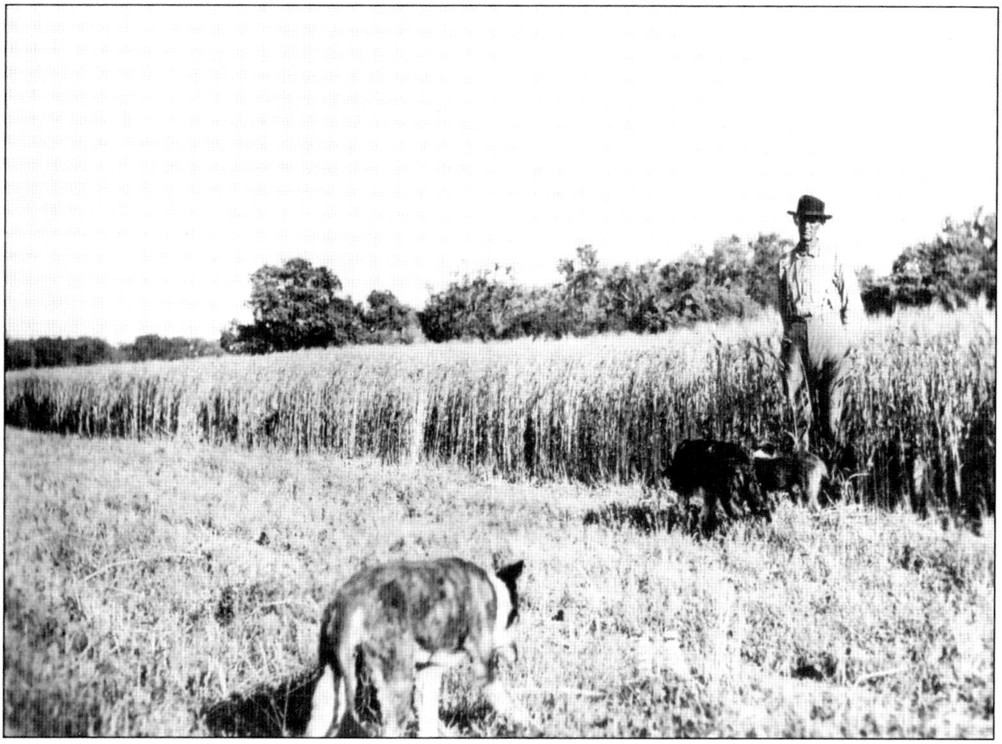

Here, Jacob Myers is shown by a field of wheat with the family dog. Jacob's farm was located on the north side of the river and to the west side of the county road. Jacob conducted dry land wheat farming on the property. The land is the current site of Jacob Myers Park.

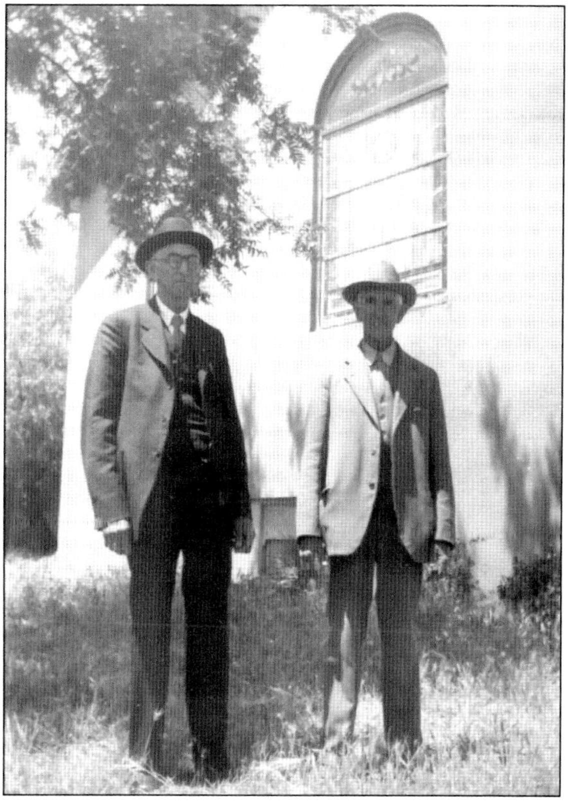

Fred and Jacob Myers were both prominent members of the Methodist church on the corner of Atchison Street and Highway 108.

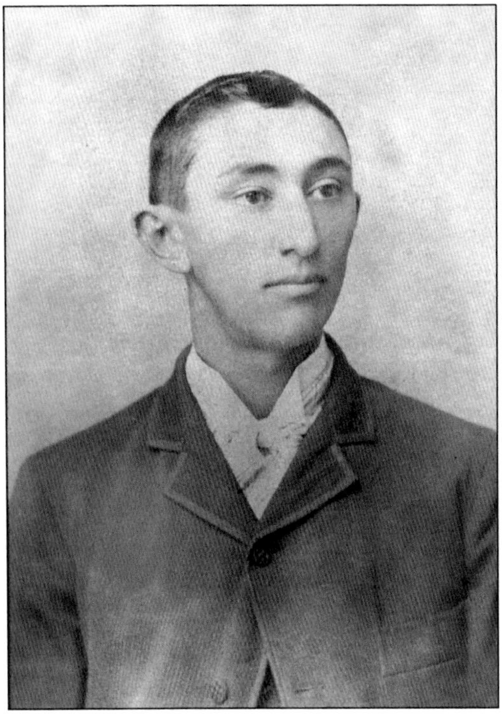

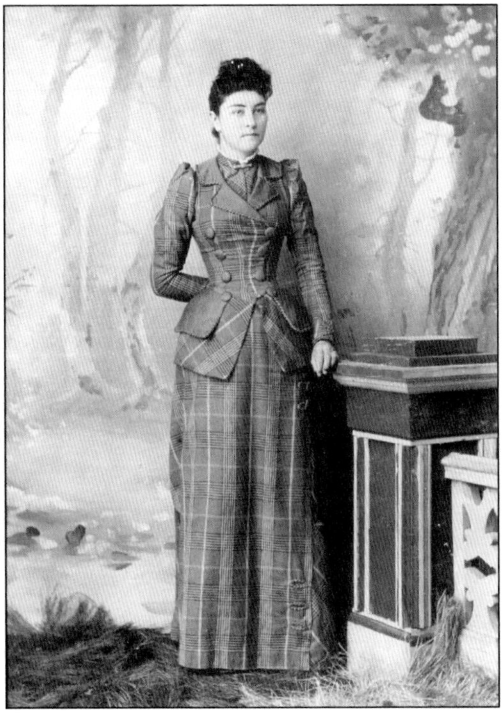

Jacob and Annie Myers's land was later donated to the City of Riverbank in order to build a public park.

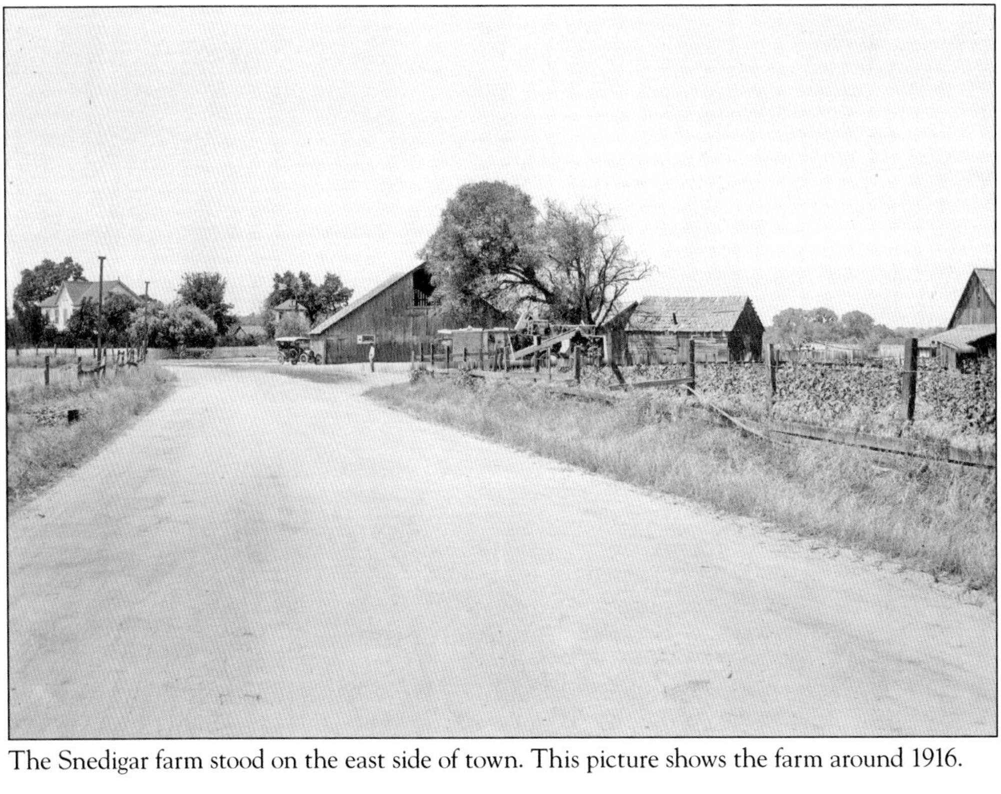

The Snedigar farm stood on the east side of town. This picture shows the farm around 1916.

Two

THE RISE OF RIVERBANK

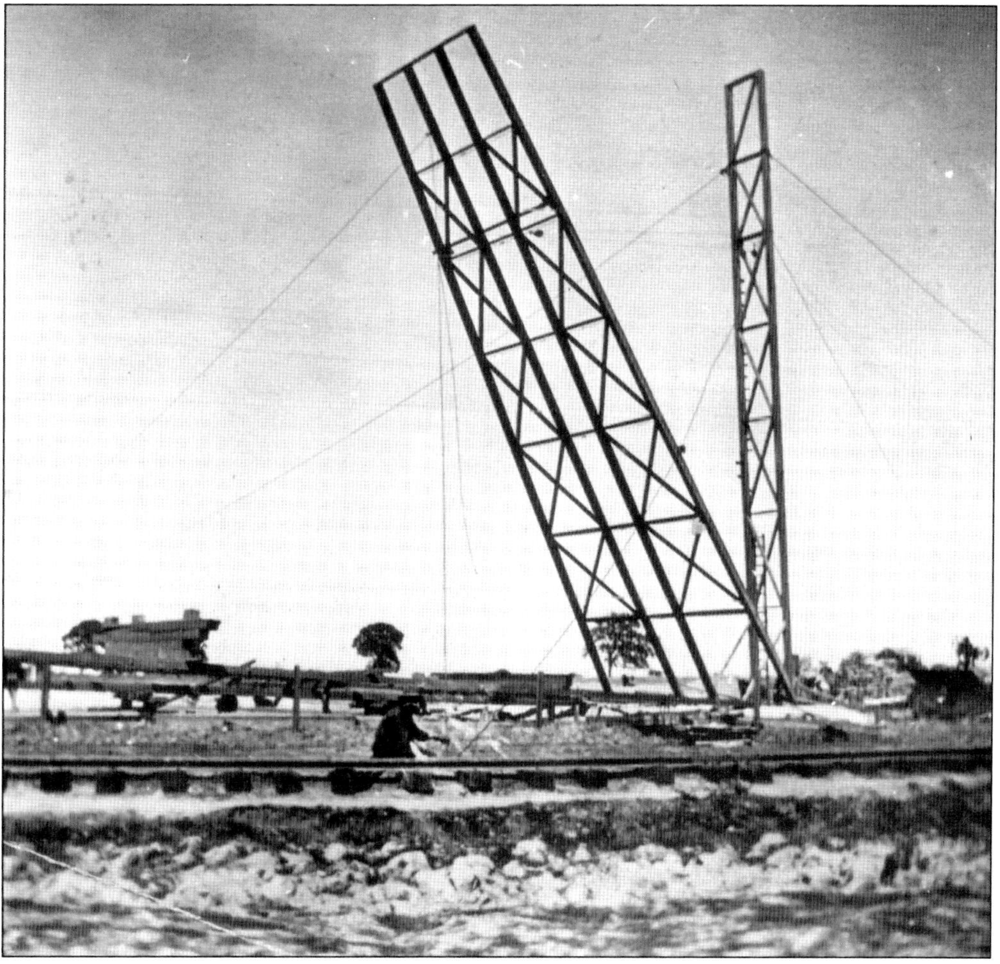

In the mid-1890s, there were very few railroads running through the Central Valley of California. The San Joaquin Valley Railroad was established on July 22, 1895. In 1900, the Santa Fe Railroad took over the line, and in 1905, a station was constructed in Riverbank so trains could carry passengers to San Francisco. In the picture above, the construction of the railroad roundhouse is shown.

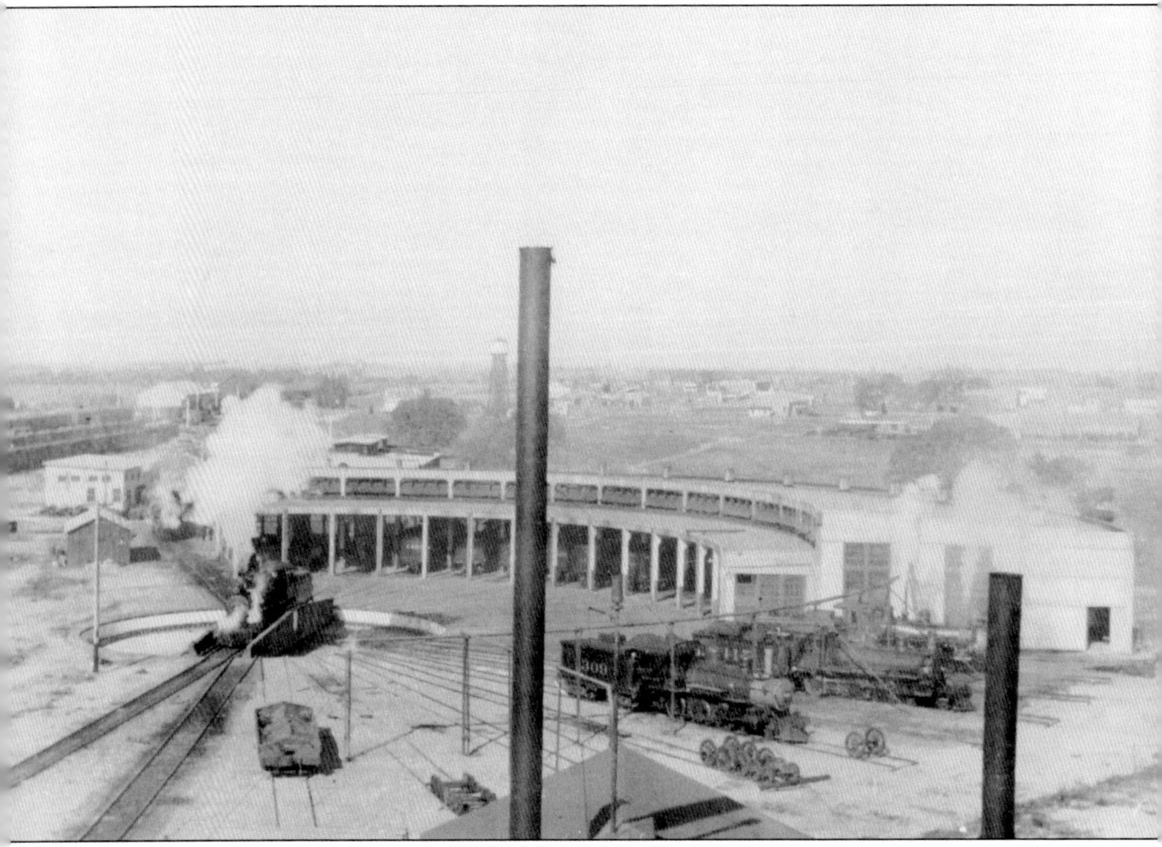

In 1910, Riverbank became a division terminal for the Santa Fe Railway. At a cost of $1 million, machine shops, a roundhouse, water towers, and oil storage tanks were built along the tracks and its spur lines. Seen here is the Riverbank Roundhouse in 1914.

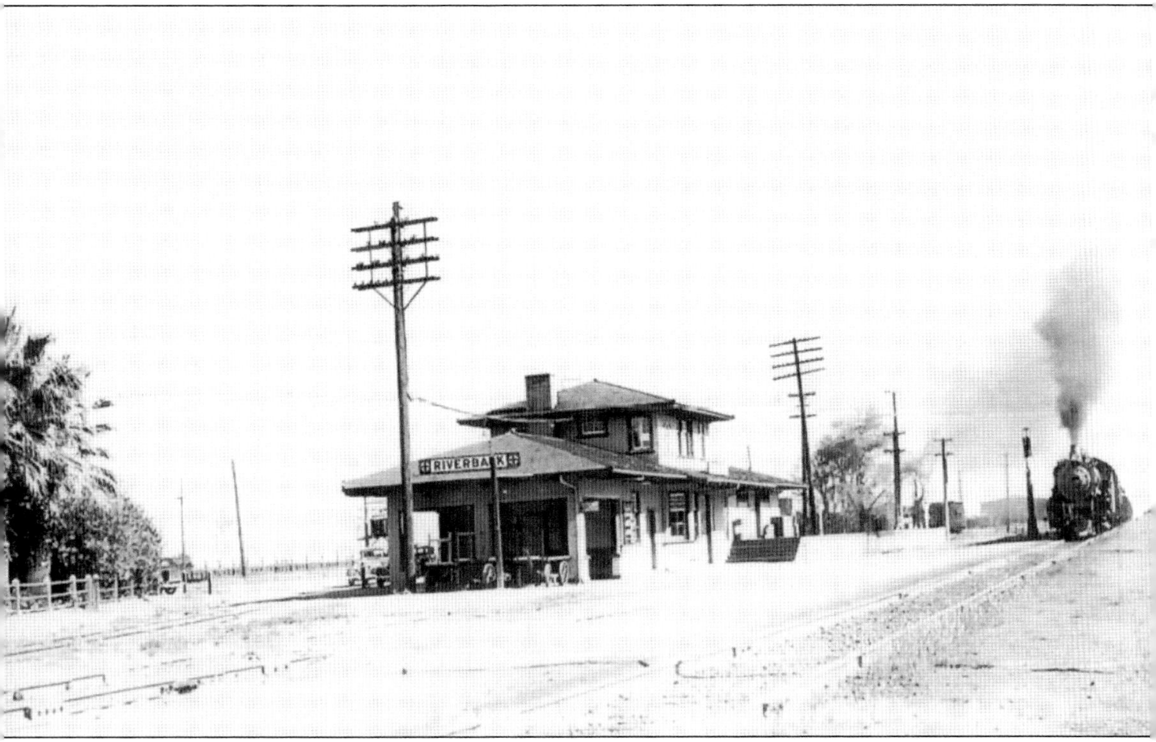

Originally, the town of Riverbank was to be called Wilbur, but as another location along the Santa Fe Railroad line already had this name, the area became known as Riverbank. Originally, the station was located off of Talbot Street, close to the railroad yards and shops, which are seen in the background here. Later, the station was moved across the tracks and further north.

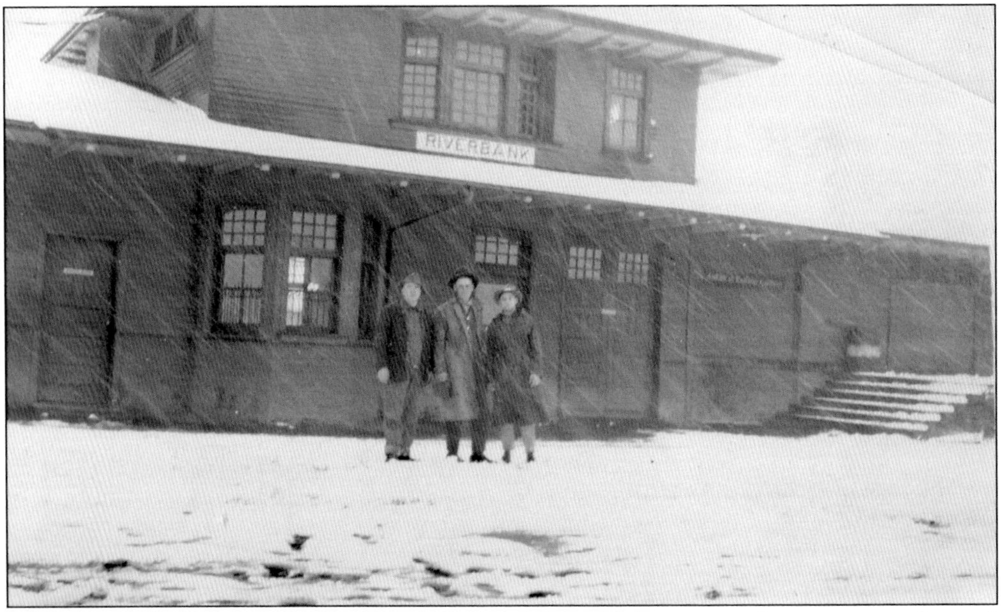

Here, the station is shown in the early part of the 20th century during a rare Central Valley snowstorm.

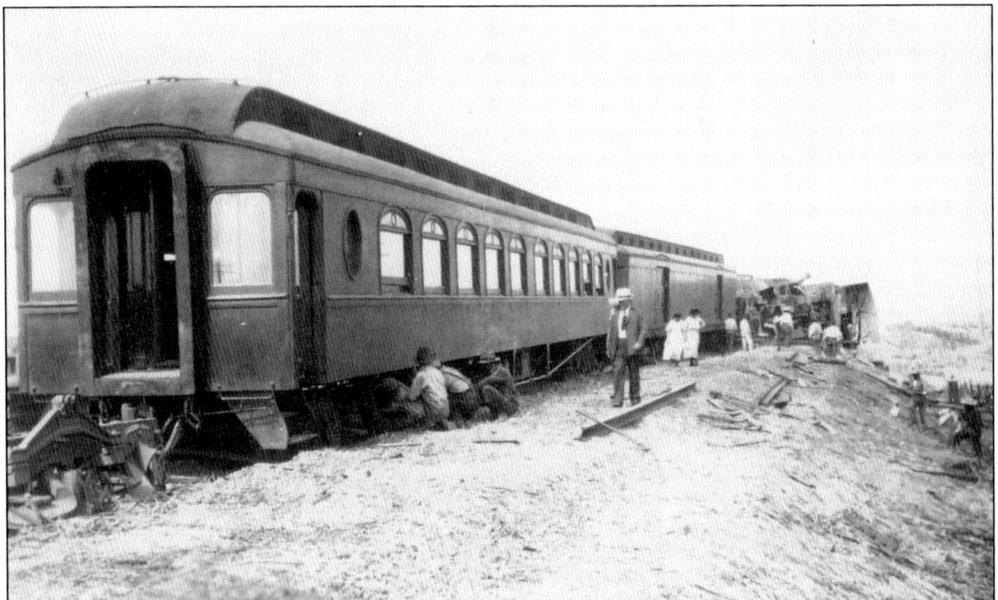

Although fast, train travel was not always safe, as is shown in this picture of an early wreck that occurred between Riverbank and Stockton in the early 1900s. By the 1920s, Riverbank had 26 passenger trains and 18 freight trains passing through on a daily basis.

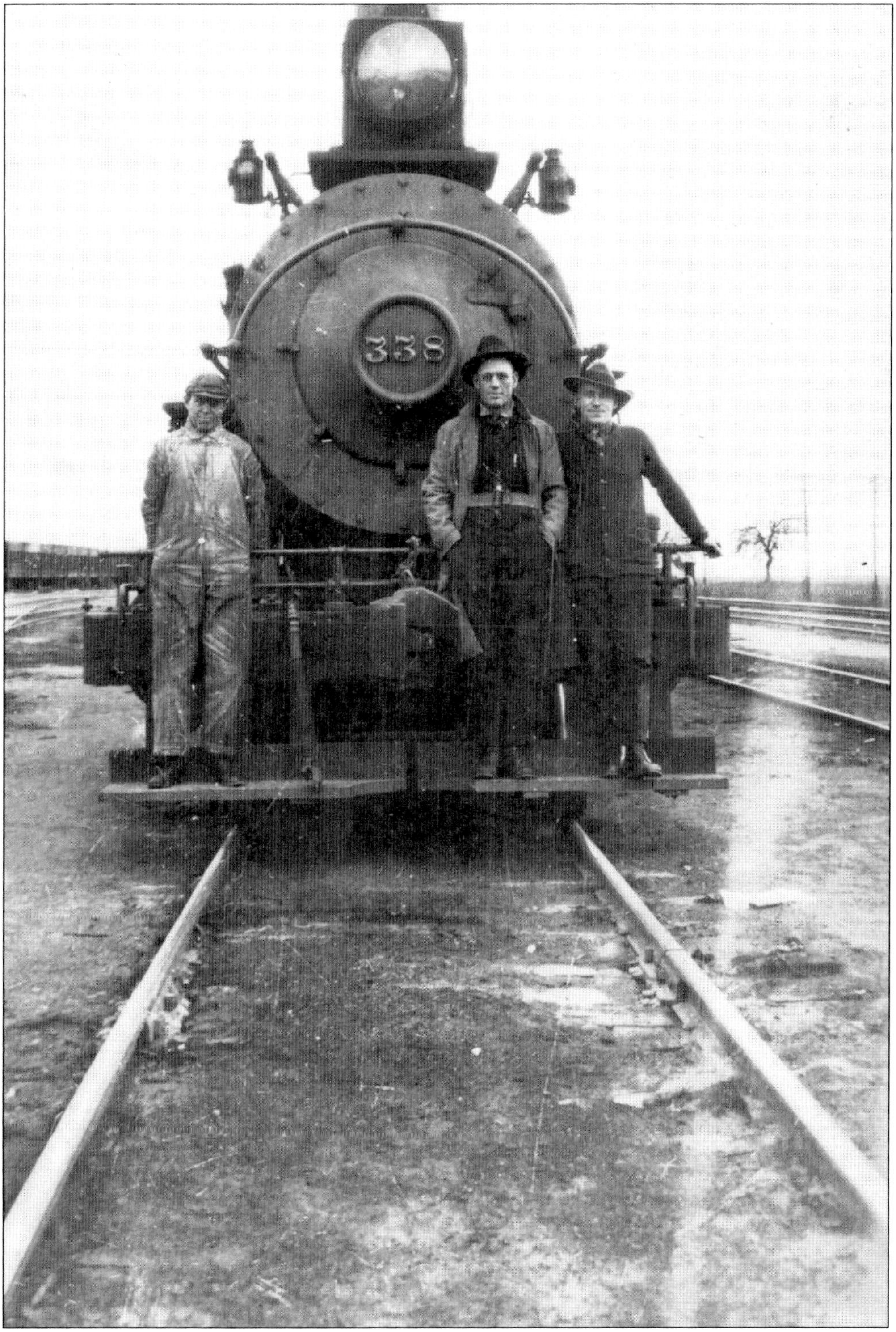

Pictured here is engine no. 338 with its three-man crew. The engine was used as a switching train in the Riverbank yard.

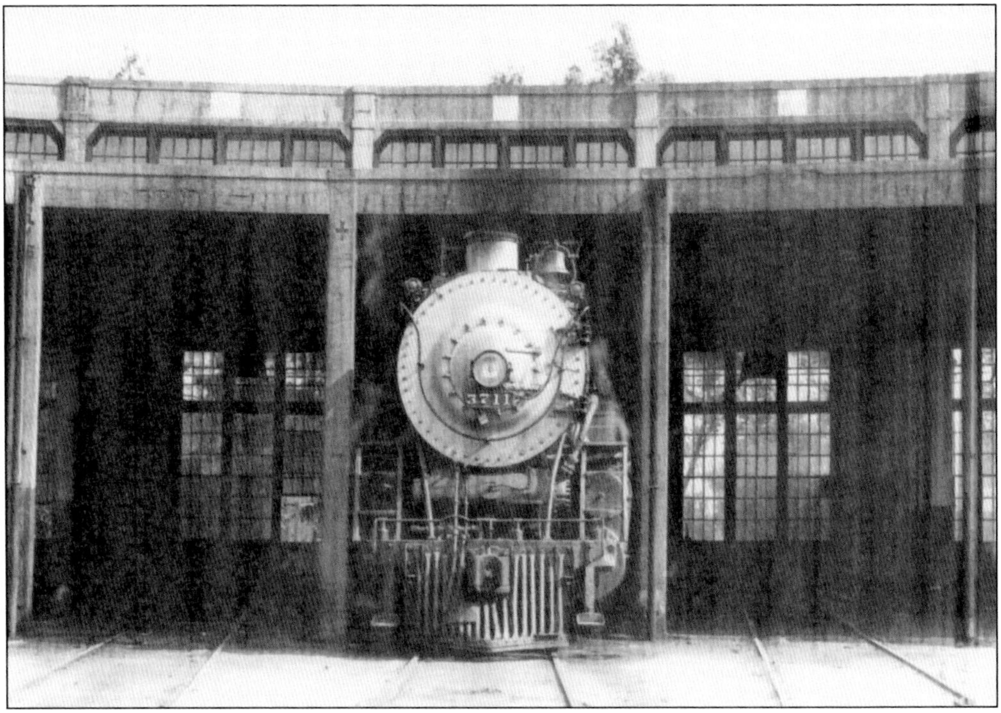

The roundhouse held up to 14 trains in a semicircular pattern, and no train left the terminal stop without being fully inspected. If problems were found, the train did not leave Riverbank. This picture shows engine no. 3711 leaving the roundhouse.

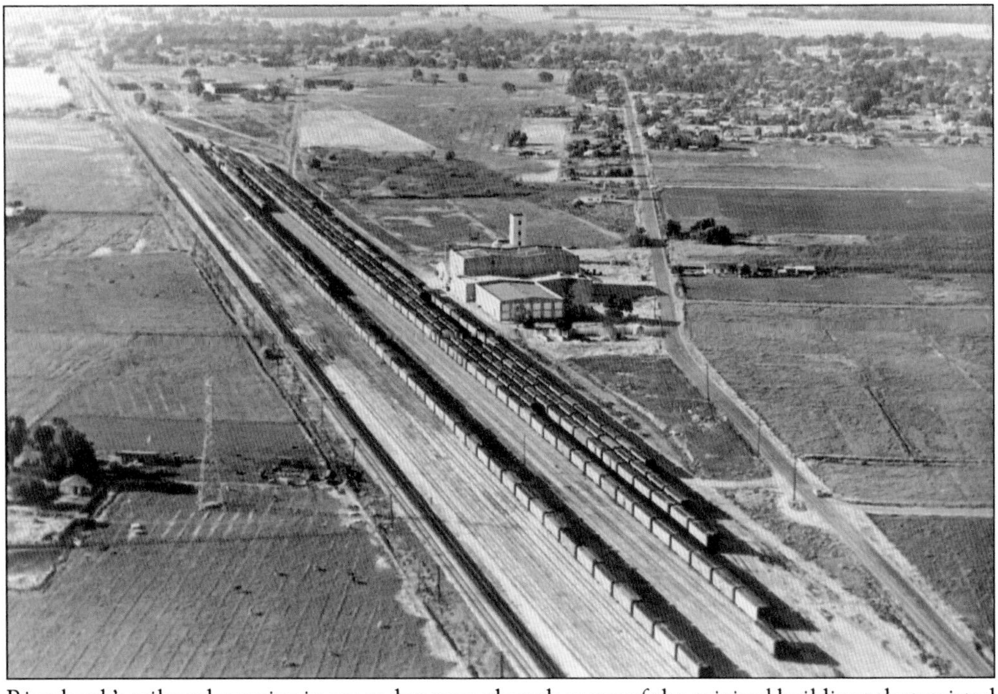

Riverbank's rail yard remains in use today, even though many of the original buildings that existed in its beginning are now gone.

Up until World War II, the Riverbank Station was on Talbot Avenue, situated on the east side of the tracks. During the war, it was moved closer to town and switched to the west side of the tracks. Today, the Riverbank Historical Society uses a train for its logo.

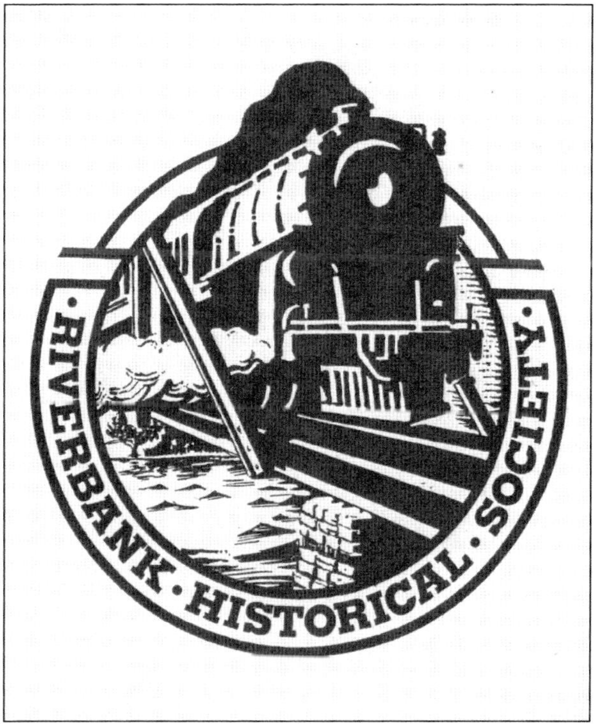

In 1916, the citizens of Riverbank realized how dangerous the crossing at the county road and railroad tracks was. In 1916, a road viaduct was built over the tracks. This view looks south, and in the background on the right-hand side of the viaduct, the Riverbank Cannery is visible.

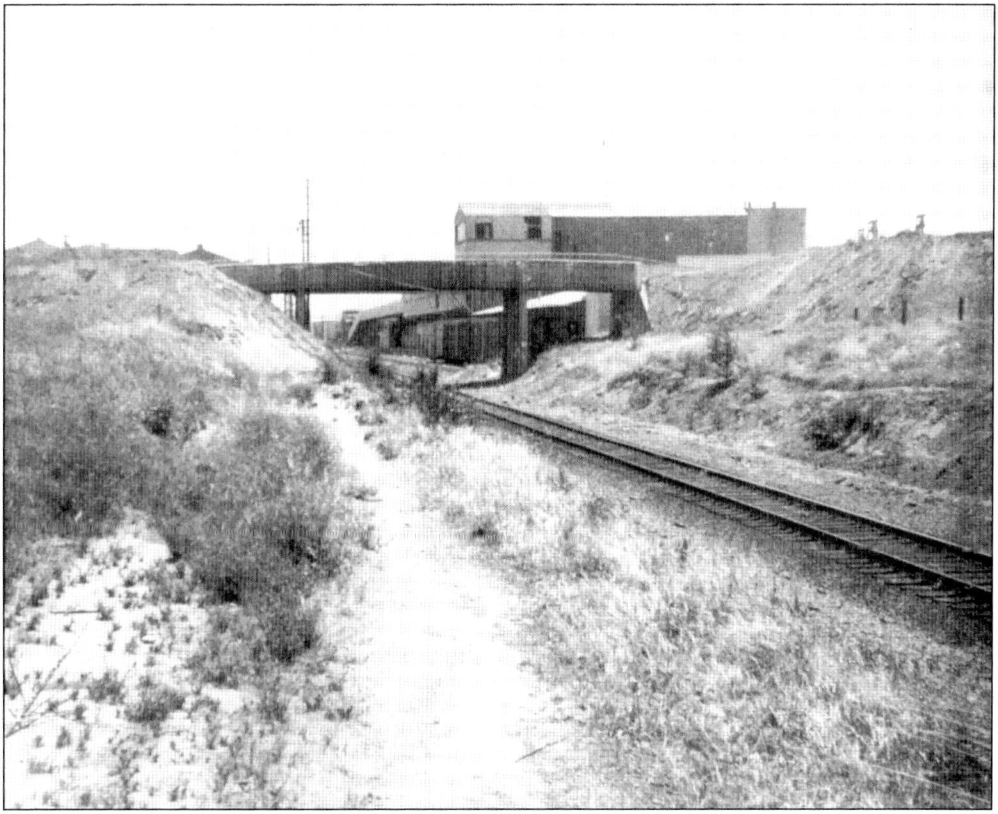

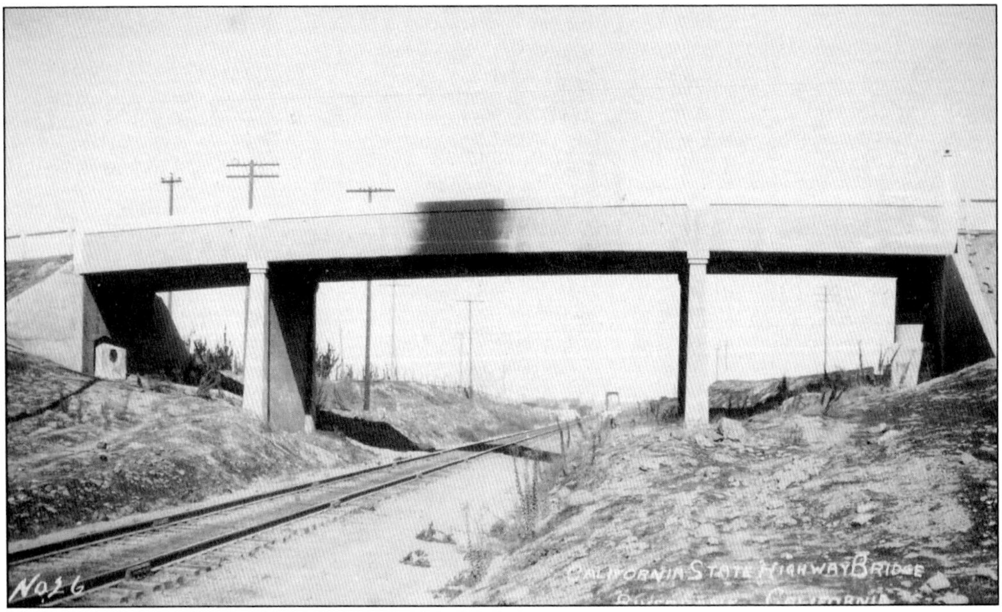

Sept. 1912

48 → SANTA FE EMPLOYES' MAGAZINE ←

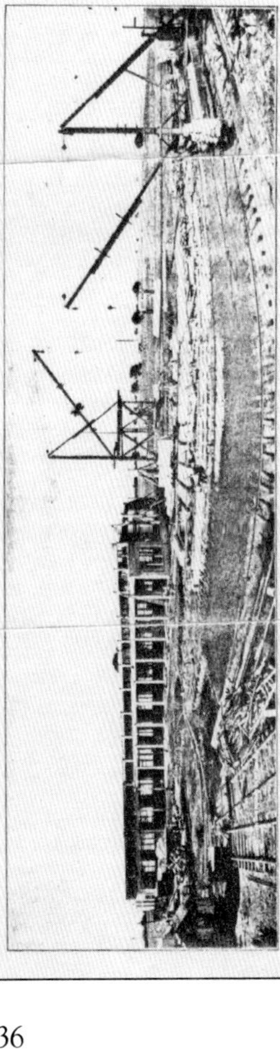

THE ROUNDHOUSE AND YARDS AT RIVERBANK, CAL.

A STURDY NEW TOWN

Over a barley field in the most bountiful part of the generous San Joaquin Valley of California a modern wizard waved the wand of a practical dreamer. That was a year ago.

Since then from the barley field has leaped a little city. It is neither a toadstool nor a mushroom, but a substantial real town with a purpose and a payroll. When the Santa Fe decided to make a new division point in the San Joaquin Valley it cast the spell of prosperity over this barley field and from it has risen Riverbank, a lusty youngster destined to have much money spent on it. Already $200,000 has been spent there by the road.

The big roundhouse of steel and cement is finished and engines are now being turned like clockwork. Twenty lines of business are represented, and the whole business situation is healthy. Only one complaint is made, and that is of the scarcity of business buildings and of homes. Recently a special meeting of the Riverbank Business Men's Association was addressed on this subject by Guy M. Rush, the Los Angeles real estate dealer who has had much to do in developing Riverbank and steps were taken to remedy the situation.

All the rich land surrounding Riverbank is to be given water enough to raise anything and everything, for, by a special ruling from the engineer in charge of the Oakdale irrigation district, canals and laterals through the Riverbank irrigated farms are to be surveyed immediately. The little farms under good cultivation and with plenty of water will produce nearly everything in the way of foodstuffs and fruit, and their development means a big traffic for Riverbank.

Riverbank eventually will have a $25,000 payroll each month from the railroad industry alone. In fact the present payroll is large and is increasing each month.

Just to show the spirit of the people in Riverbank this story is illuminating: They needed a church, and so all the able bodied men got together one day and by nightfall the church was built and finished with the first coat of paint. Now the church is completed and in use.

Here is an image of the completed concrete viaduct. Even after its construction, the area around the cannery and the switching yard was still dangerous. Often, children on their way to and from school would duck in between trains in the yard or near the cannery, which was very dangerous. Crossing the viaduct was not easily done either, as trains would blow their whistles right underneath one's feet. Many school lunches were lost as a result of being dropped in fear.

In 1912, the growing town of Riverbank had a population of over 400 people that mainly included railroad employees and their families. *Santa Fe Employees' Magazine* proudly advertises the new town and its fertile land, which was to be well irrigated by the water company. It also describes the industrious nature of the townspeople, who practically built a Methodist church overnight.

The town of Riverbank was designed by surveyors and engineers and was somewhat unique in its design. The city was laid out in a north-to-south grid pattern. This is contrary to the majority of towns on the Santa Fe line, which are laid out in an east-to-west pattern.

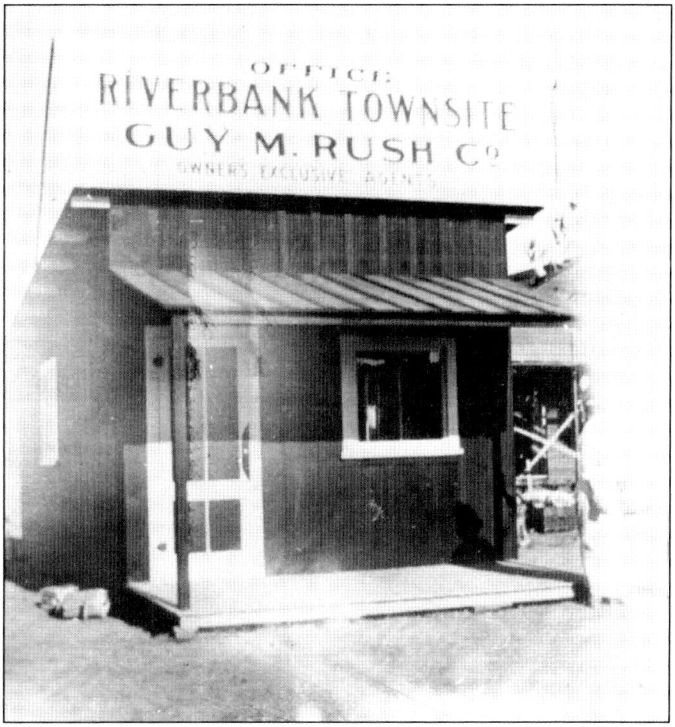

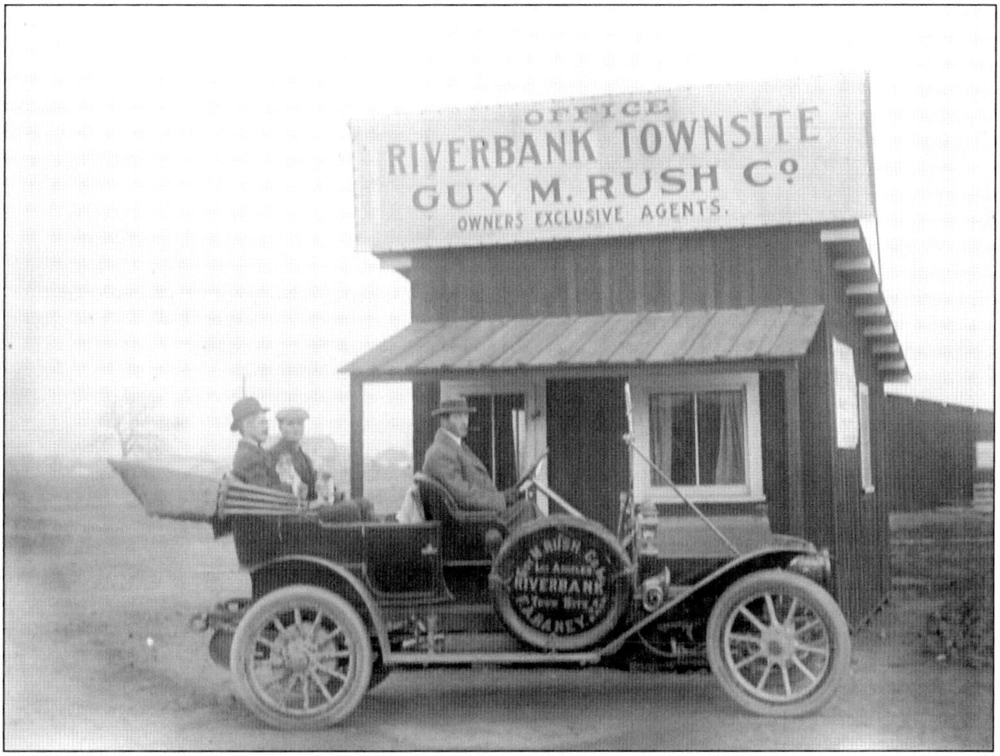

Guy M. Rush had a touring car to carry potential land buyers around the area of Riverbank. His name and business information can be seen on the cover for the spare tire in this image.

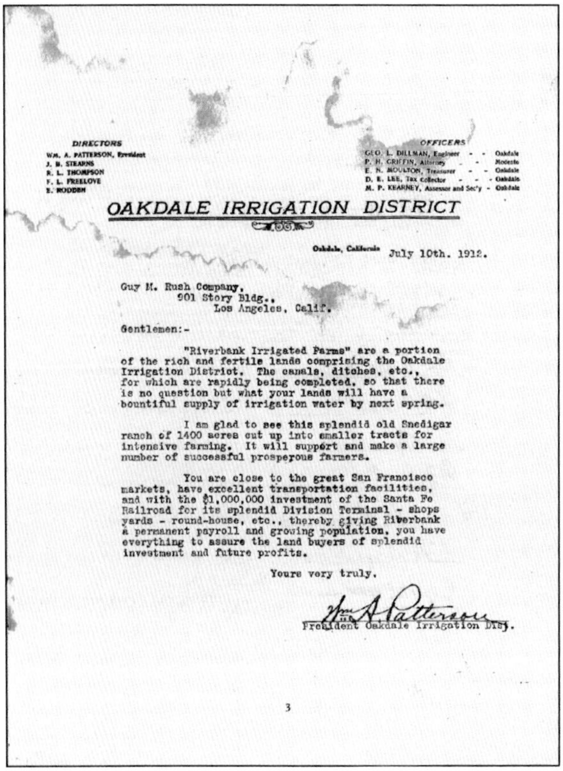

DIRECTORS
Wm. A. PATTERSON, President
J. B. STEARNS
R. L. THOMPSON
F. L. FREELOVE
E. RODDEN

OFFICERS
GEO. L. DILLMAN, Engineer - - Oakdale
P. H. GRIFFIN, Attorney - - Modesto
E. N. MOULTON, Treasurer - - Oakdale
D. E. LEE, Tax Collector - - - Oakdale
M. P. KEARNEY, Assessor and Sec'y - Oakdale

OAKDALE IRRIGATION DISTRICT

Oakdale, California July 10th. 1912.

Guy M. Rush Company,
901 Story Bldg.,
Los Angeles, Calif.

Gentlemen:-

"Riverbank Irrigated Farms" are a portion of the rich and fertile lands comprising the Oakdale Irrigation District. The canals, ditches, etc., for which are rapidly being completed, so that there is no question but what your lands will have a bountiful supply of irrigation water by next spring.

I am glad to see this splendid old Snedigar ranch of 1400 acres cut up into smaller tracts for intensive farming. It will support and make a large number of successful prosperous farmers.

You are close to the great San Francisco markets, have excellent transportation facilities, and with the $1,000,000 investment of the Santa Fe Railroad for its splendid Division Terminal - shops yards - round-house, etc., thereby giving Riverbank a permanent payroll and growing population, you have everything to assure the land buyers of splendid investment and future profits.

Yours very truly,

Wm. A. Patterson
President Oakdale Irrigation Dist.

3

A letter from the Oakdale Irrigation District expounds upon the well-watered region around Riverbank. Rush also collected letters from local residents stating how well their crops grew to entice people from far away to relocate to the new, growing town.

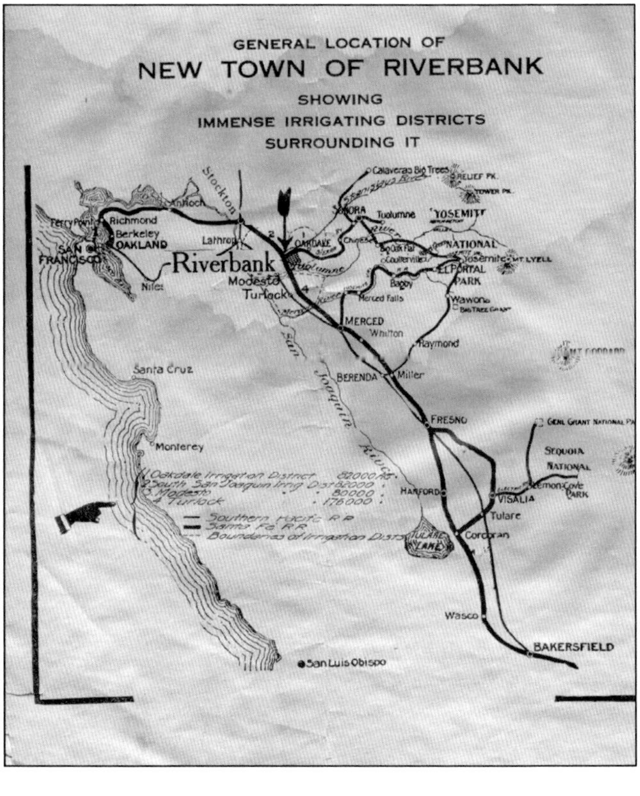

This map gives an idea of the general location of Riverbank to other surrounding cities and sites.

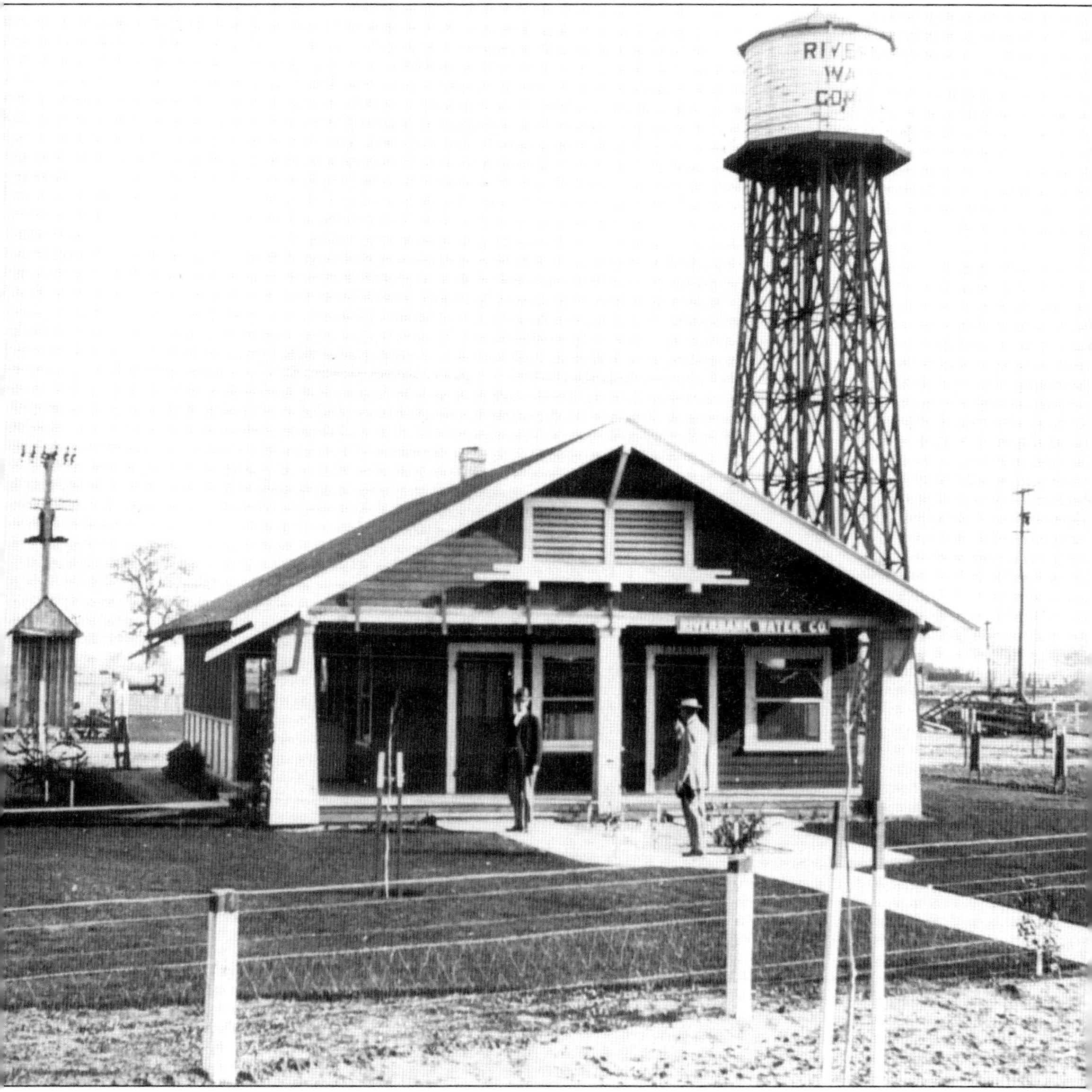

The Riverbank Water Company stood beside Guy M. Rush's office. The first water tower was replaced in 1931. The building is now a residence.

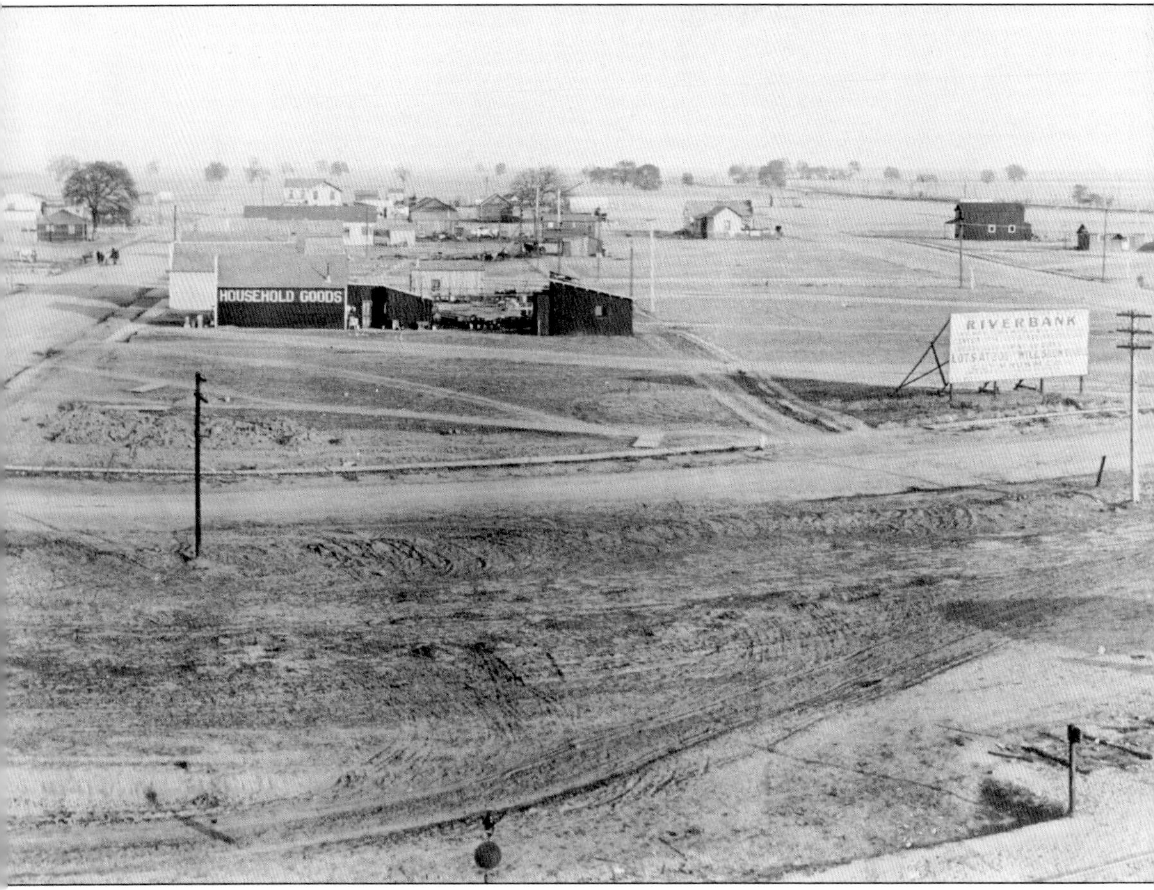

In this picture, which was taken on December 10, 1912, a sign can be seen advertising tracts for sale in Riverbank. The town stood in the center of 160,000 acres of fully irrigated land that sold for $200 a lot through the Guy M. Rush Company.

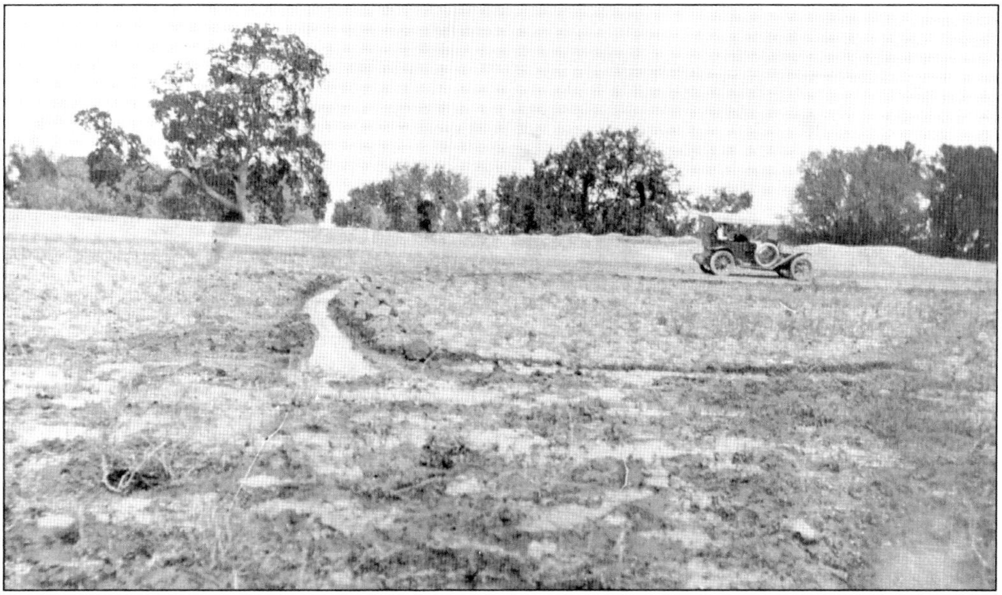

The center of lot 132 looks north toward the Stanislaus River from the 3800 block of Topeka Street between Claus and Eighth Streets. Irrigation water is being delivered left of center. Lot owner Berg's car can be seen in the distance on a warm August day in 1913.

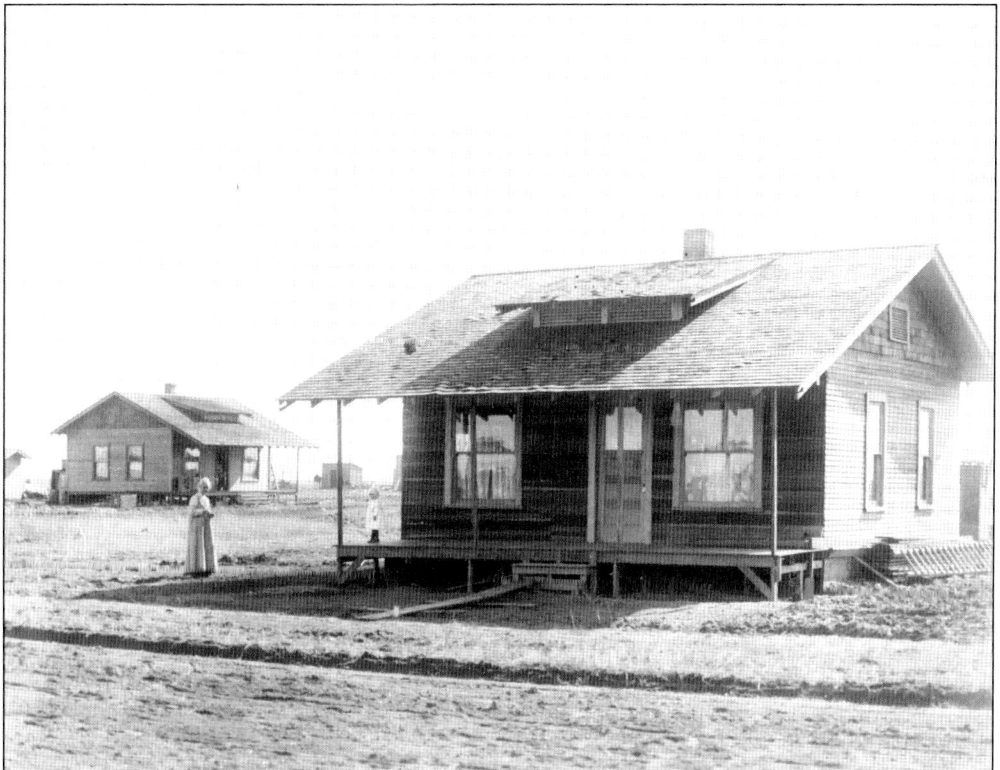

Homes on the west side of town, built mainly for the railroad workers, were often small and similar in their style. In the 1920s and 1930s, most small lots could be bought for a sum of around $1,800.

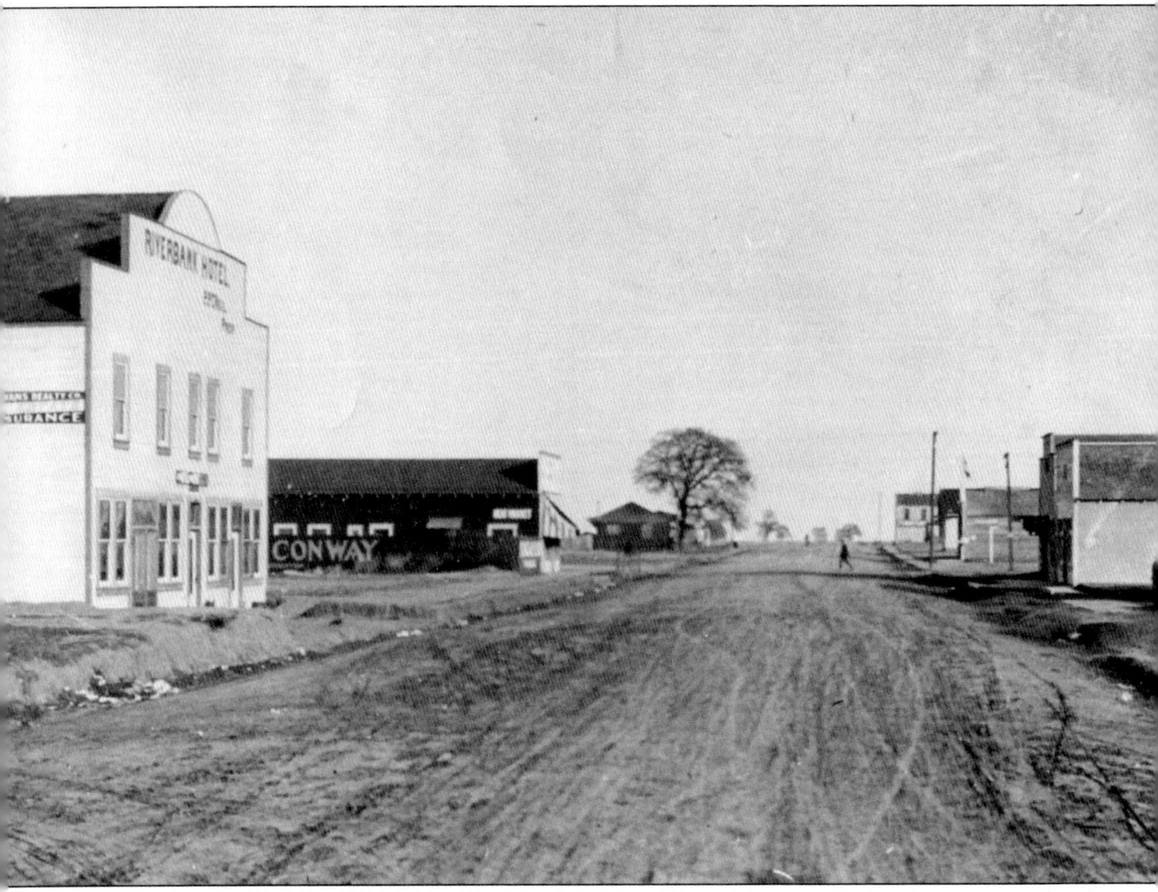

Naturally, not every worker on the railroad could afford to buy a lot to build a house upon. Riverbank also needed places to stay for those who were just passing through the town, whether for business or pleasure, as well as boardinghouses and apartments. The Riverbank Hotel, pictured at left, built about 1912, was once a highly regarded place to stay while travelling through Riverbank. When it was torn down, any salvageable lumber, the windows, and door frames were all used to construct a home on the southwest corner of Santa Fe Avenue and Claus Road.

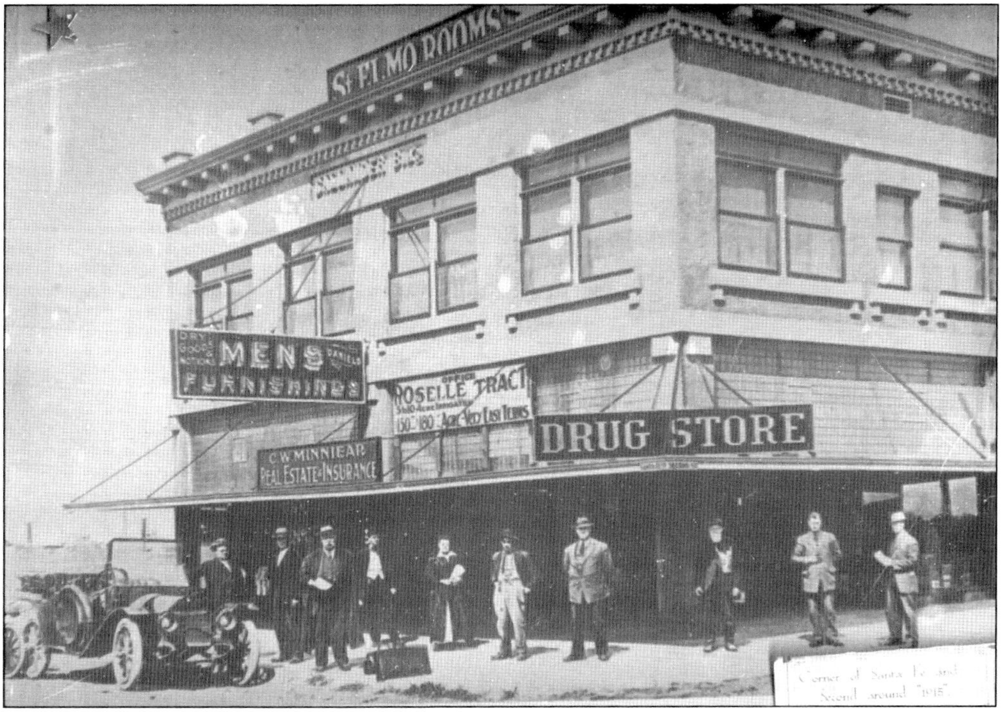

The Callander Building was constructed in 1912 and stood on the corner of Second Street and Santa Fe Avenue. Its first floor contained a drugstore, Daniels Dry Goods and Notions, a real estate office, and an insurance office. The St. Elmo Hotel, run by a Mrs. Scheela, was on the second floor.

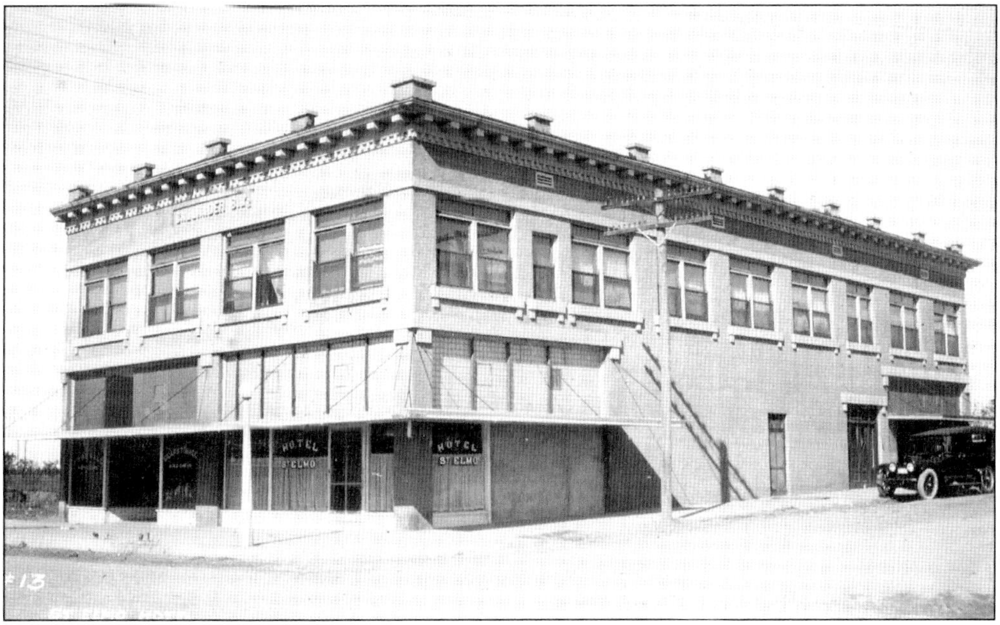

Here is a full view of the Callander Building. Over time, the building's windows have been gradually blocked up. It is presently being used as the Masonic lodge, but none of the original windows remains.

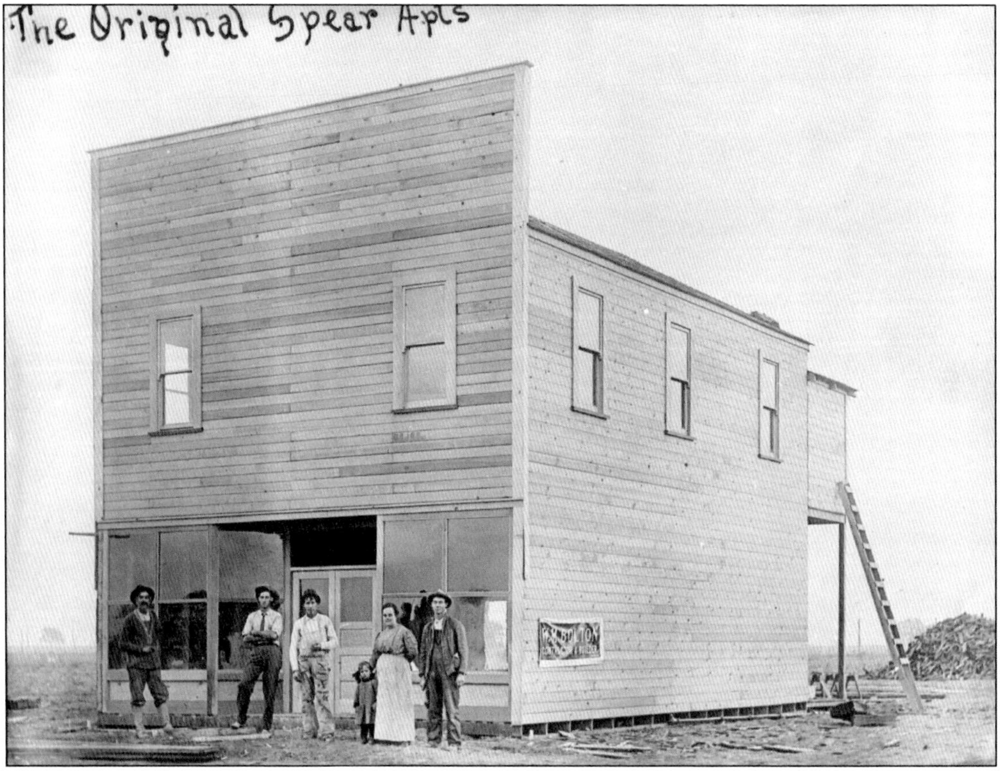

The Spears Apartments were one of the earliest places in town to stay. The building was constructed by W.M. Bolton to house railroad workers.

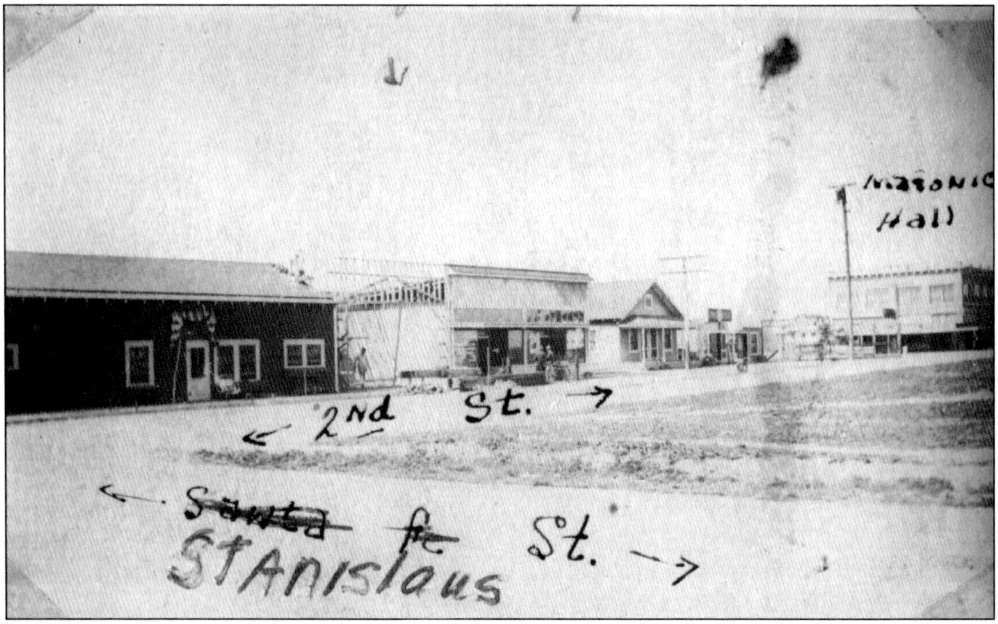

The Jackson family owned not only a boardinghouse but also an insurance office next door and a hardware business down the street. The building being constructed in this picture is a candy shop also owned by the Jacksons.

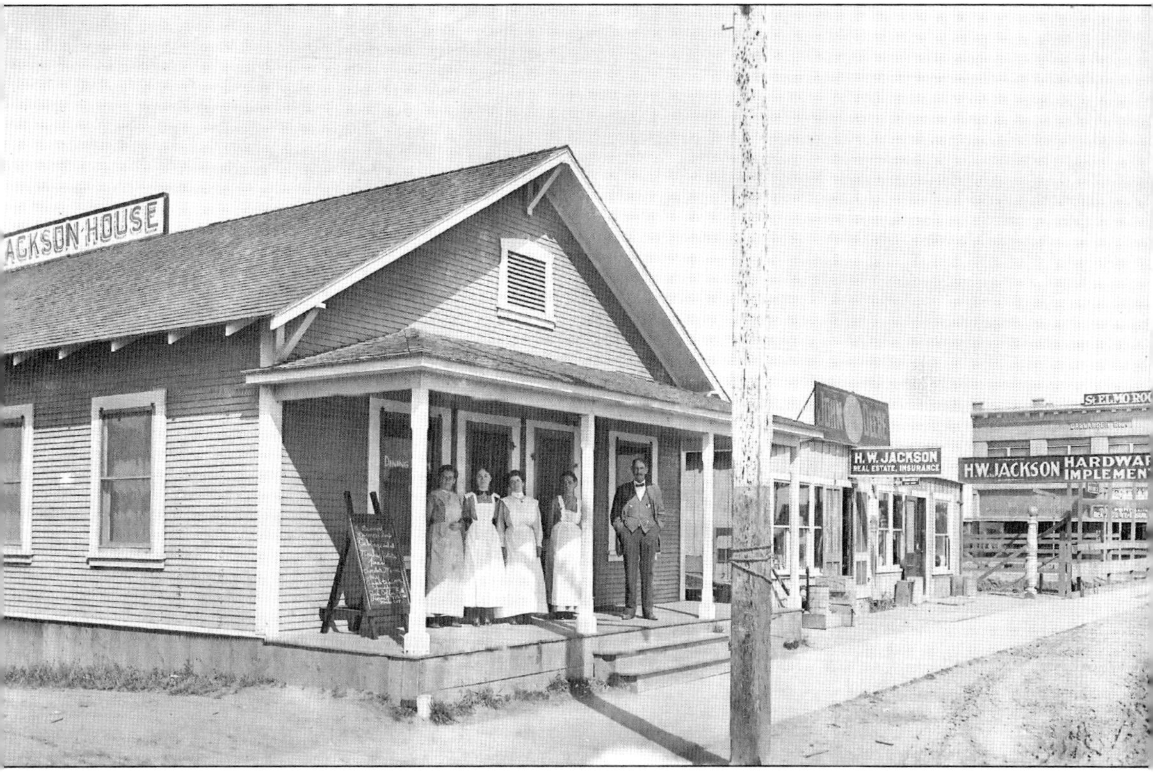

The Jackson Boarding House also contained a restaurant. In 1913, the Jacksons lost the property, along with other businesses, due to a raging fire.

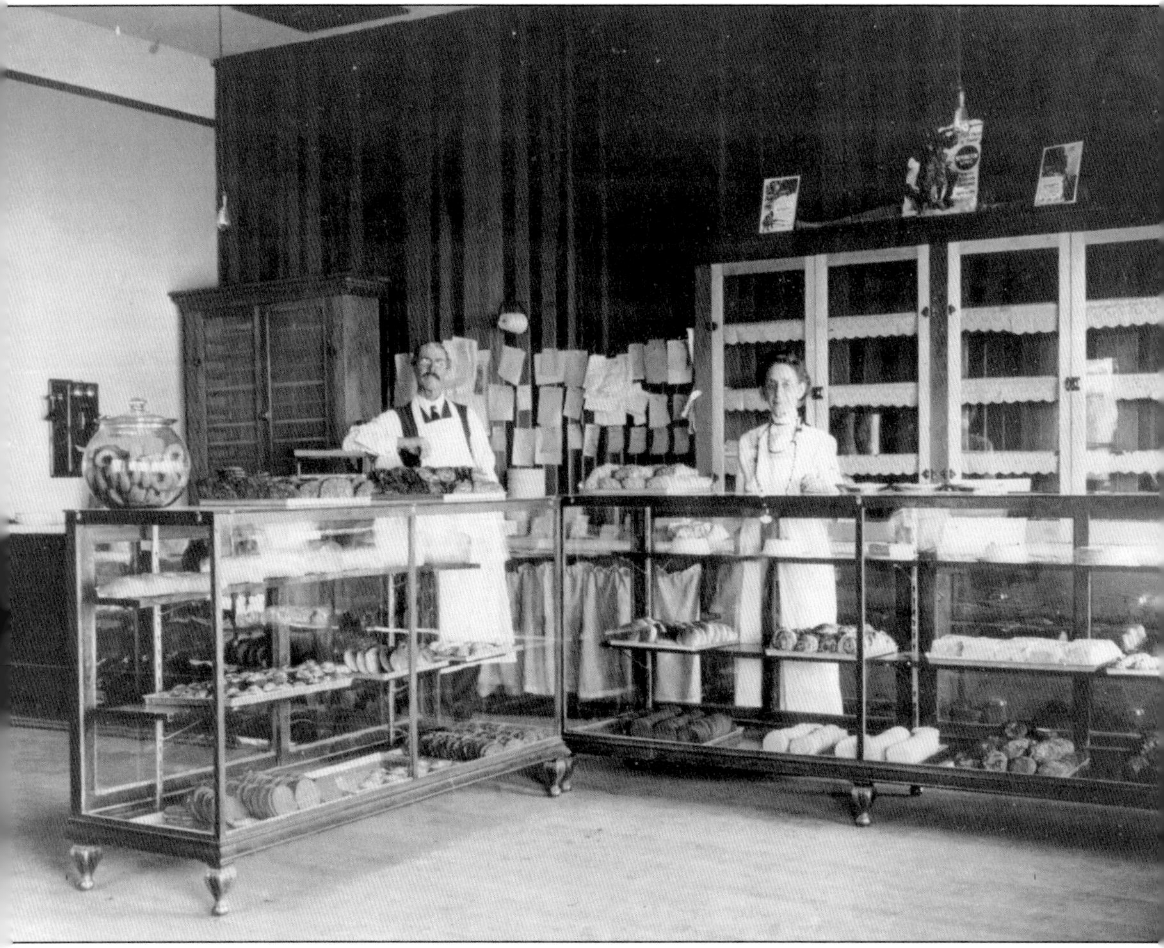

Many people remember stopping by the Jackson Bakery on their way home from school. When they asked Alice Jackson if they could have a treat, she would respond, "Only if you have been good!" Some desired the baked sweets and candies while others craved the freshly baked, buttered bread.

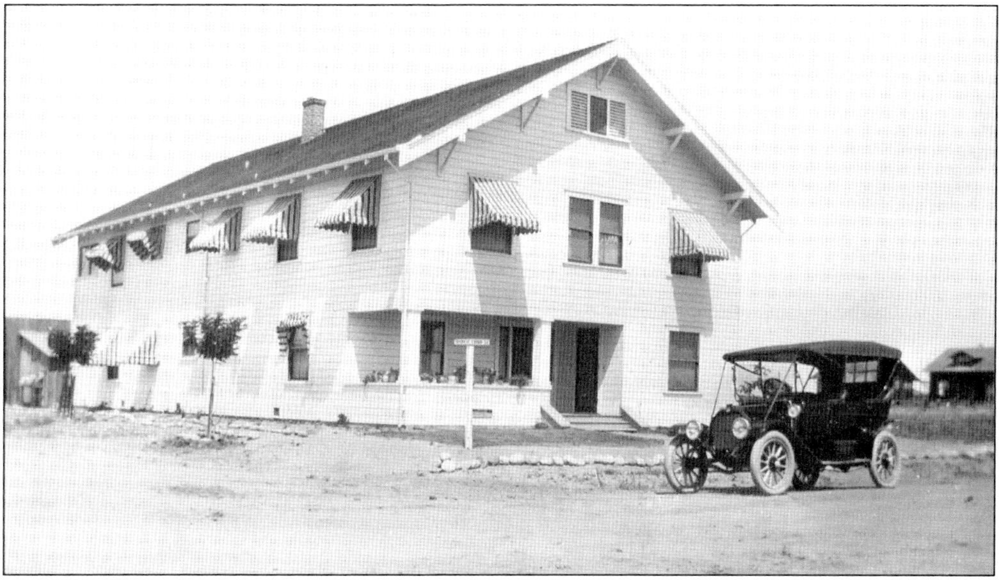

Those who were high up in the railroad hierarchy might have chosen to stay at the Ditman Apartments, which were constructed in 1913 on the corner of Third and Topeka Streets. Bed linens were changed on a daily basis, and the lodging featured electricity as well as carved mahogany furniture. The front porch shown in this picture was later enclosed after the building was bought by the Snyder family. George Wesley Ditman's Hupmobile is shown in front of the building on Third Street.

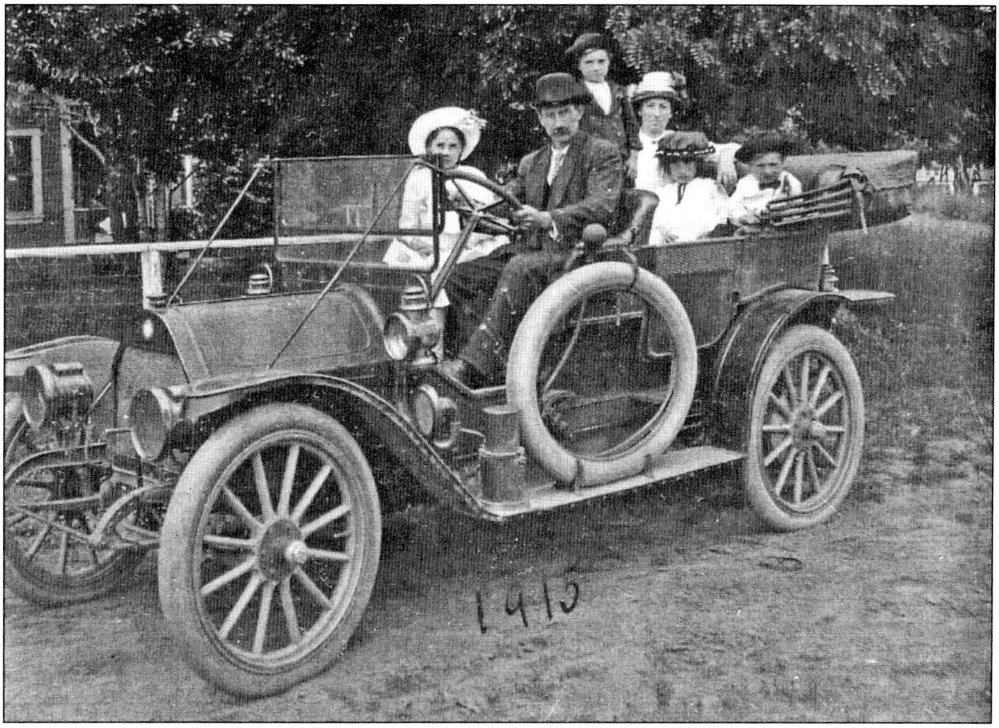

The driver of this vehicle is George Wesley Ditman, owner and builder of the apartments. The other people in the picture are unidentified but could be either Ditman or Fisher relatives.

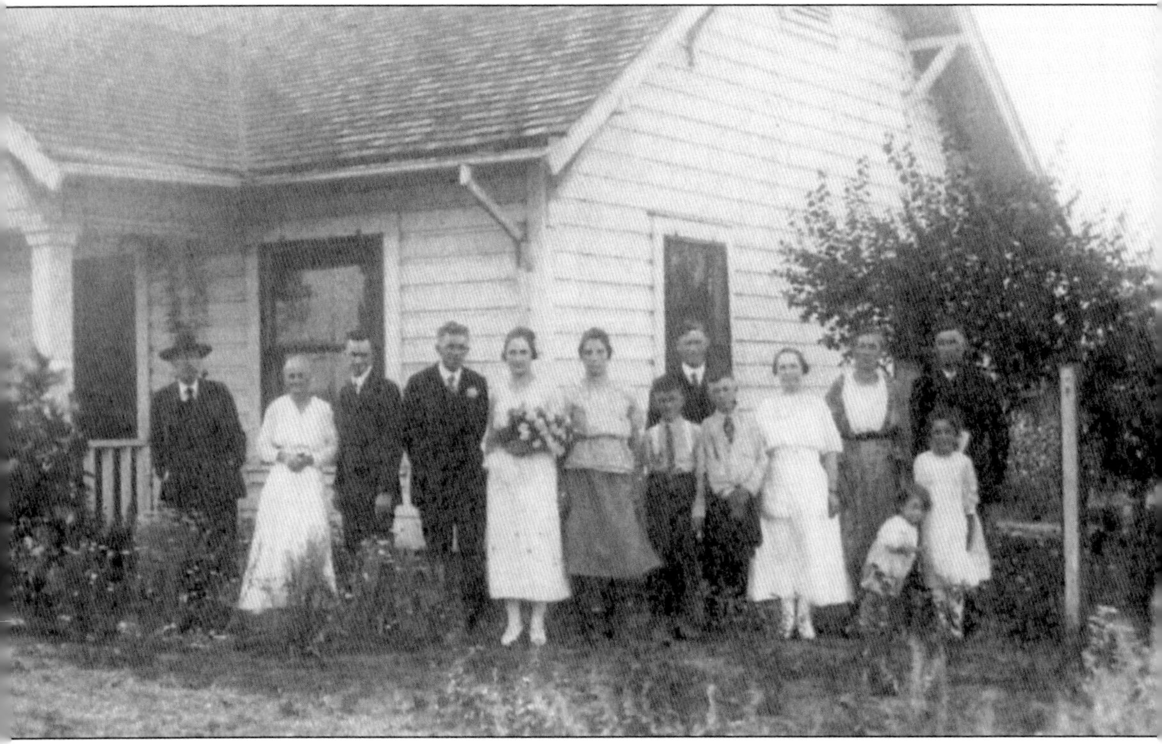

In 1920, the Ditman family and the Harris family were joined in marriage. The Harrises are well known in the area for running a photography studio.

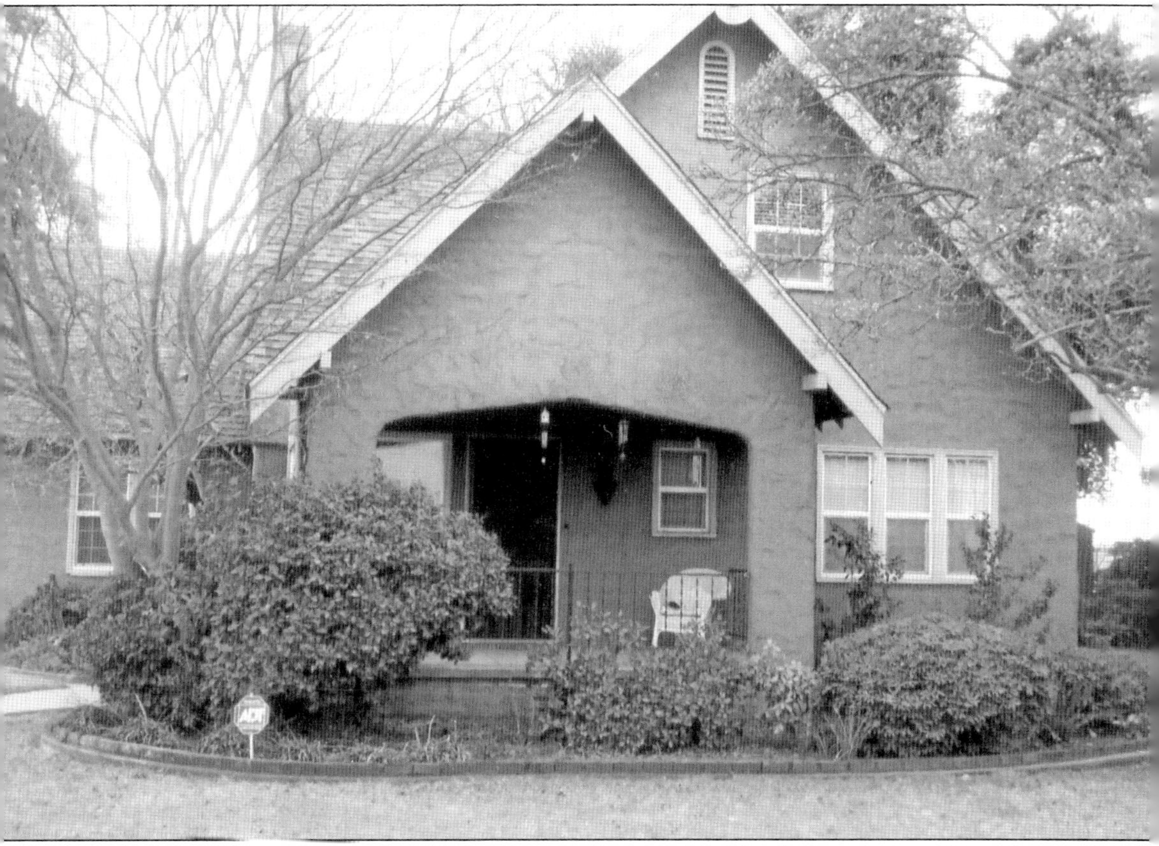

Gerald Staley, who owned the home above, was a judge in Riverbank during the 1950s, when city hall was on the corner of Third Street and Santa Fe Avenue.

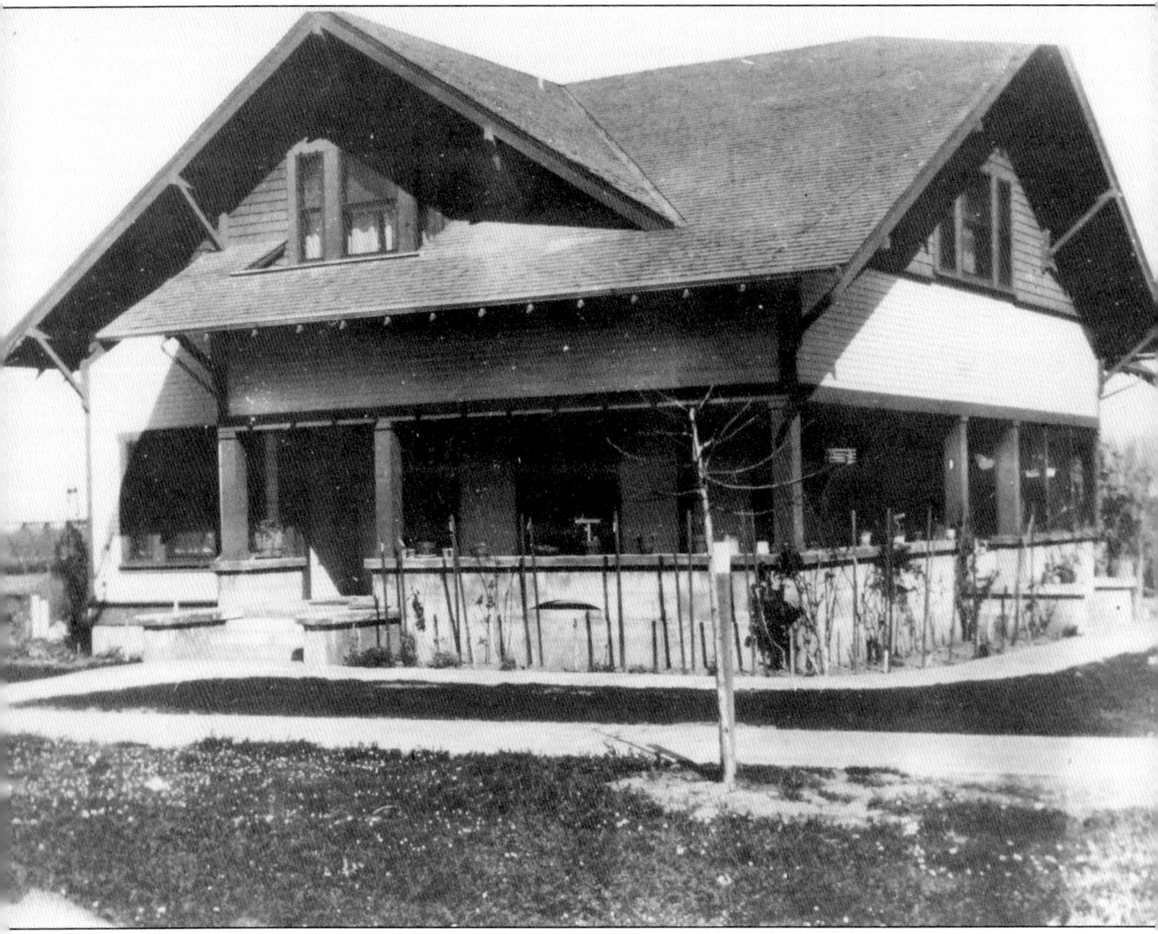

Hans Harder built the house pictured here by himself. It had a fireplace in every bedroom and a boiler in the basement, which Harder had built with his own hands. The valve on the boiler had to be turned off on occasion by Hans to avoid a buildup of pressure. He used to park in the same spot by the bank when he came downtown, so everyone knew when he was around.

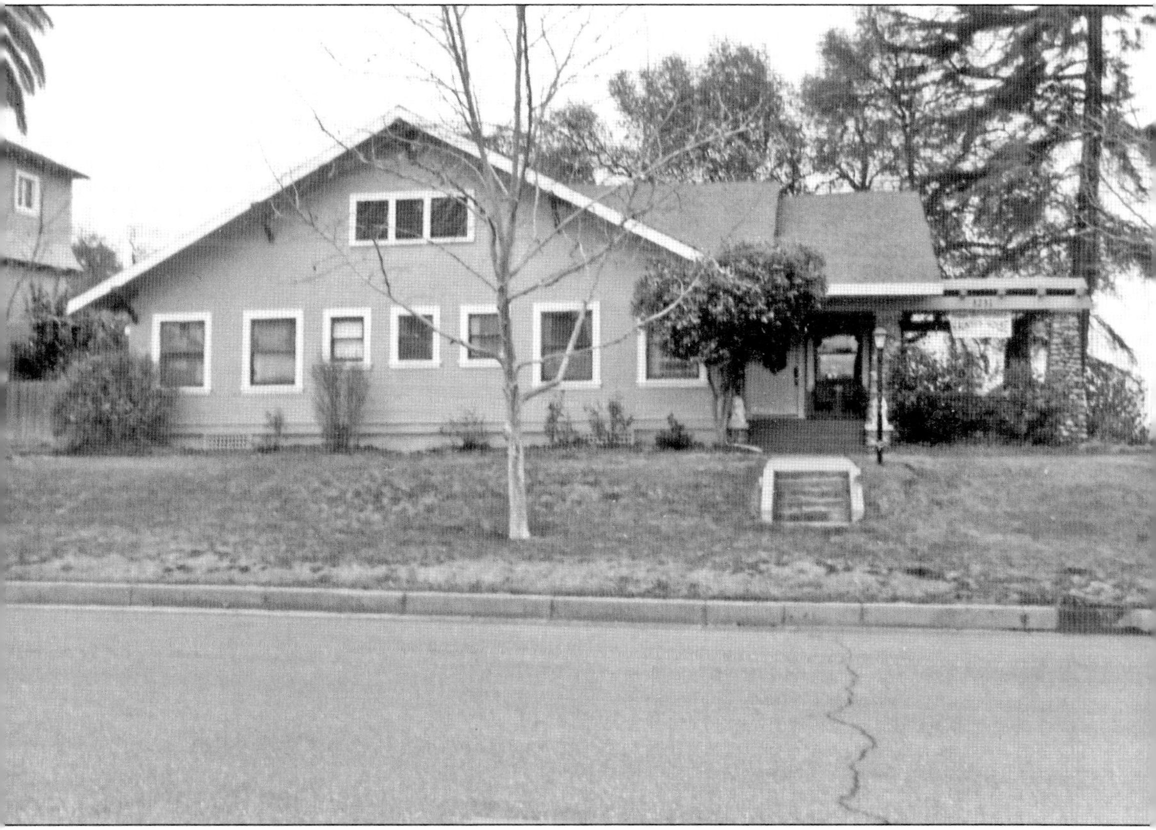

This home on Riverside Drive, originally owned by a railroad superintendent by the name of Sanjule, was built in 1912. Later, the home was owned by Felix Raney. The home is well known for being haunted; it is one of four houses in Riverbank known for its paranormal activity. Another well-known house rumored to be haunted is the Zerillo Mansion. Two others houses stand along Topeka Street.

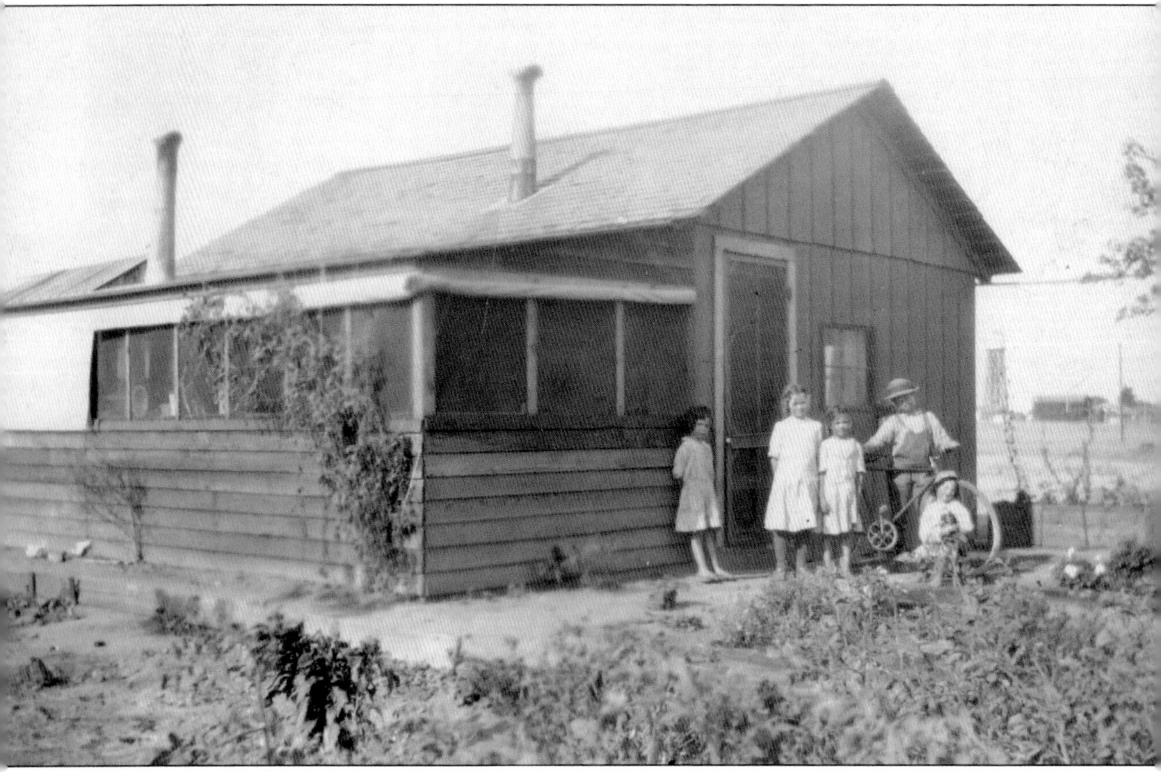

The Perrin family was regarded as important in early Riverbank. One of the family daughters, Vera, helped raise the first flag over the first school in the town. The Perrin children also established a tennis club.

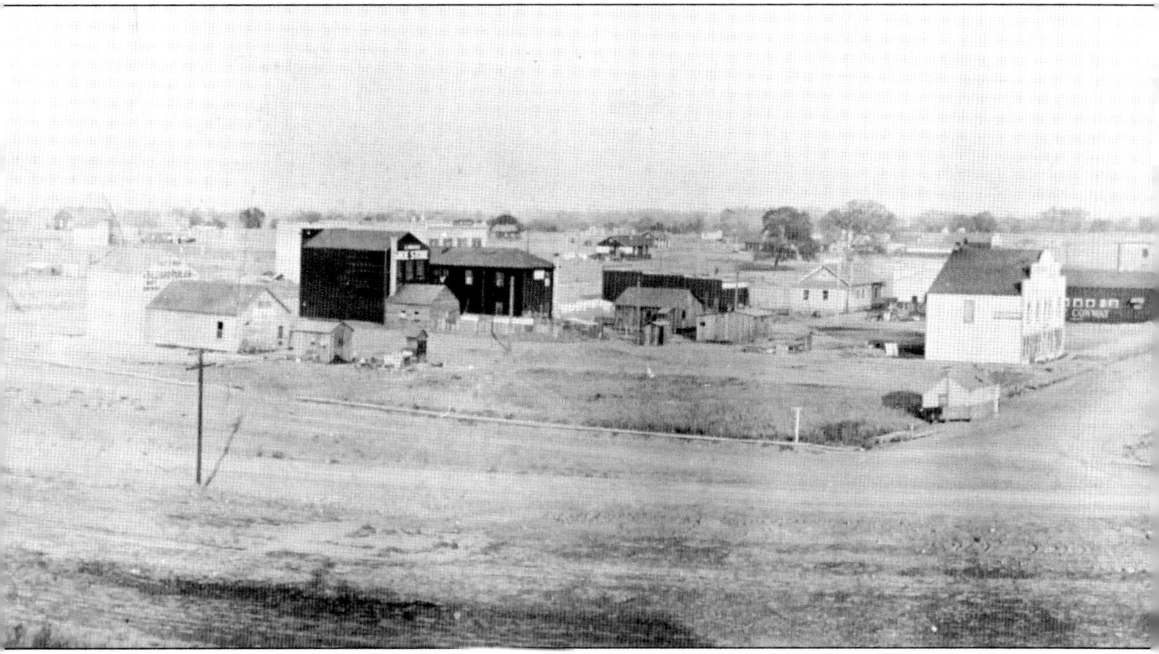

This early view of Riverbank shows the Riverbank Hotel, a shoe repair shop, and a billiard parlor.

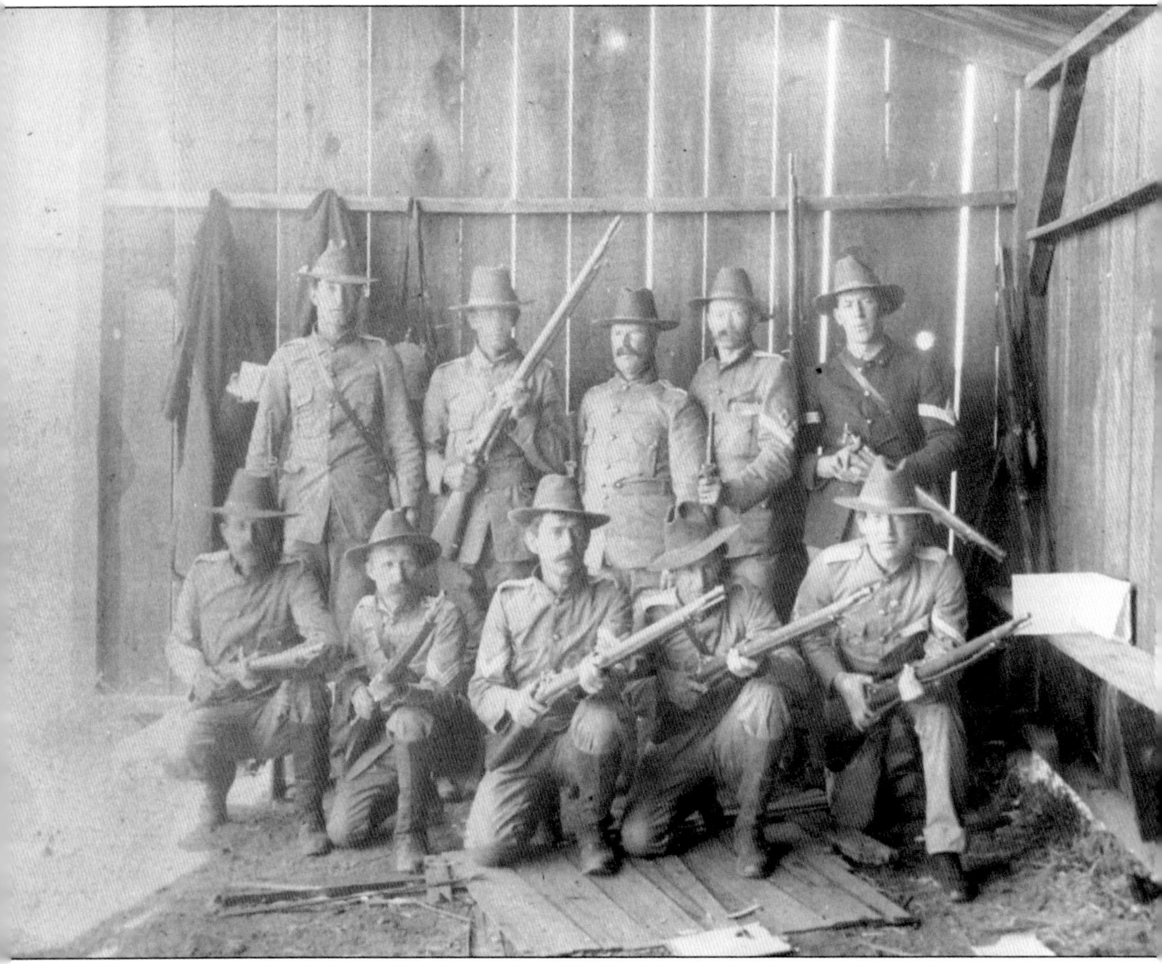

As in many towns across America in 1918, the peace and quiet of Riverbank was destroyed by war in Europe. Shown here are some of the brave men who went overseas to protect freedom in the States and Riverbank.

Three

THE BOOM OF BUSINESS

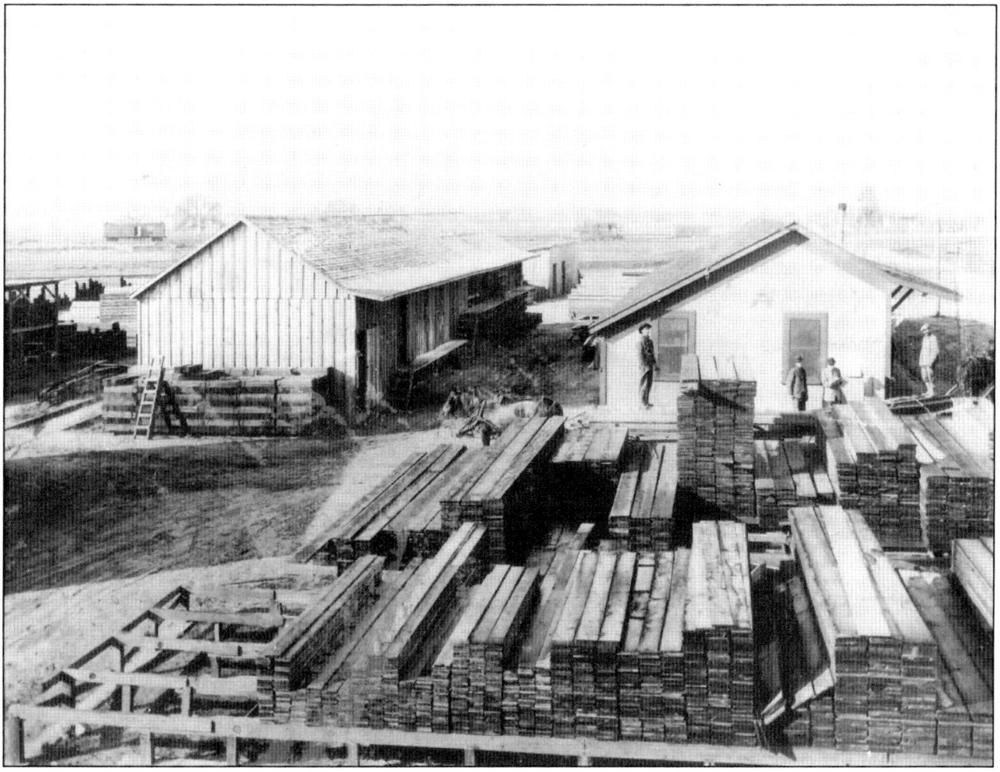

On July 3, 1911, the first load of lumber came into town; it was ordered through Riverbank Lumber Company, one of Riverbank's first businesses. The order was made by A.W. Jackson, who planned to open a restaurant. The lumberyard had steady business in the early years as homes, hotels, businesses, a water company, a bank, and other necessities were built and added to the new town.

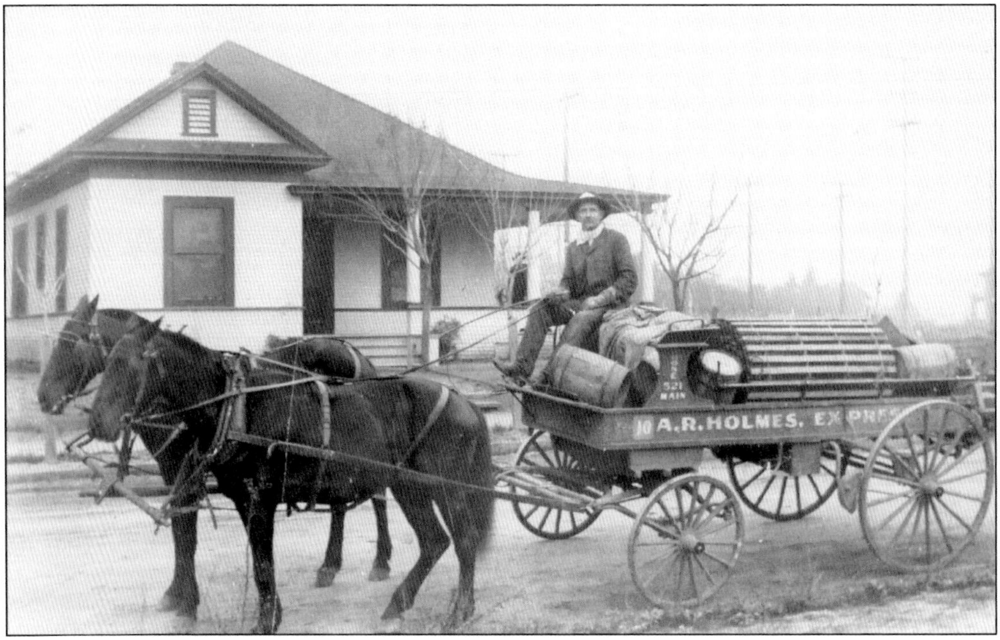

Once a lot was purchased and construction began, businesses such as A.R. Holmes's delivered goods to further enhance the comforts of the new home.

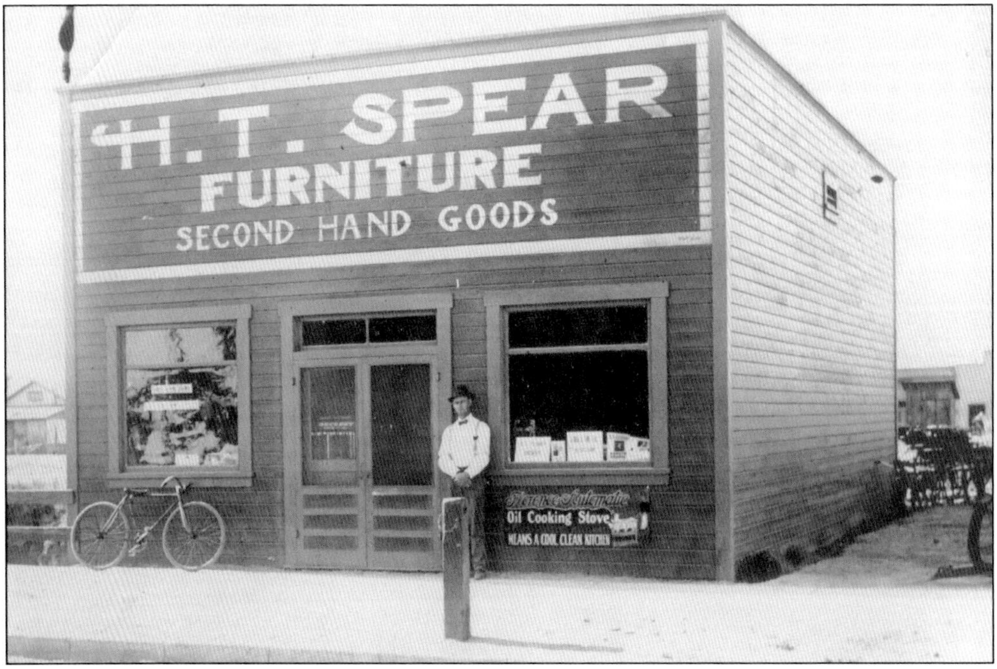

In addition to running apartments, the Spear family also ran a furniture store with some of the latest conveniences. On the front of the building is an advertisement for an oil cooking stove.

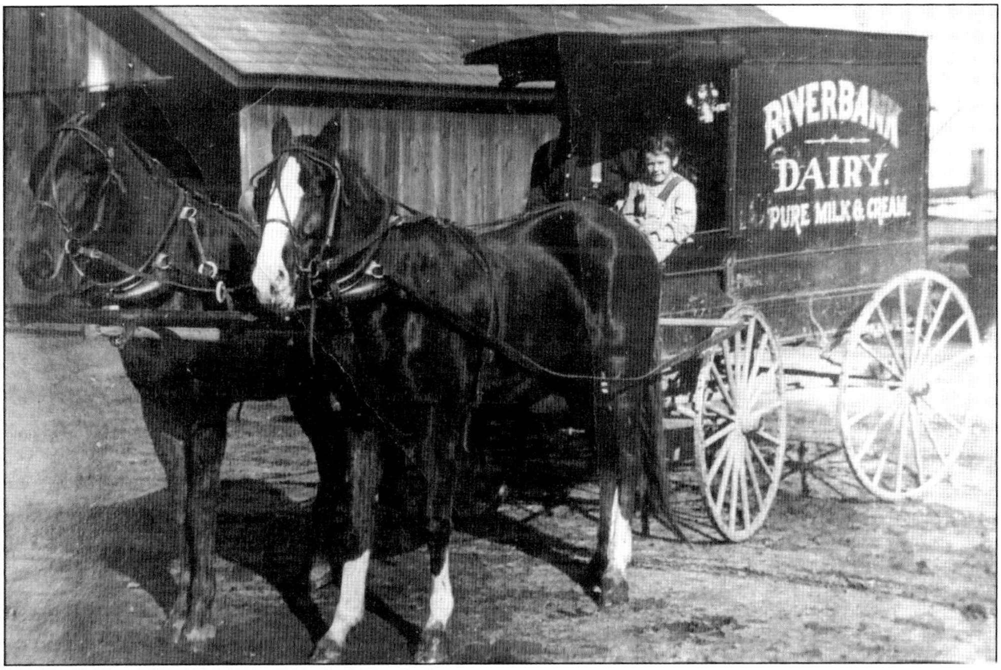

Myron Kline delivered milk from his dairy on the corner of Patterson and Coffee Roads in the early 1900s. His hat can just be seen under the cart's visor. The boy is Myron's son Pinky, who took over the business from his father later on. The Klines had another son named Arlo. Descendants of the family can still be found today in Riverbank.

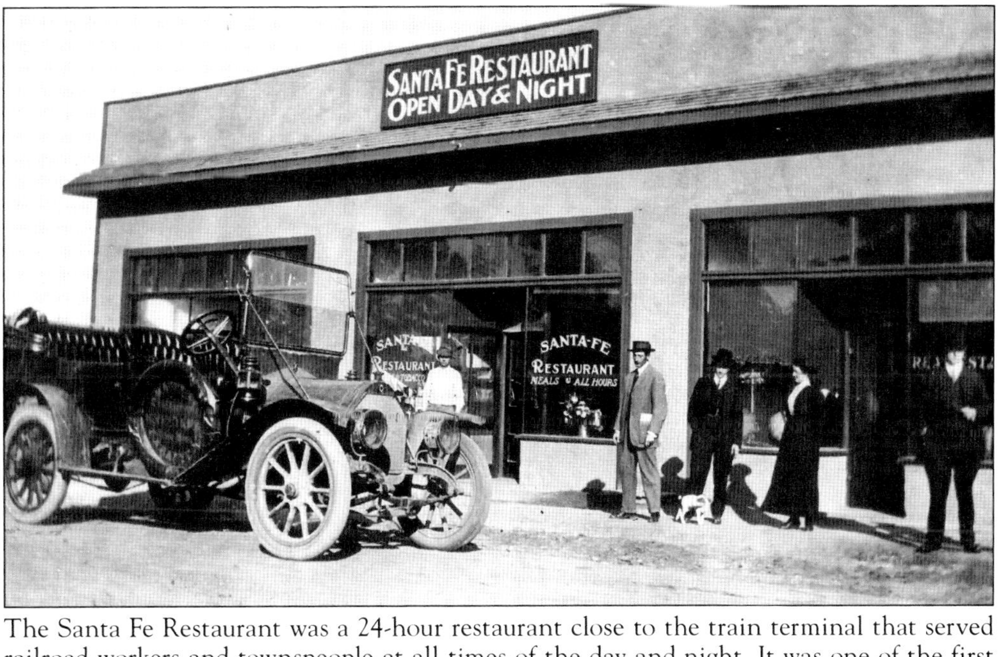

The Santa Fe Restaurant was a 24-hour restaurant close to the train terminal that served railroad workers and townspeople at all times of the day and night. It was one of the first businesses in town.

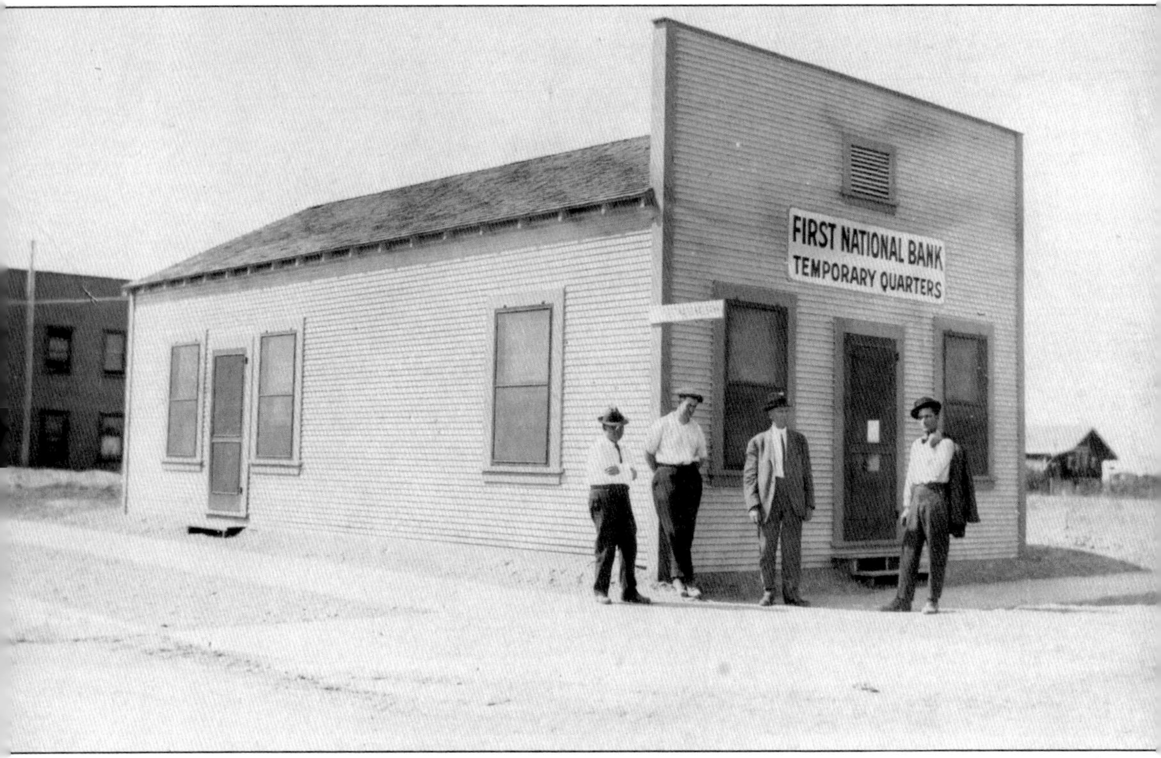

The first bank building is pictured here. The bank handled the railroad payroll, which amounted to $50,000.

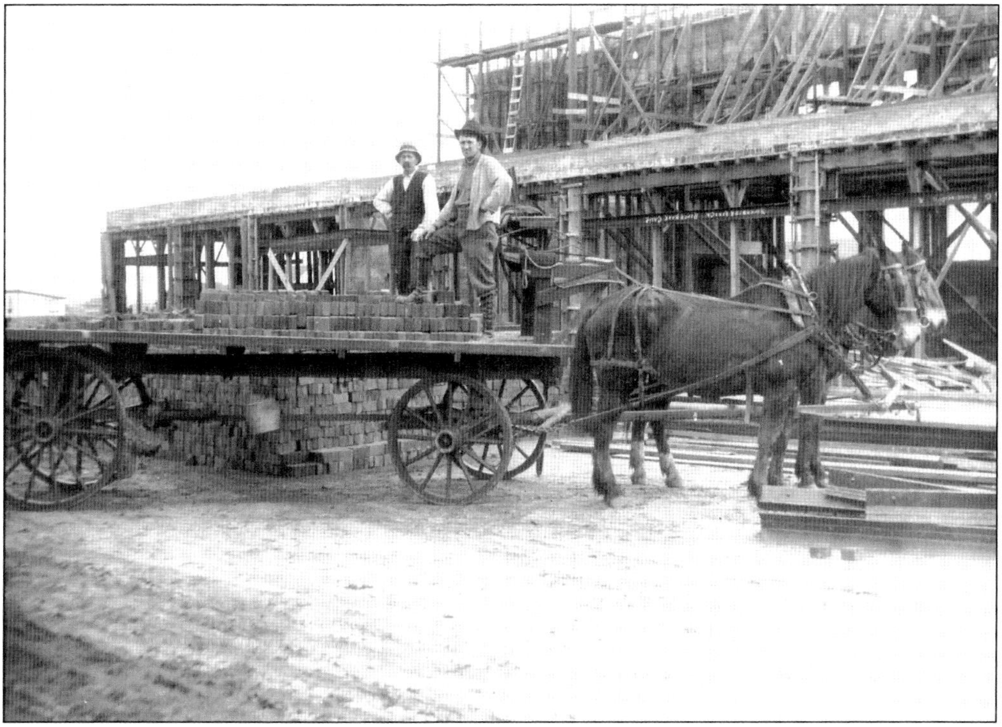

In 1913, a brand new brick bank building was constructed on the corner of Third Street and Santa Fe Avenue. The interior included marble columns, floor tiles, and fancy grillwork. Sadly, the bank president absconded with the bank's funds in 1927 and ran away to South America. His actions caused the bank to close.

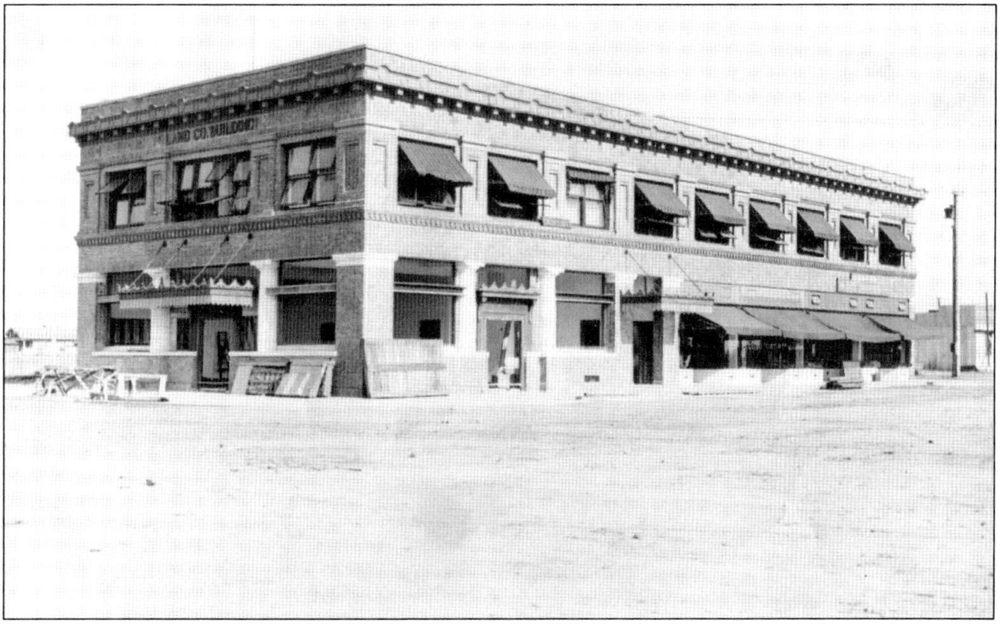

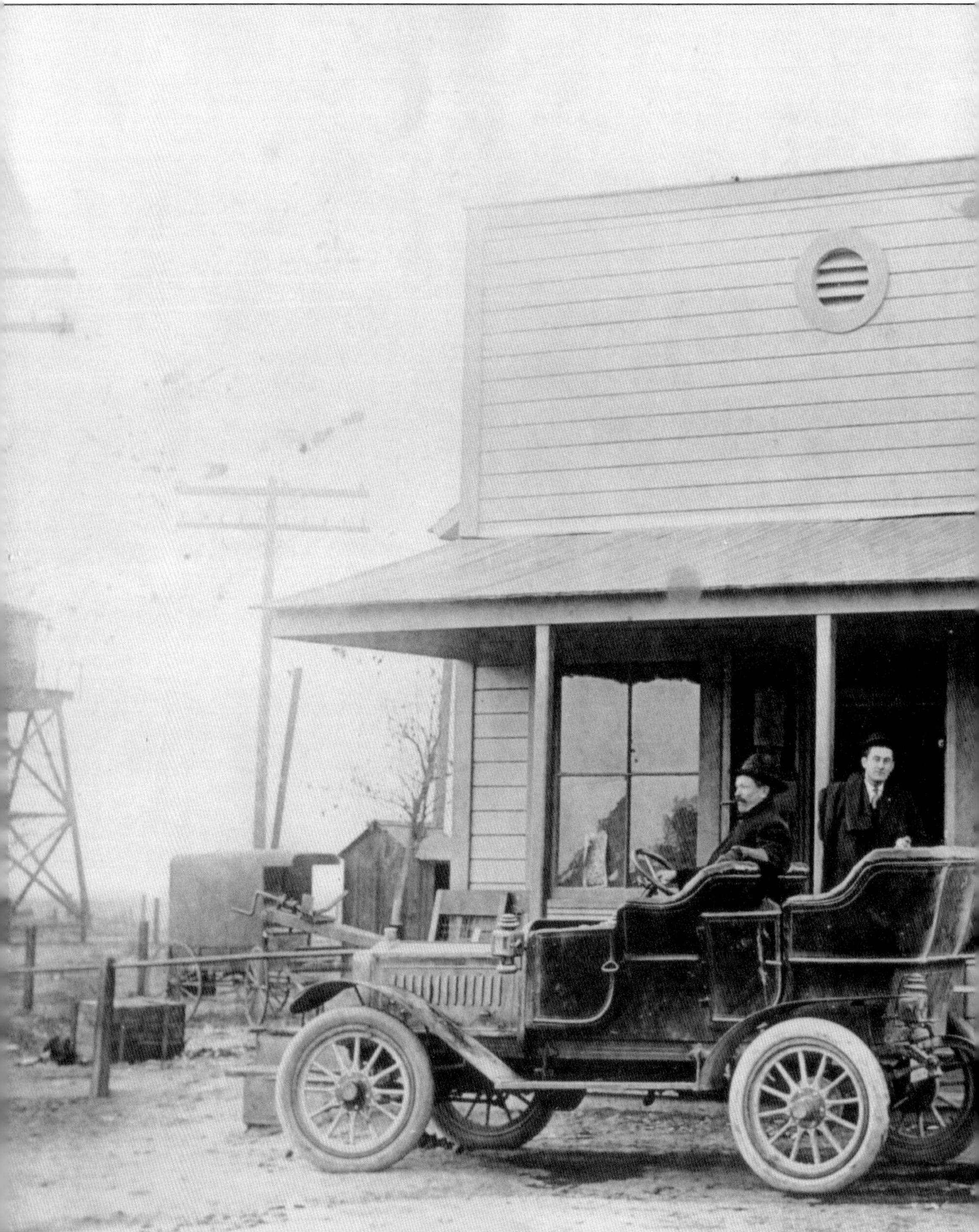

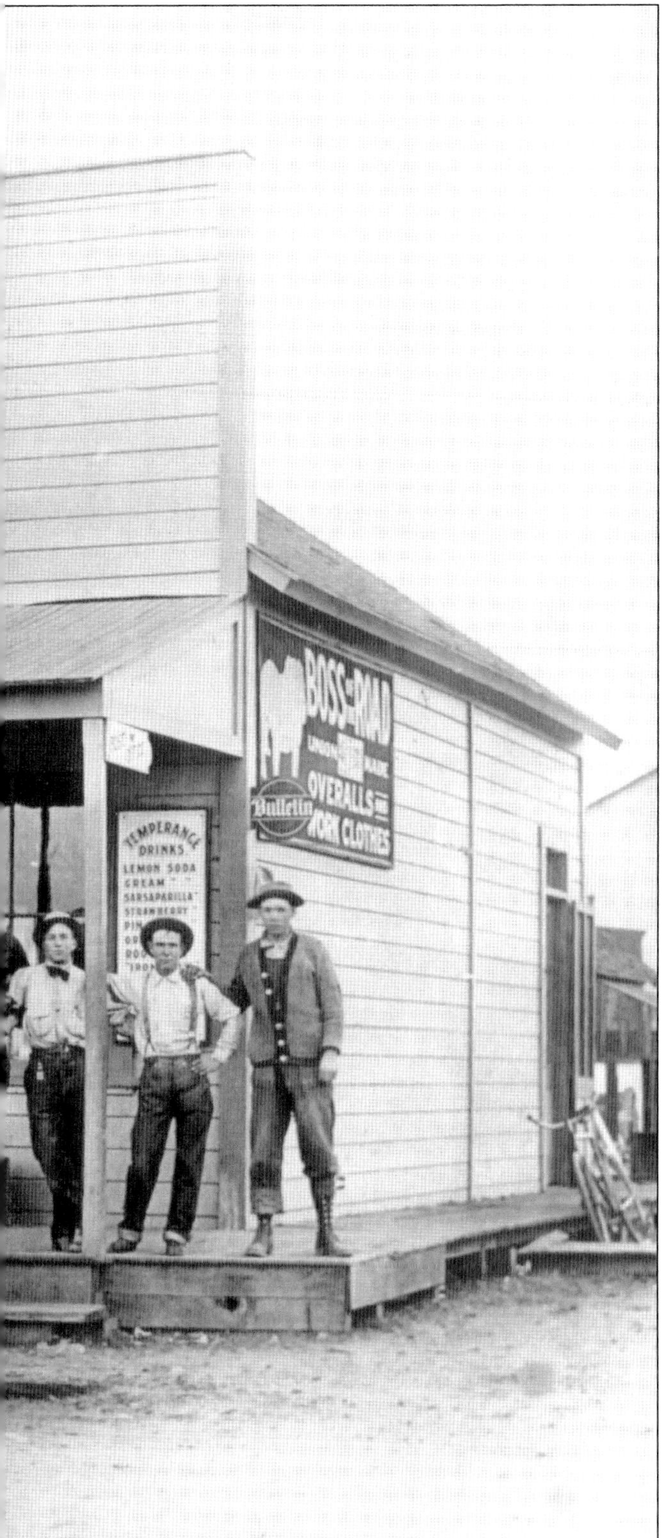

Although many businesses such as the one seen here sold temperance drinks during Prohibition, the town of Riverbank did have a speakeasy on Santa Fe Street. Some townspeople avoided paying for drinks entirely by creating bathtub gin and kept liquor stashed in cabinets and other areas of the house to defy the temperance movement.

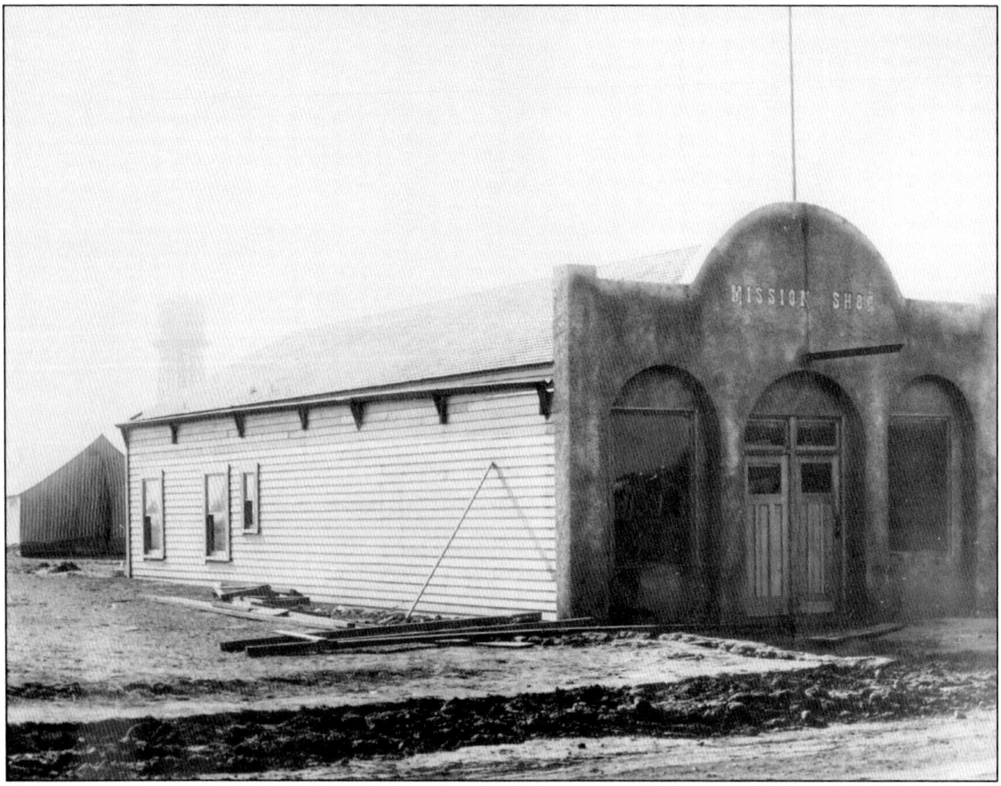

The Mission Shop functioned as a stationery store, library, and the town's telephone exchange, although at the time of its construction, the town only had about 15 phones in operation. In 1921, the library books were moved into a larger building on Santa Fe Street.

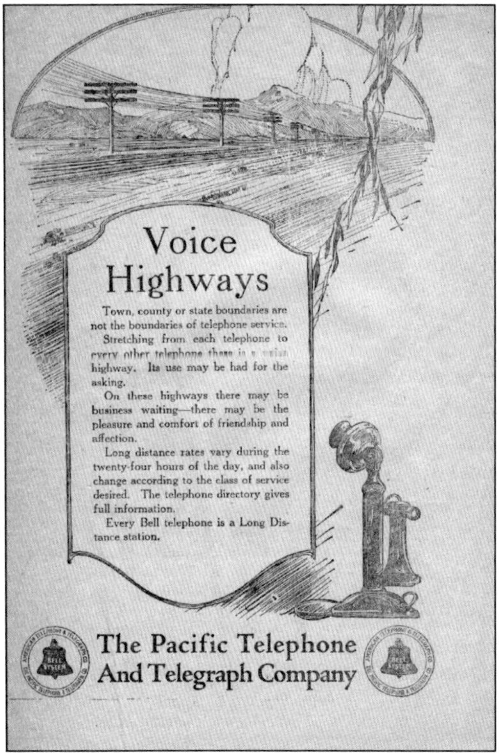

This Pacific Telephone ad ran on July 7, 1922, in an effort to increase telephone usage in Riverbank. It encourages people to join the "Voice Highway." Many amenities such as telephones and water and at times even electricity were done without in outlying areas.

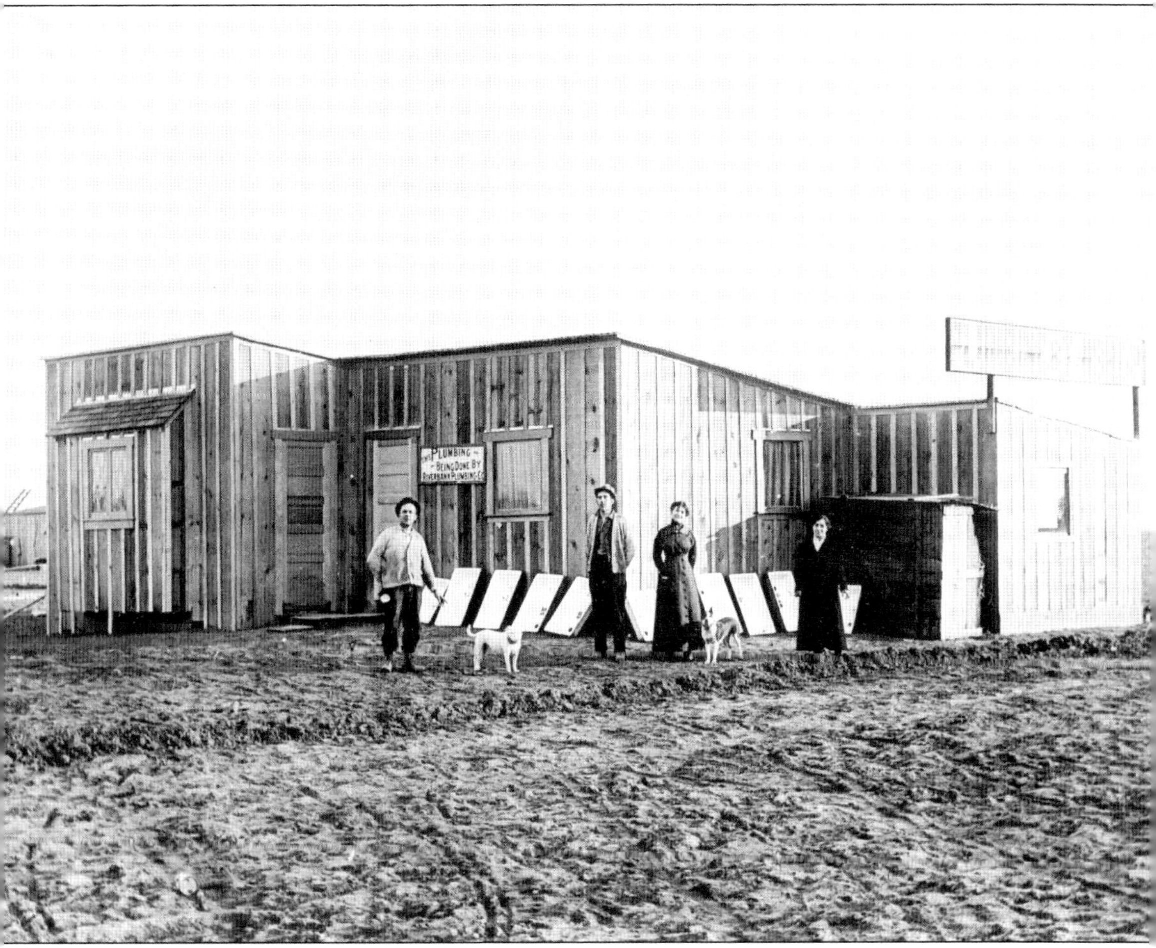

The Reichmann Brothers Plumbing and Tinning Shop on Santa Fe Street provided homes with sink basins, as can be seen against the building in the picture, as well as roofing materials. The brothers also built the Legion Theater, which started out as a place to see vaudeville acts and later became a country western gathering spot.

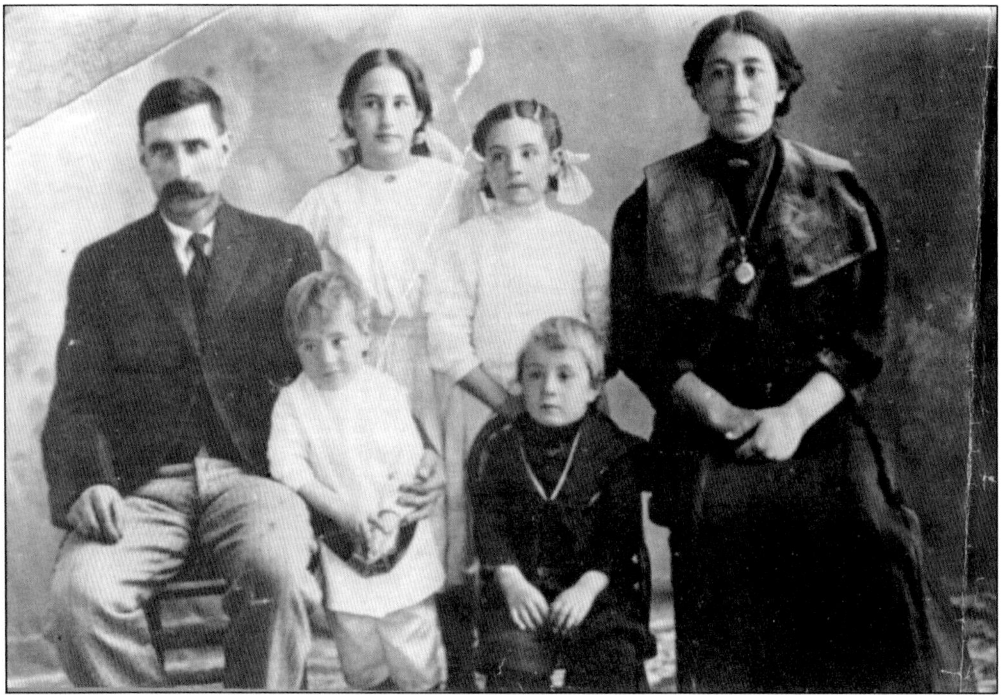

The owner of a photography studio, Eleazar Harris is seen with his wife, Leathey Anne, who processed his film. The eldest girl in the background is Claria Harris, who later married Manford Ditman and ran a real estate business on Atchison Street after her husband's passing. Eleazar passed the photography business on to his son Lee, the eldest boy on the left next to his brother Merle. Lee eventually passed the photography shop on to his son Ed. Lee was famous for taking pictures of elementary school classes in front of the town fire truck as well as many events in town.

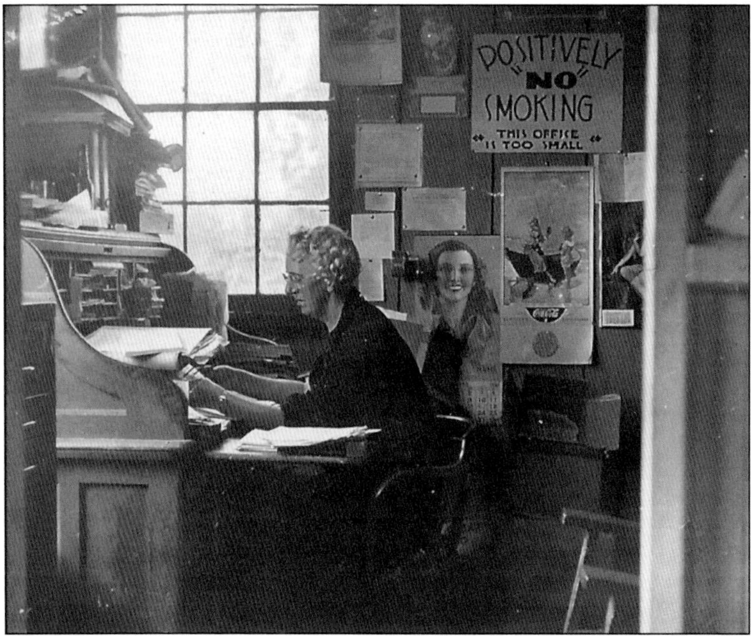

The woman at left is believed to be May Case, who established the first newspaper in town, known as the *Riverbank Review.* The paper only lasted a period of six years before May took a job in Clovis. The Bessac family started a second paper, the *Riverbank News*, which is still in publication today.

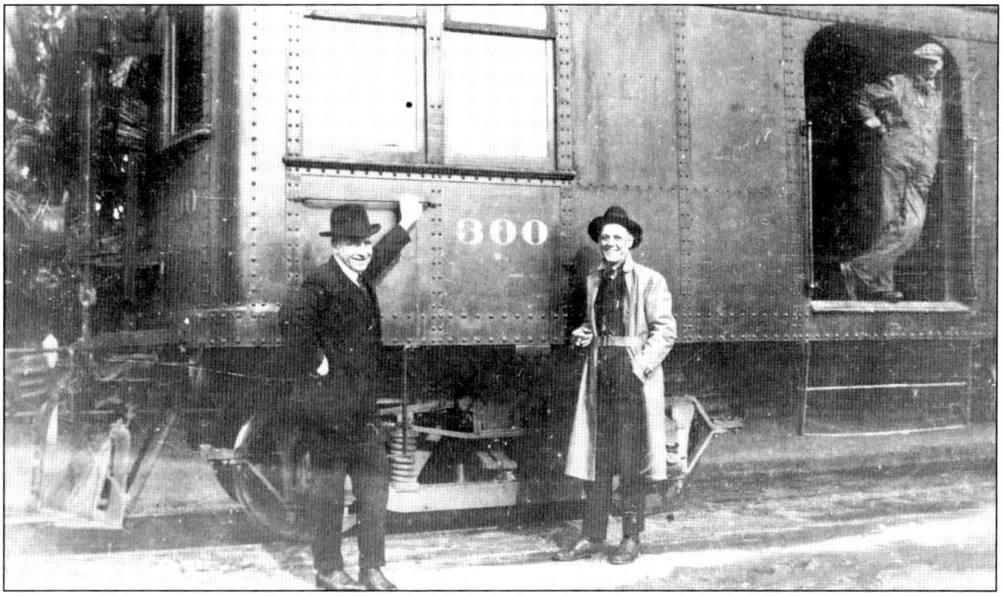

The Santa Fe Railroad ran a line into Oakdale that carried passengers and mail. In the 1940s, a Bugg car carried passengers along this route.

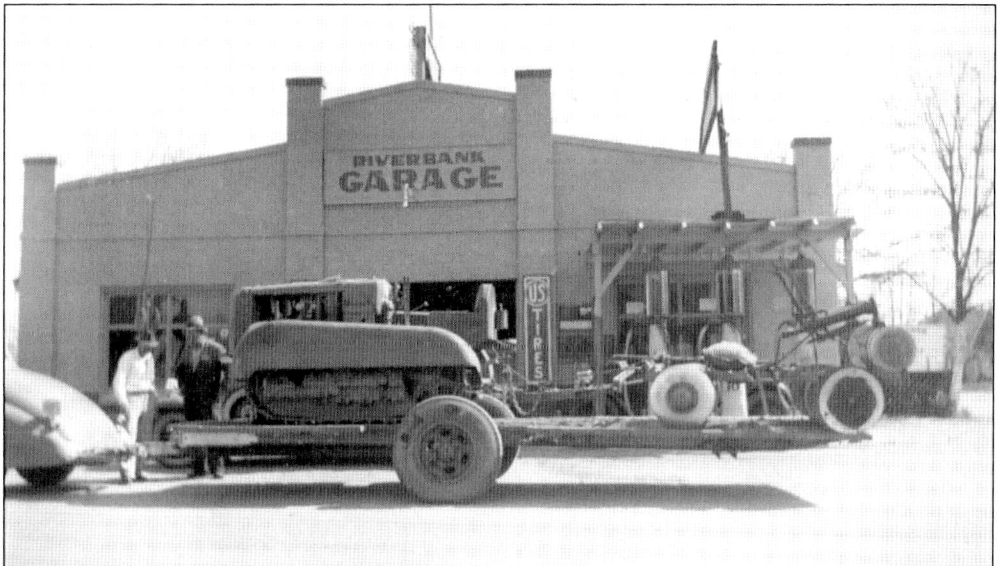

The Riverbank Garage serviced both cars and farming equipment in the 1930s and 1940s.

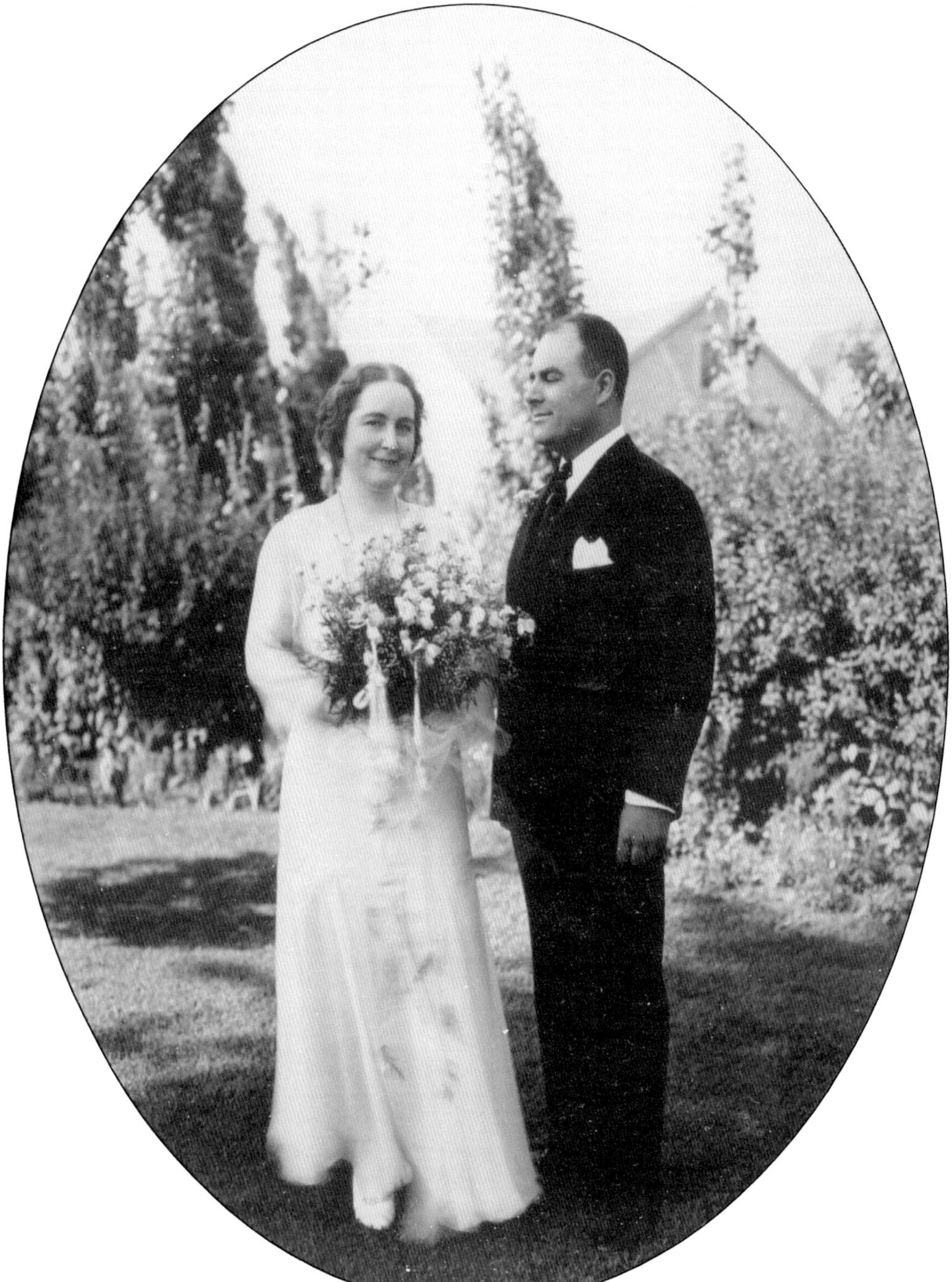

This image was captured at the wedding of Lorenzo and Frances Getty Zerillo. Lorenzo came to California in 1921 and purchased what was then the Riverbank Canning Company, turning it into a larger operation that employed between 1,500 and 2,000 people. A variety of fruits and vegetables were processed at the plant. His wife, Frances, was a former opera singer from the New York area. The newly purchased cannery renewed the Santa Fe Railroad's interest in the town when its days as a terminal stop were coming to an end.

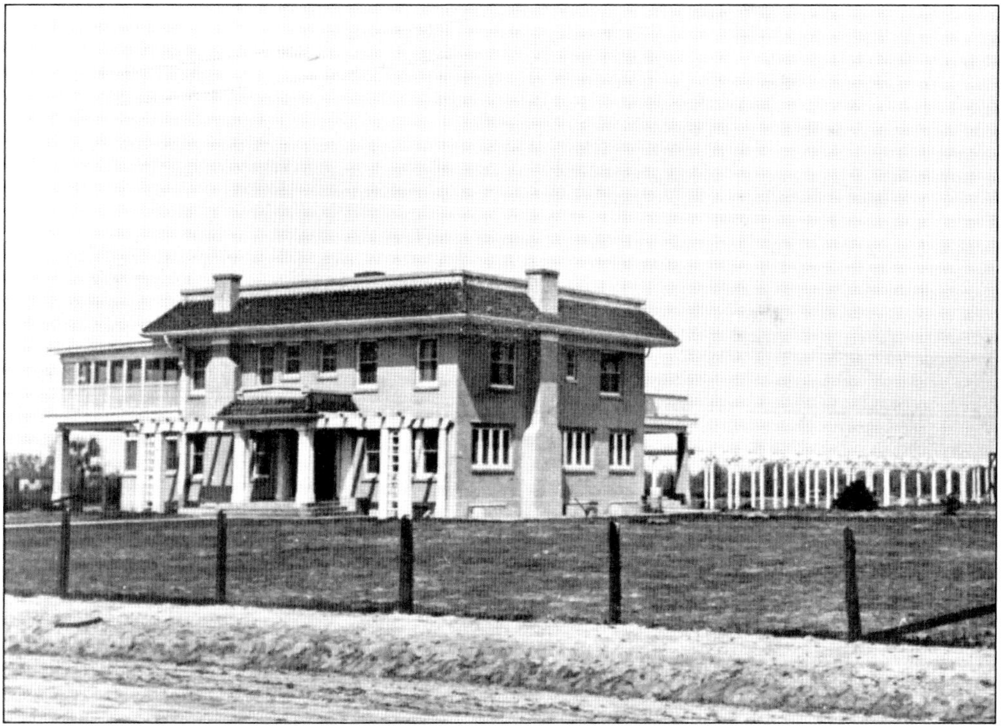

The Zerillos purchased a home at Topeka Street and Highway 108 and turned it into a beautiful Italianate mansion. Frances's sister listed the house in a state register of names, calling it Casa Felice. The upper enclosed porch no longer exists, but many of the mansion's original features remain to this day.

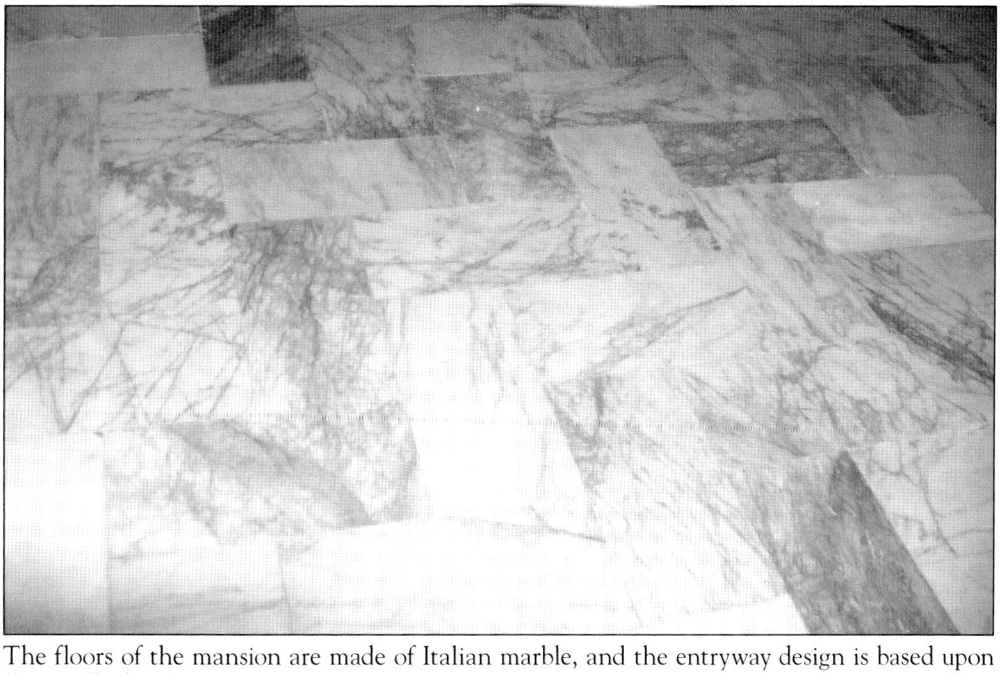

The floors of the mansion are made of Italian marble, and the entryway design is based upon the Zerillo family crest.

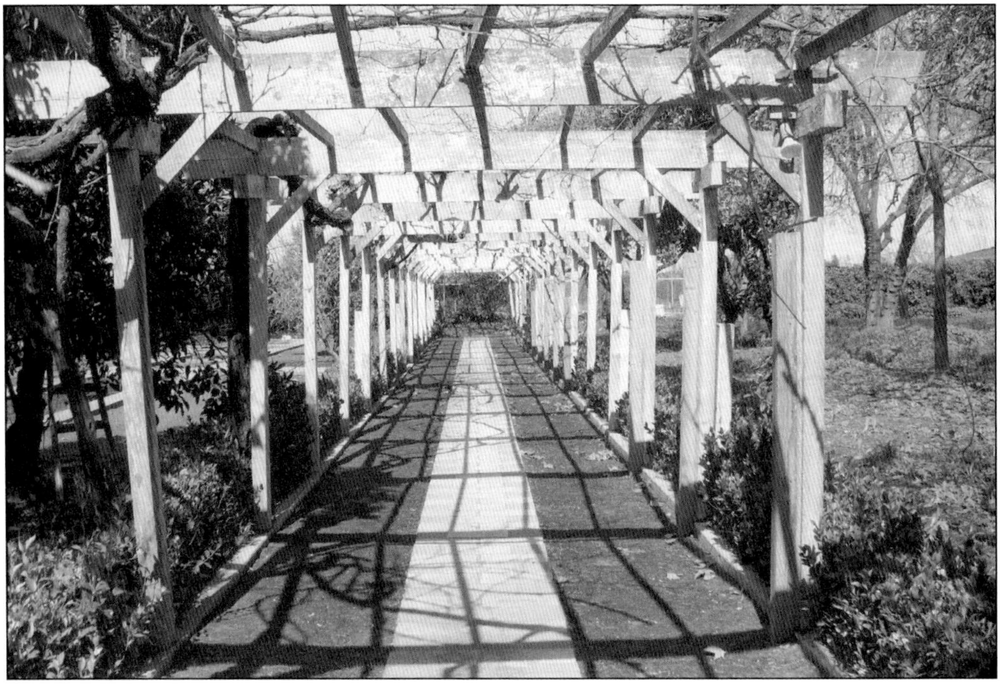

An arbor in the back of the house once led to a swimming pool that had to be drained and cleaned when it was in use. The pool was filled in long ago, and an adjoining changing room was torn down.

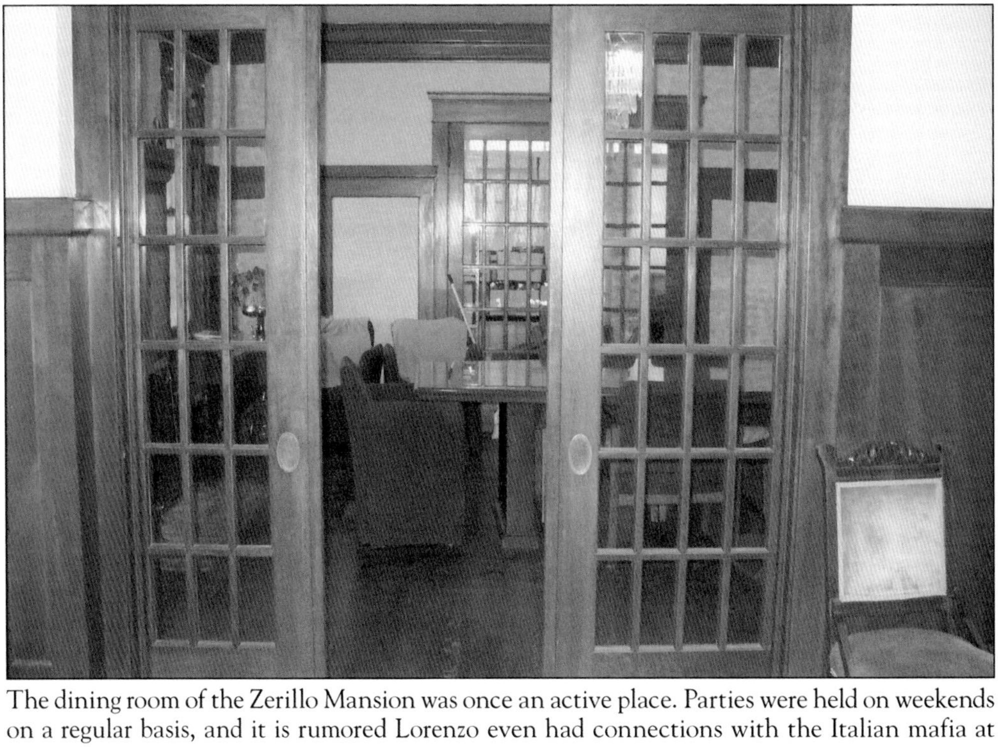

The dining room of the Zerillo Mansion was once an active place. Parties were held on weekends on a regular basis, and it is rumored Lorenzo even had connections with the Italian mafia at one time.

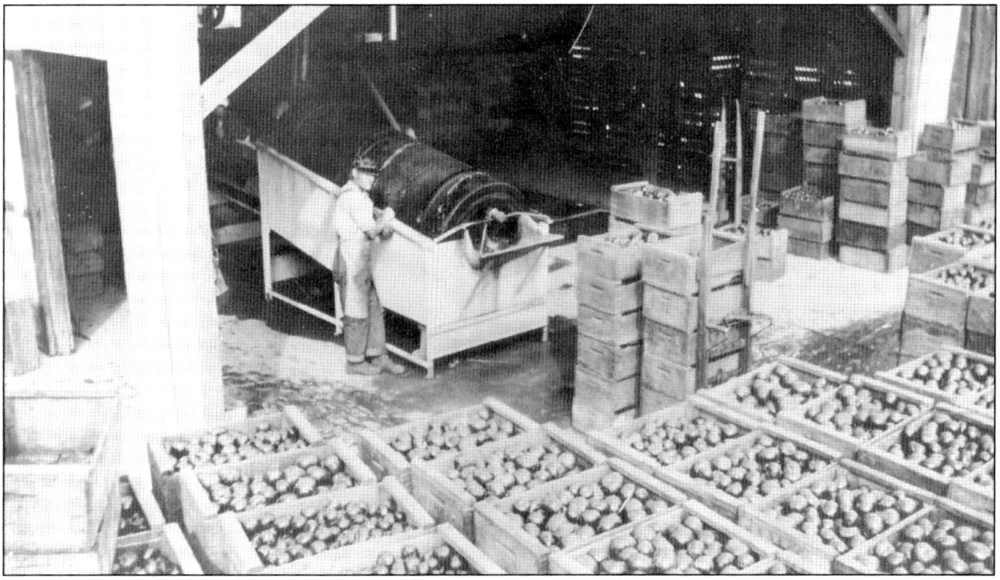

One of the most popular fruits to be processed at the Riverbank Cannery was tomatoes. Zerillo sold both tomato sauce and wine under the Madonna label to markets all over the United States and even sold such fruits such as apricots in Western European markets under the name.

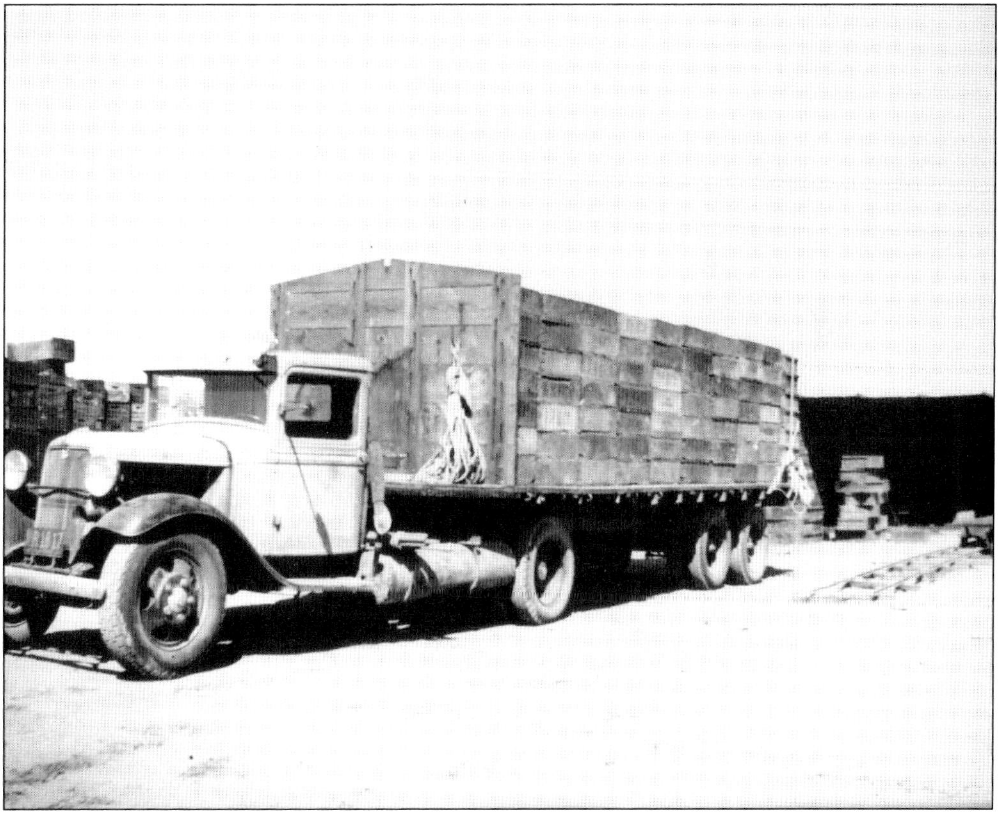

The tomatoes were shipped by both trucks and train to reach markets in Stockton and San Francisco. Some, when they reached the ports, would also travel to other countries.

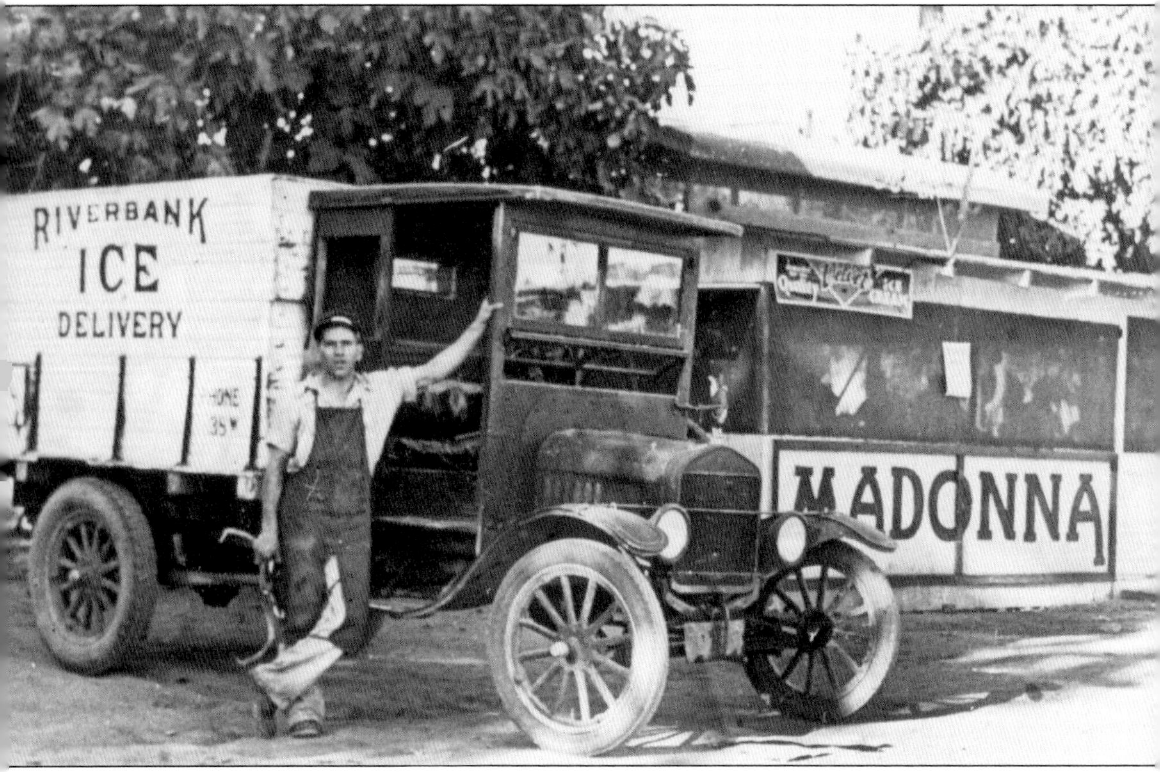

Allen Holbrook ran an ice delivery service in town. Here he is seen delivering ice to a Madonna fruit stand.

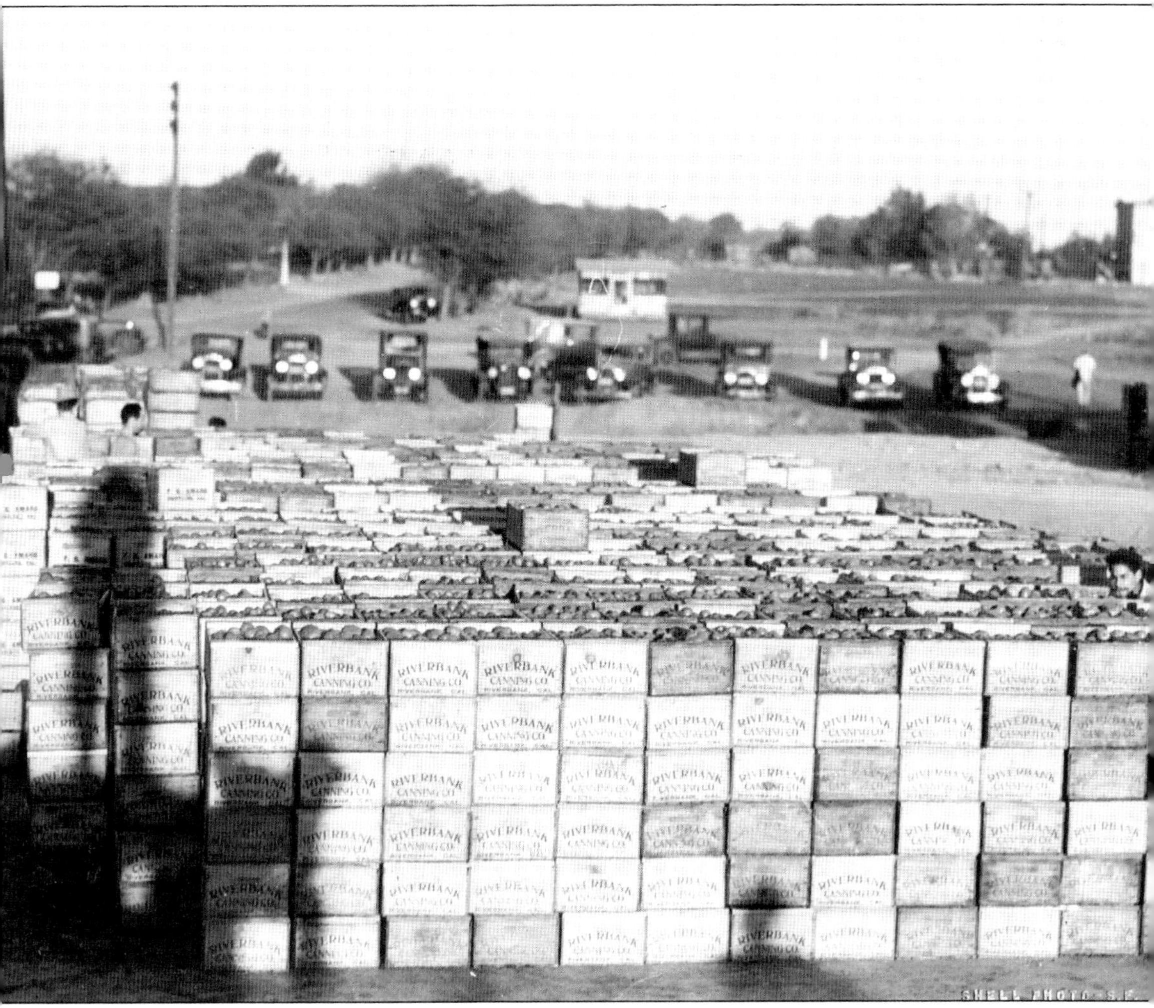

The Riverbank Cannery was famous for being the largest tomato processing facility in the United States at its time. Here, cannery boxes full of products are ready to be delivered in the 1920s. In the 1950s, the cannery was bough by Contadina Foods, which owned the land into the early 2000s.

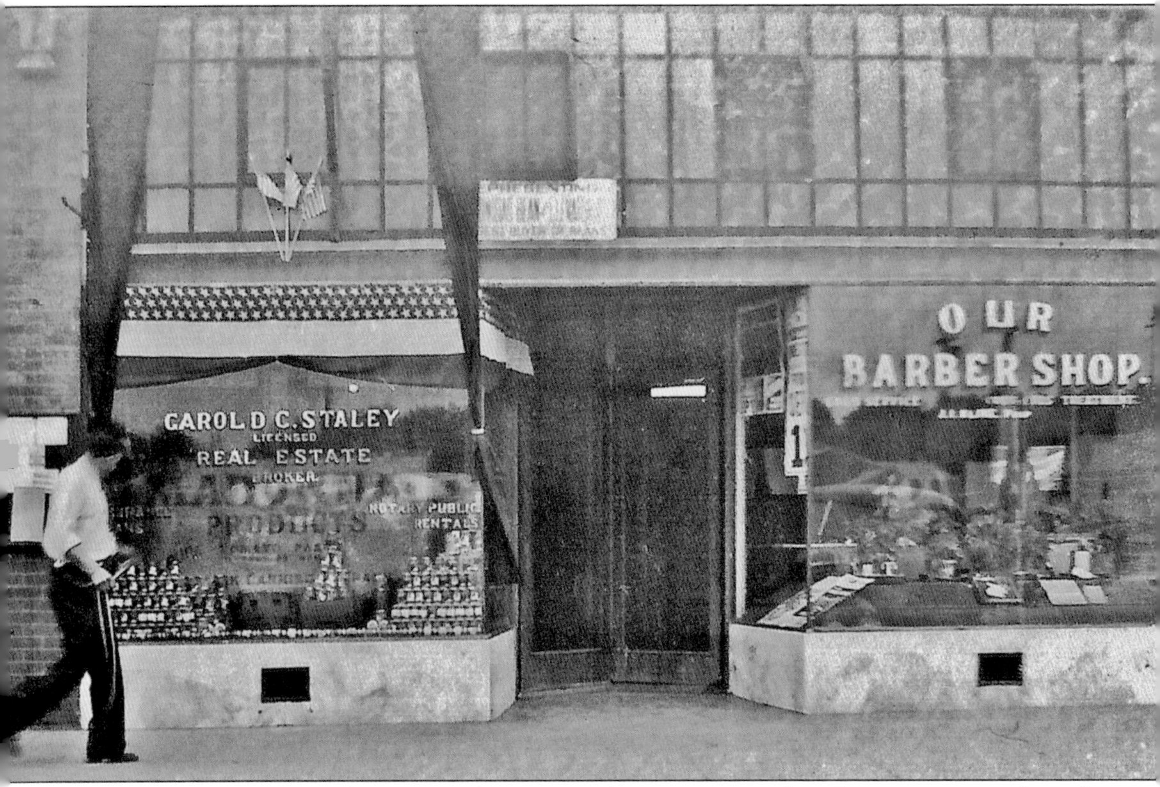

When the railroad era began to end, many people in town turned to the cannery to make ends meet. The popularity of the Madonna brand back east, and even in foreign markets, caused the Santa Fe Railroad to take new interest in Riverbank and the products it sold. Of course, Madonna products were also sold in town and proudly displayed in store cases, such as the one seen here in the mid-1920s.

During the mid-1920s, the *Riverbank News* was connected to the cannery, printing labels for the cans and recipes suggesting how to use tomatoes in cooking. During World War II, the paper lost many of its workers to the draft, and supplies became more difficult to buy. Eventually, the publication was suspended in 1945. The newspaper was started up again when the war died down. This time, in order to make additional money, the newspaper printed books. One was for Central Valley Growers, and the other provided a list of prices and owners of cows. In 1963, after Ed Bessac, the original owner, passed away, the paper was bought by one of its former workers, Howard Roberson, and in 1974, it became a part of the *Oakdale Leader*.

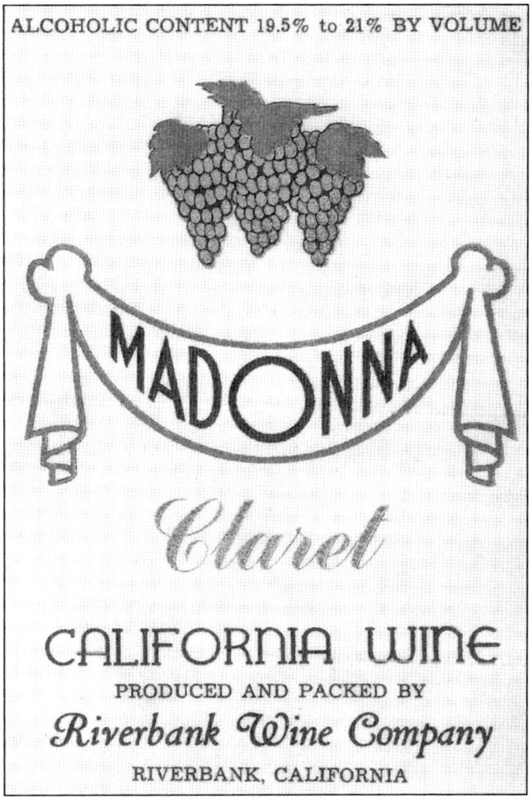

This 1940s picture of Atchison Street was taken from the intersection with Fourth Street. The viaduct can be seen in the distance.

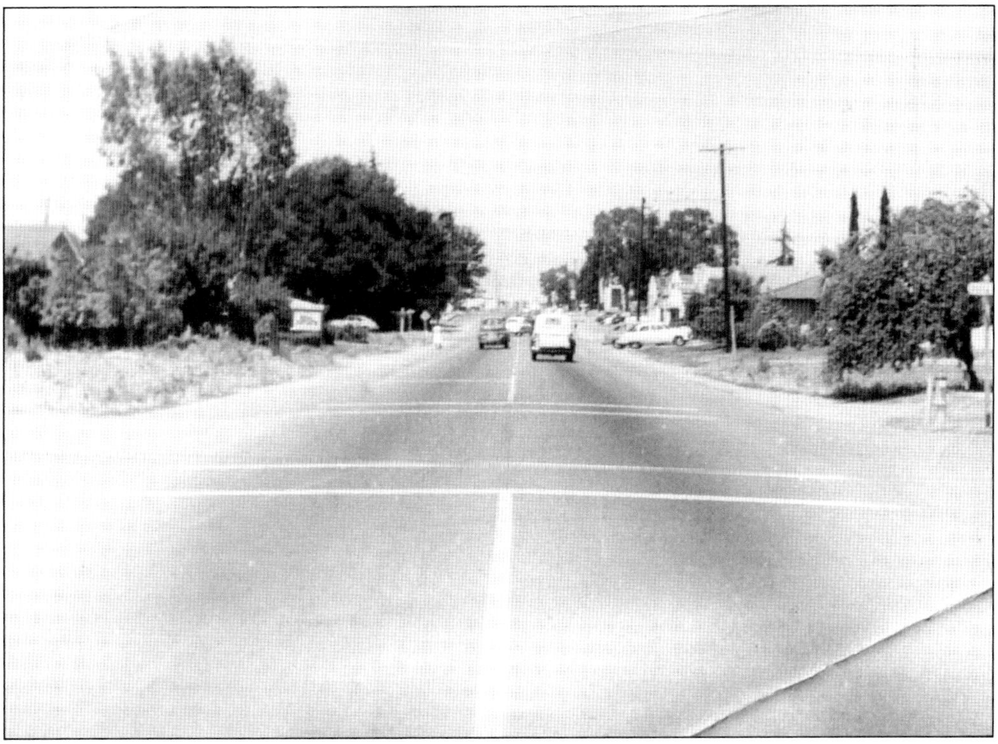

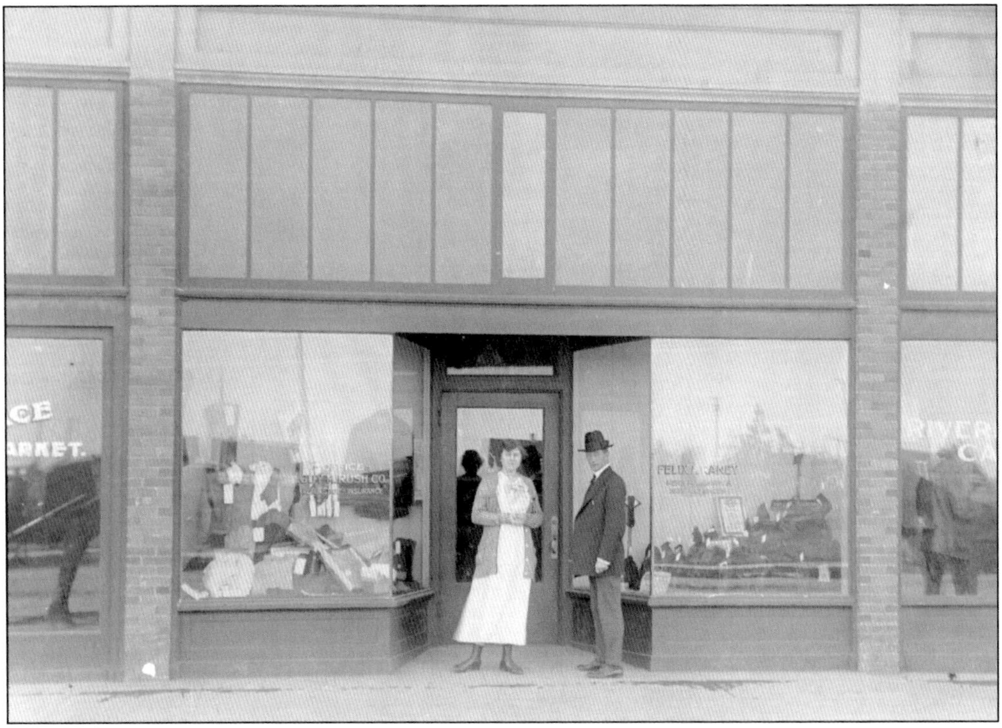

In the mid-1920s, Santa Fe Street was the thriving heart of the downtown area. Even Guy M. Rush, the real estate tycoon, had moved his office onto the street in an office behind a men's store and in between the Palace Meat Market and the Riverbank Café.

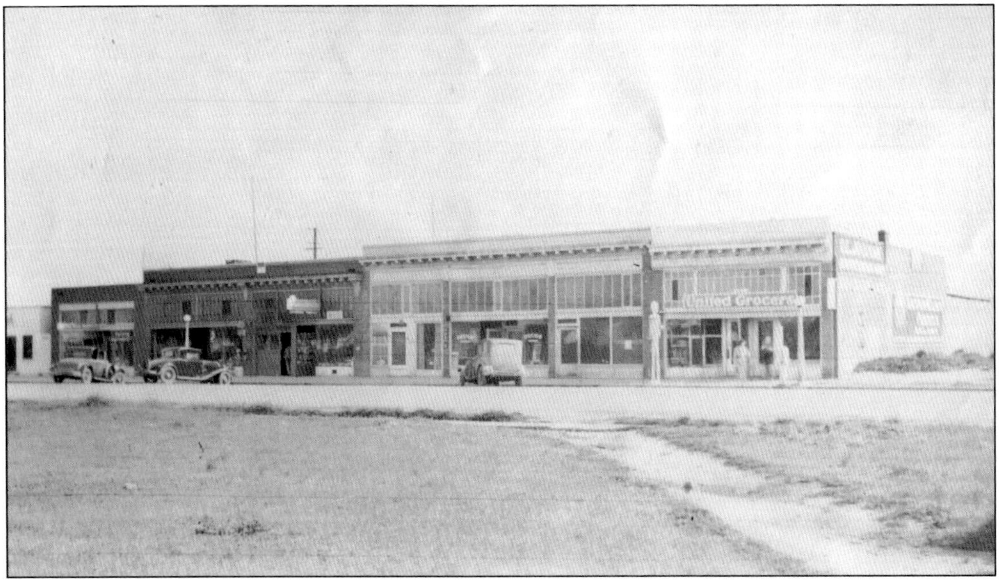

This image of Santa Fe Avenue in the 1920s shows the OK Inn, a drugstore, and United Grocery.

Four

Depression and War

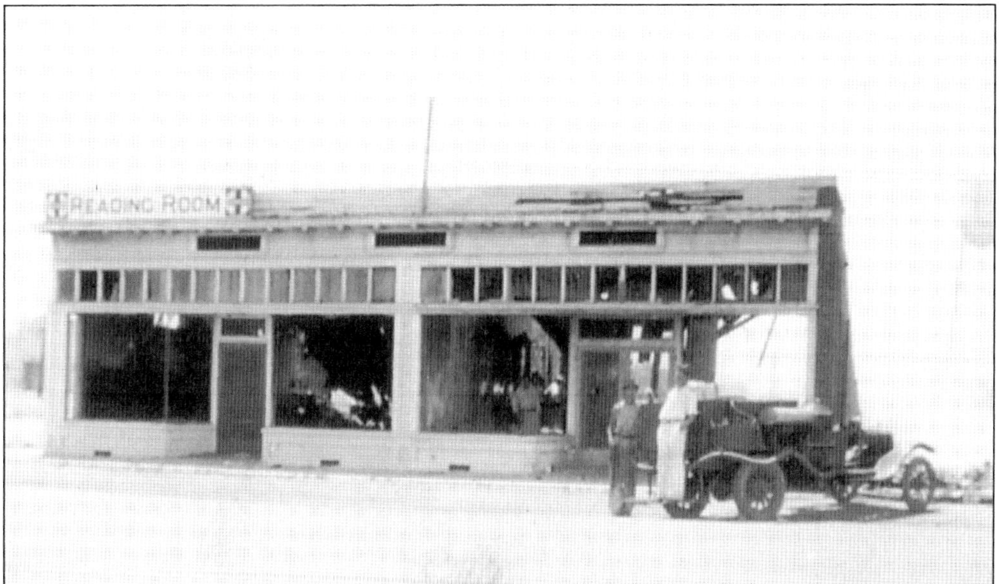

Tragically, in 1931, the events of a 1913 fire appeared to repeat themselves as another large fire devastated the commercial center of town again. One of the buildings severely damaged was the Santa Fe Reading Room, shown here. Other buildings on the street were completely destroyed by fire.

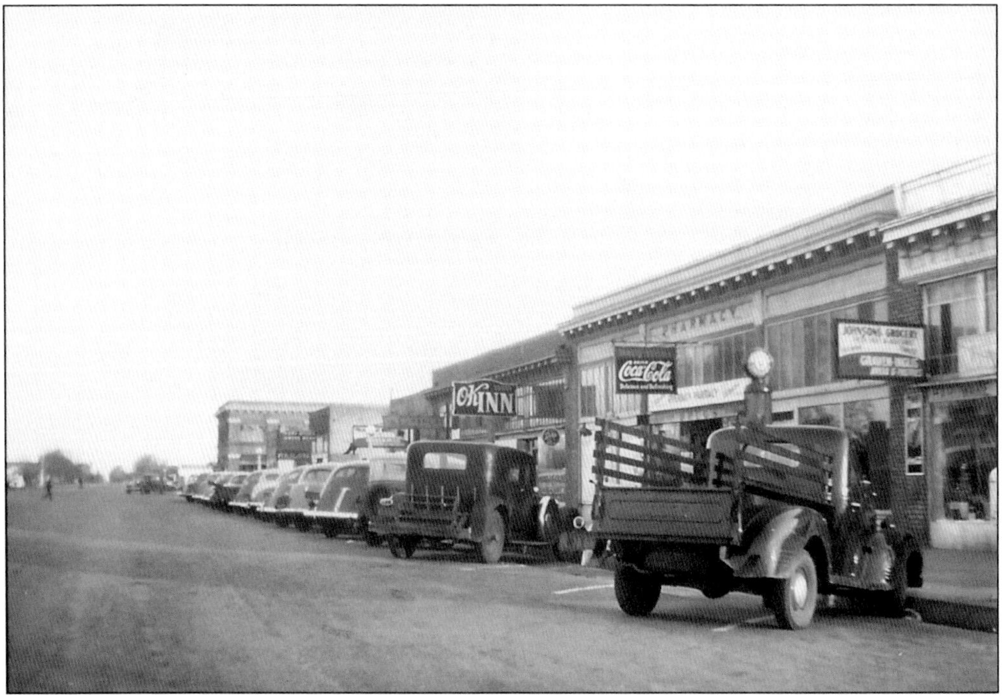

Even though the Depression hit Riverbank hard, the downtown area was again rebuilt. The high sidewalks seen in this picture were constructed as part of a Works Progress Administration (WPA) project. Most of the businesses have been rebuilt, including the real estate office.

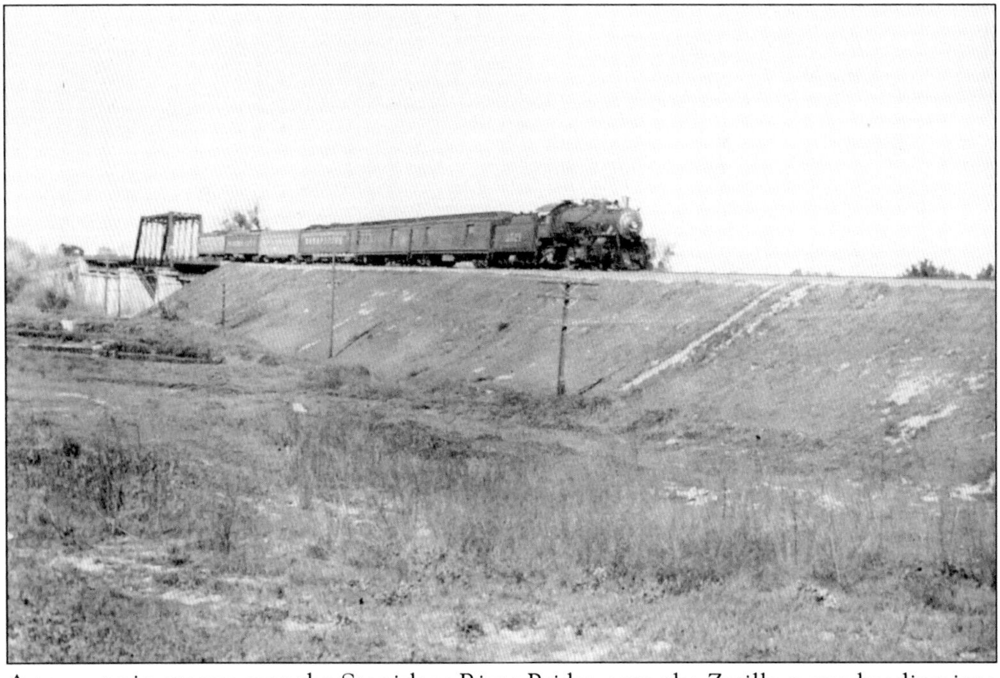

A troop train crosses over the Stanislaus River Bridge onto the Zerillo curve heading into Riverbank. At the depot, "donut girls" greeted the hungry and exhausted soldiers on their way to military bases further south.

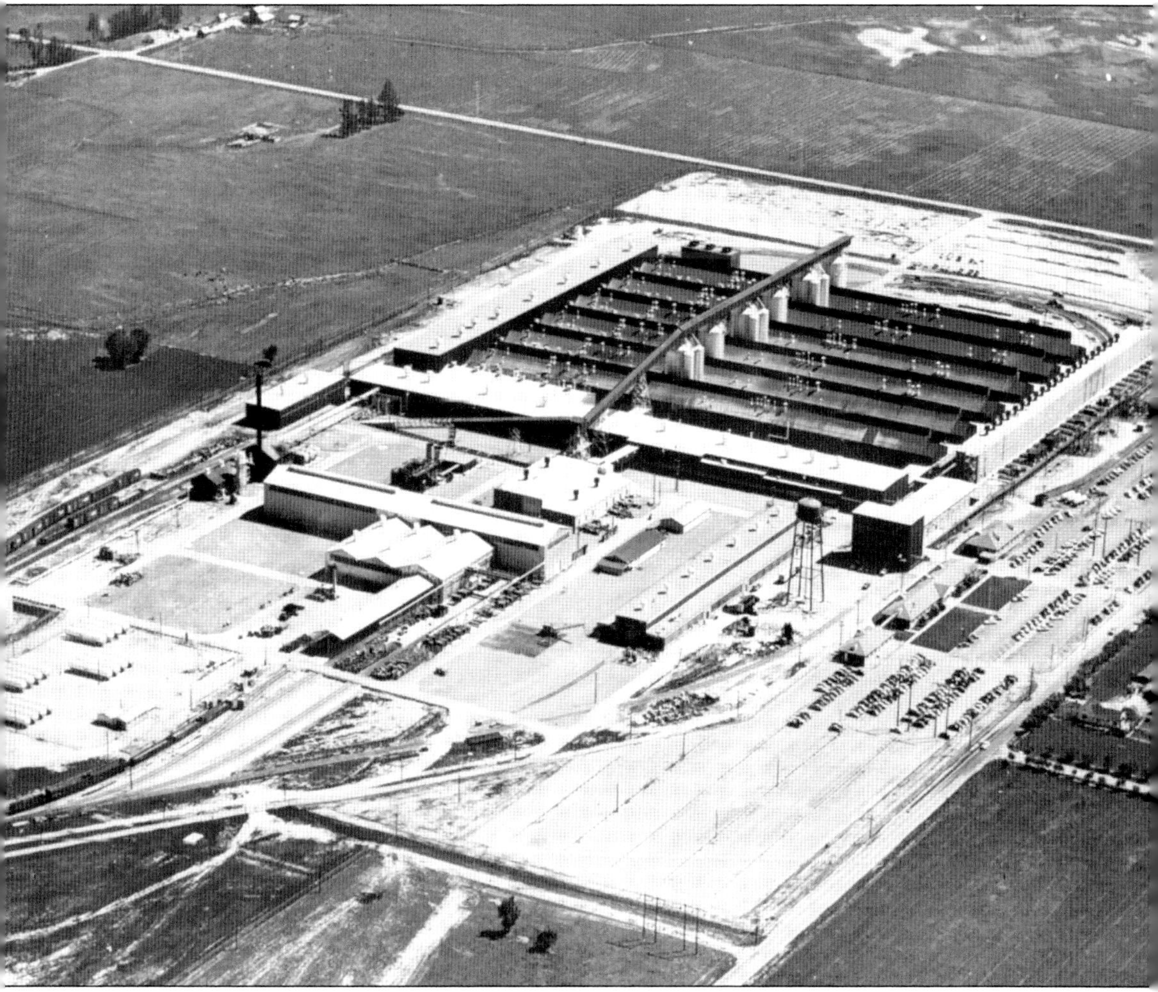

In 1943, at the height of World War II, an ammunitions plant was built that doubled the size of the town. Three hundred and twenty acres of land were purchased by the Defense Plants Corporation in May 1942 in order to construct a $12-million plant. Originally, it was designed to produce materials for aircraft. The site was chosen for its proximity to the Hetch Hetchy power system and the Santa Fe Railroad facilities. The Hetch Hetchy power line ran directly through the middle of the plant. The plant began production at midnight on May 18, 1943. About 80 million pounds of aluminum were produced by the time the plant closed on August 7, 1944, a little over a year after production began.

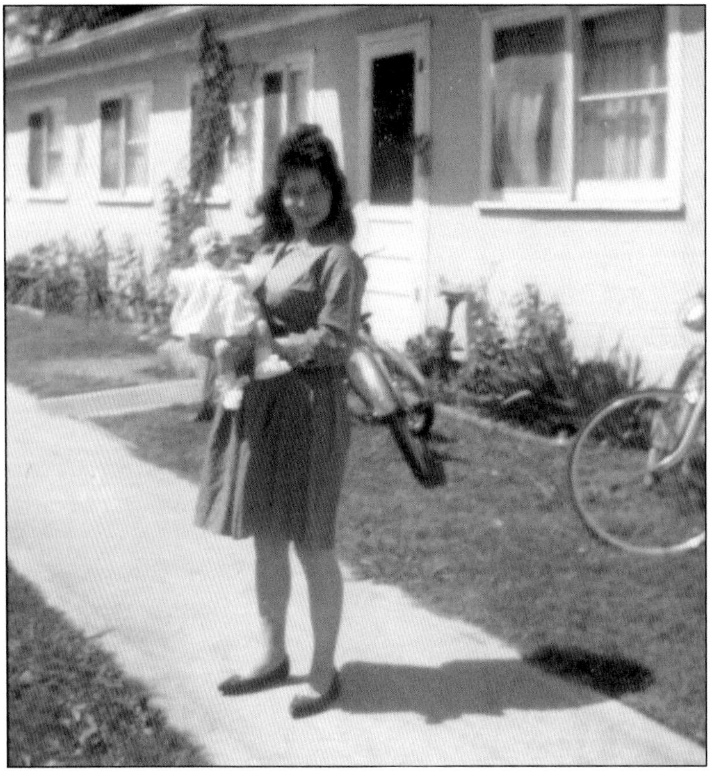

Most of the growth that occurred in the town at the same time was due to the Riverbank Housing Authority's construction of facilities to house the employees of the ammunitions plant. In January 1943, a complex known as Victory Homes was constructed off of Sixth Street. Later, another facility was built off of Eighth Street. After World War II, Riverbank changed yet again in its personality as many people sought land in California's rich soil not only to grow crops but also to find suitable land on which to build homes for their growing families in the Baby Boom.

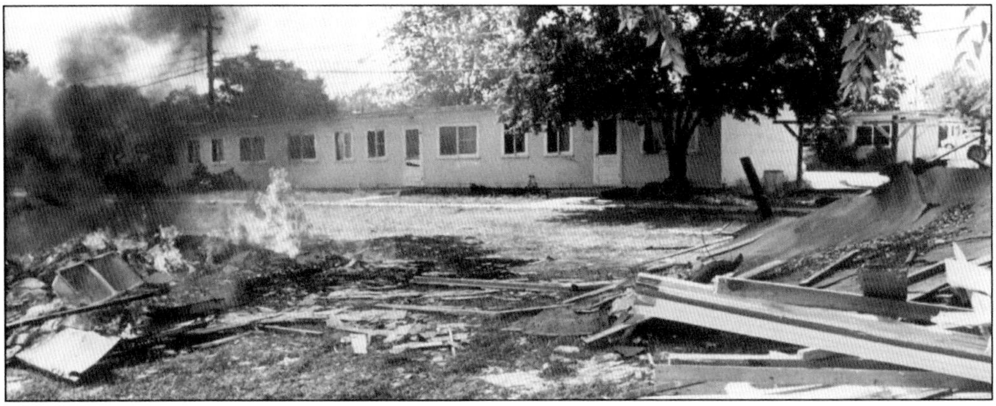

In order to make way for an expansion of Cardozo Middle School, the Victory Homes Project was eventually torn down. After the Baby Boom, the homes served as low-cost housing in the area. Many still remember having lived in the Victory Homes and the neighbors they met there.

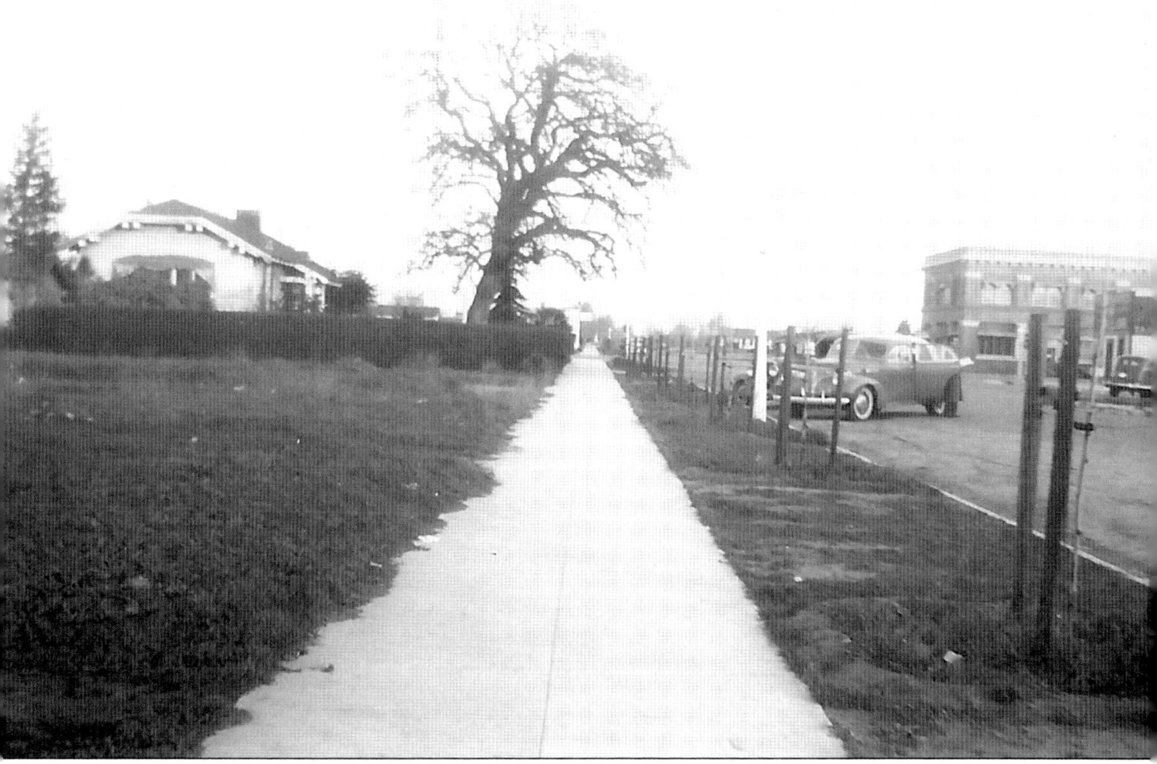

A contrast between young and old trees is seen here in the mid-1940s. In the center of the picture in front of the old library building stands an enormous valley oak tree that had been around since perhaps even before the town began. Behind the library stands a redwood dedicated to a World War I veteran. The new city trees were planted at this time. Ironically, along with the buildings, only the redwood tree currently remains.

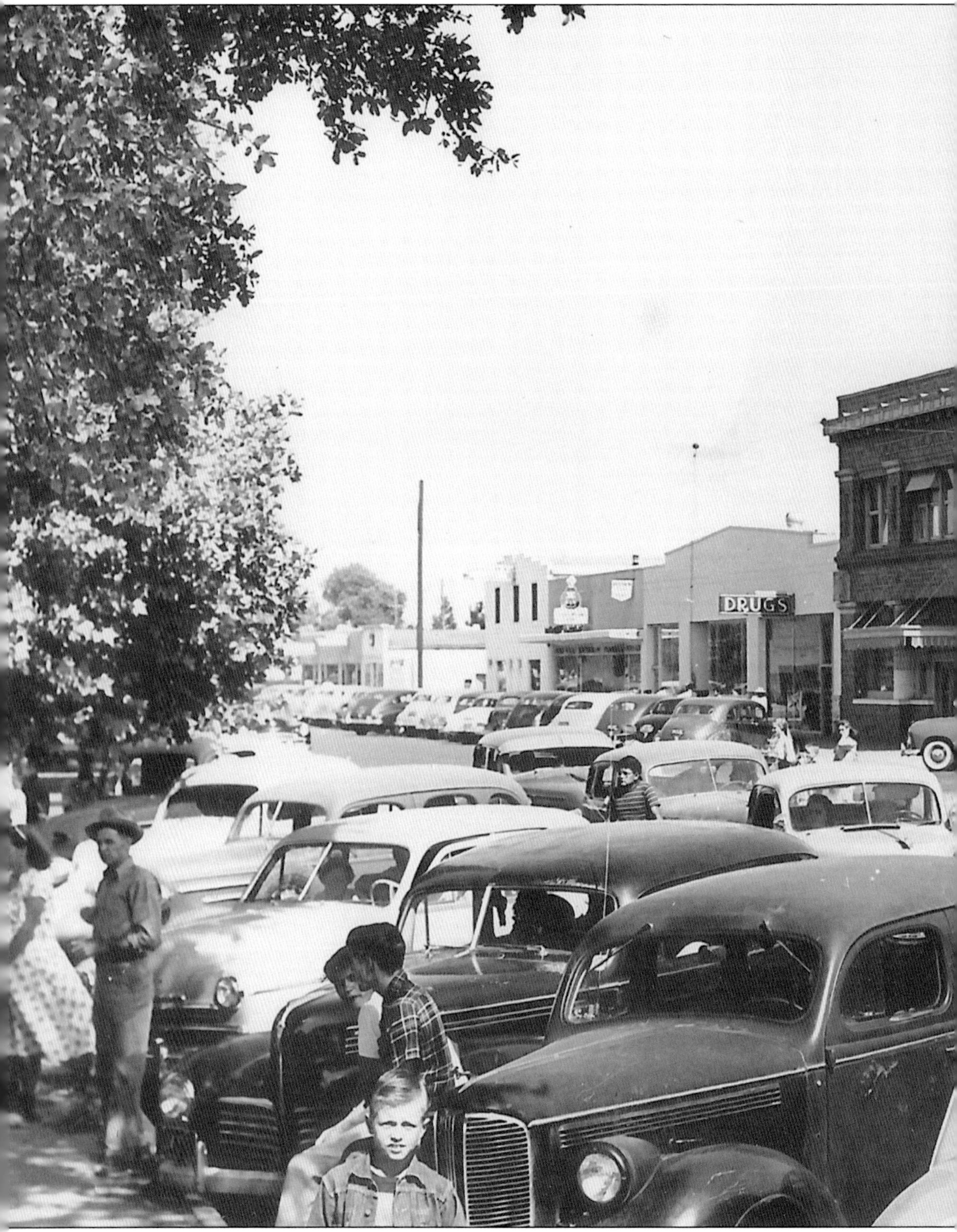

It was a busy day of activity in downtown in January 1948 when this picture was taken. A parade and carnival were taking place just down the street, sponsored by the Madonna Cannery. Large

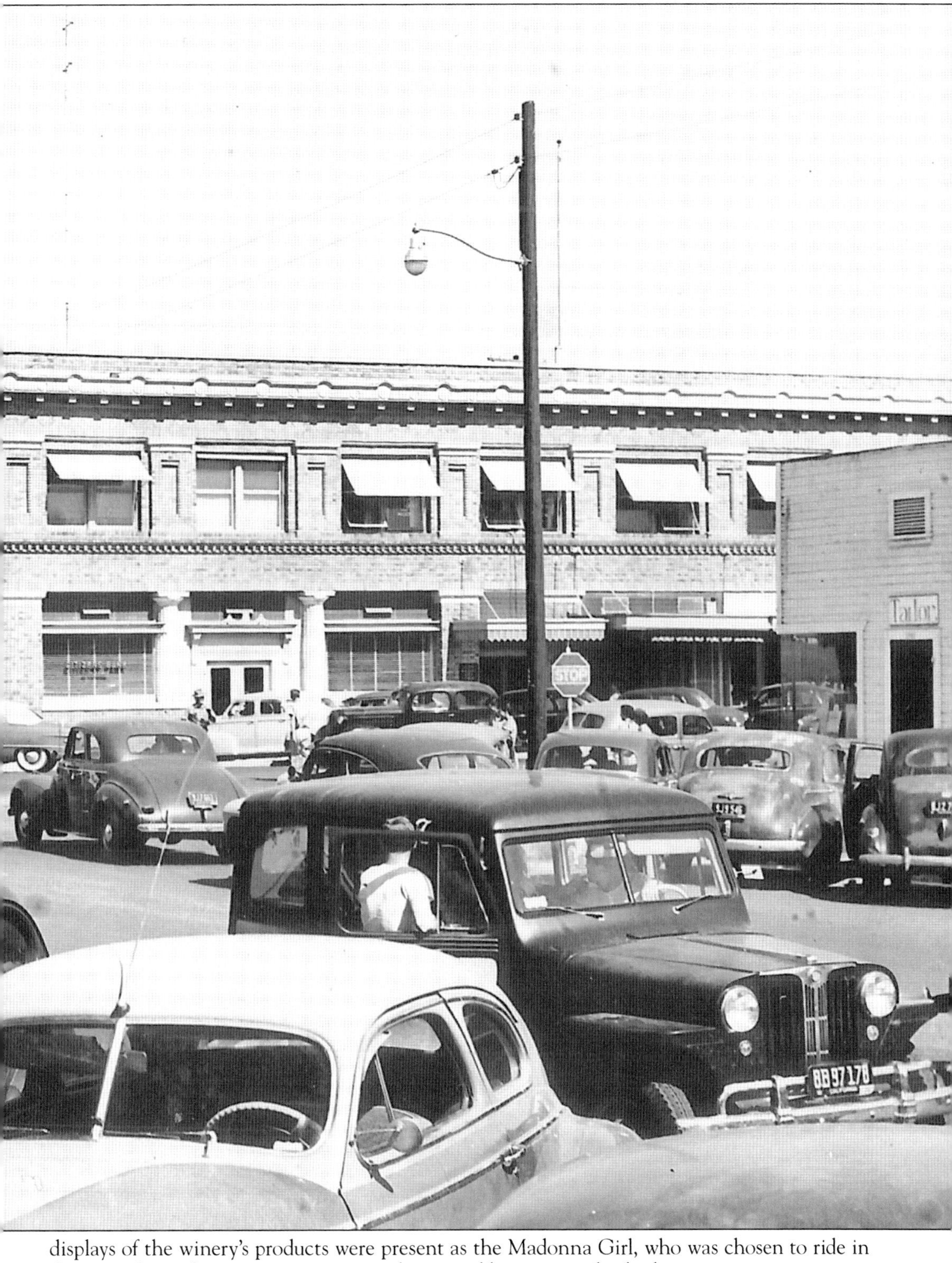

displays of the winery's products were present as the Madonna Girl, who was chosen to ride in the annual parade as a princess, anxiously awaited her turn to dazzle the spectators.

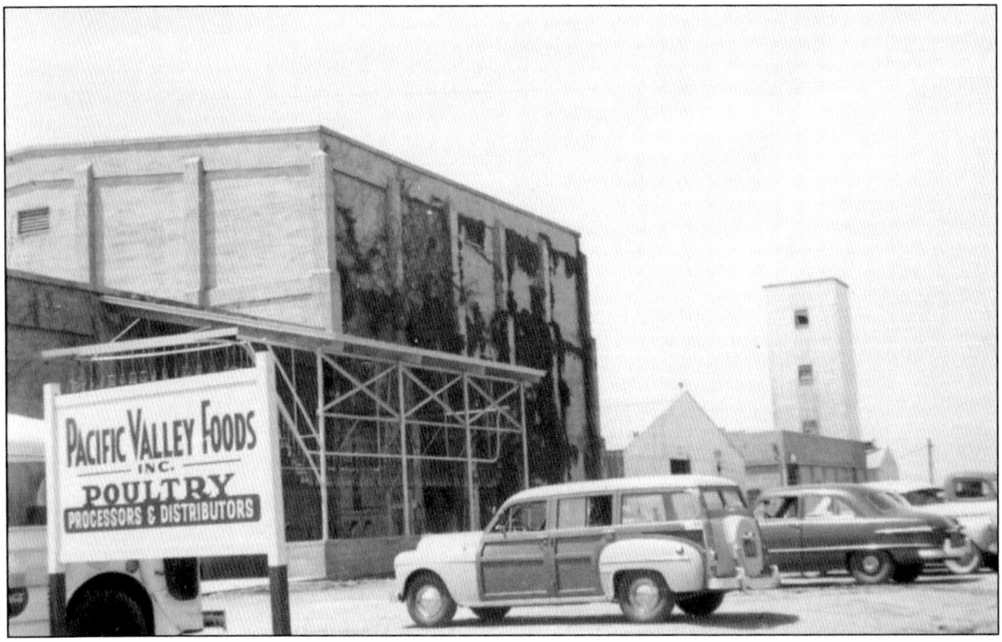

Riverbank has always been an agriculturally minded town. Many businesses centered around this industry have come and gone. This picture shows Pacific Valley Foods some time in the 1940s. The plant processed and distributed poultry from Riverbank to larger cities along the route of the Santa Fe Railroad.

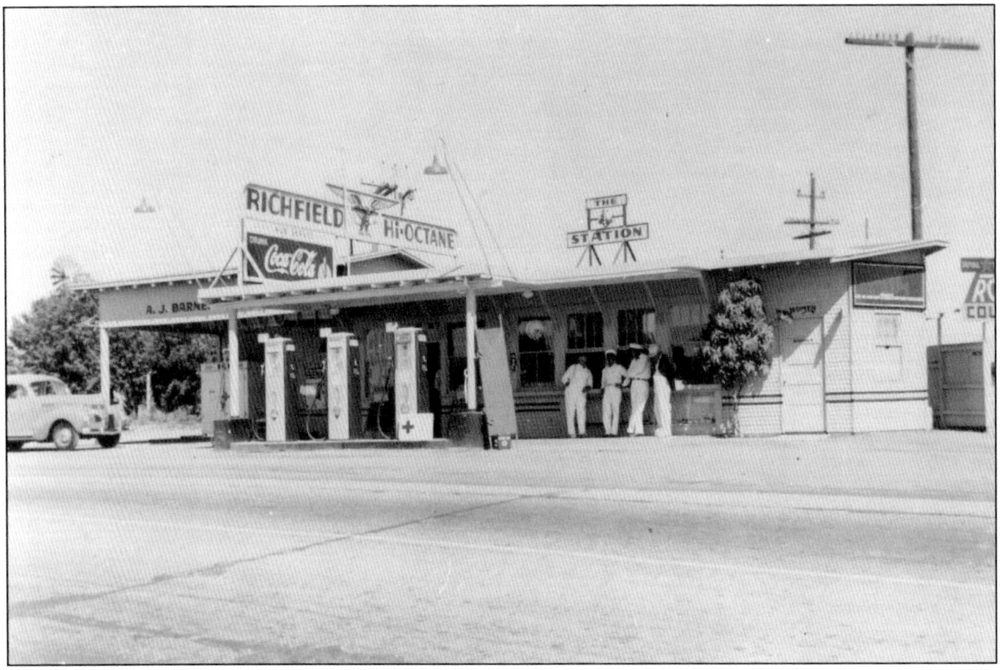

The Hub was a popular service station in the 1940s. The four gentlemen in the picture appear to be waiting for a car to enter the lot in order to perform the full service of not only gassing up the car but also checking the oil, cleaning the windshield, and performing other services for drivers without them ever leaving their cars.

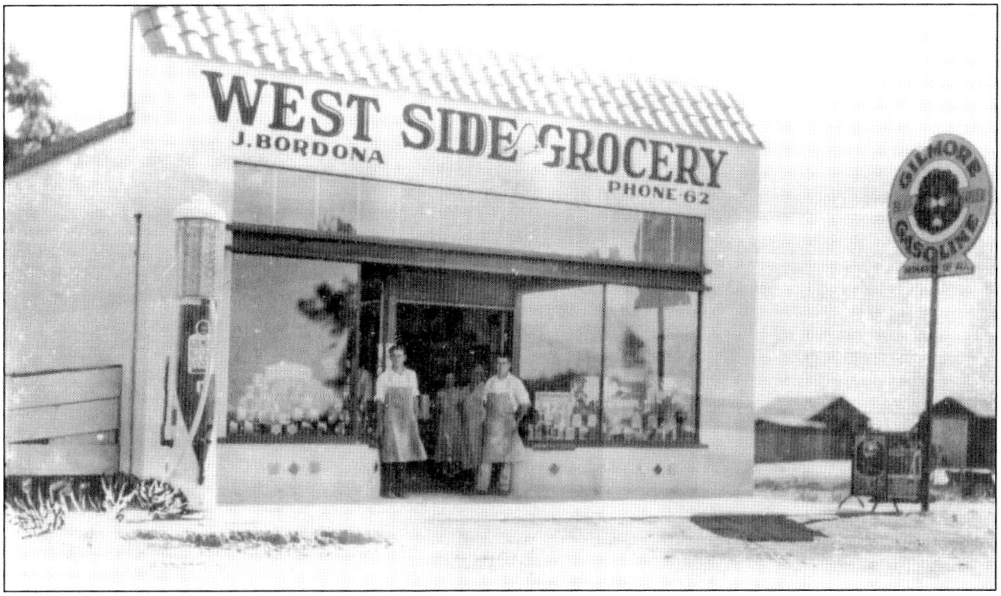

The Westside Grocery was started by the Bordona family in the 1940s. The family included Bob Bordona, Harmin, Miguel, Julian, Margarita, Martin, and Mike. It is now a Mexican market. The Bordonas currently own a furniture store off of F Street in Oakdale.

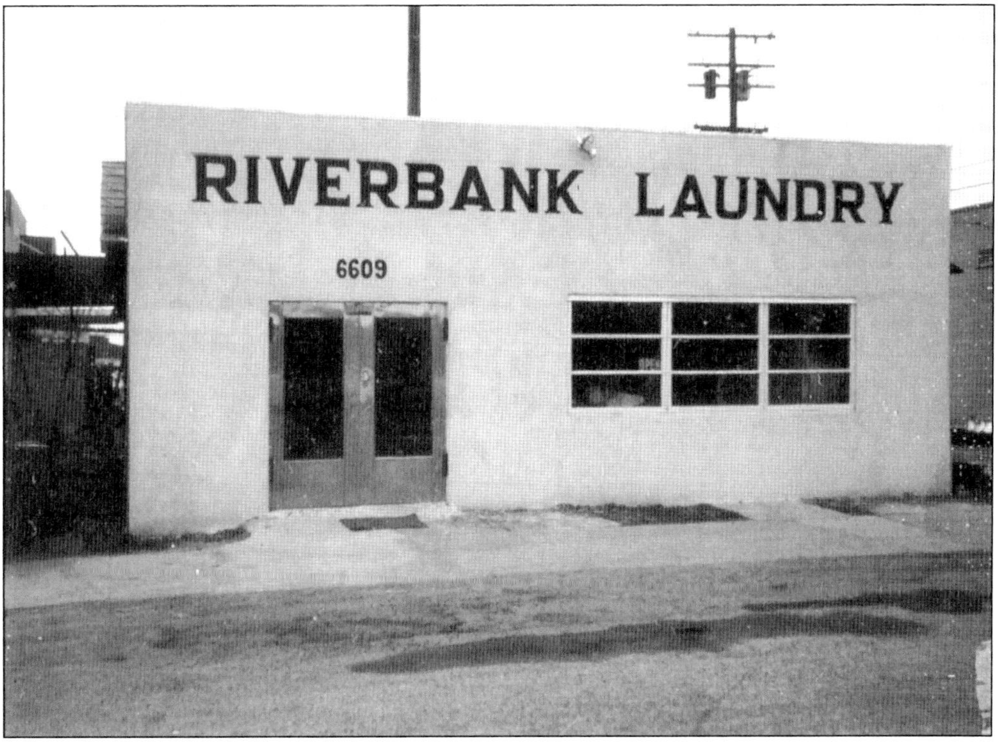

In the early days, Hop Sing belonged to the only Chinese family living in Riverbank. Hop Sing was the original owner of the Riverbank Laundry. The laundry was originally a two-story building but burned down, leaving only the frame, from which a house was constructed. The business was rebuilt and has now been around for some time.

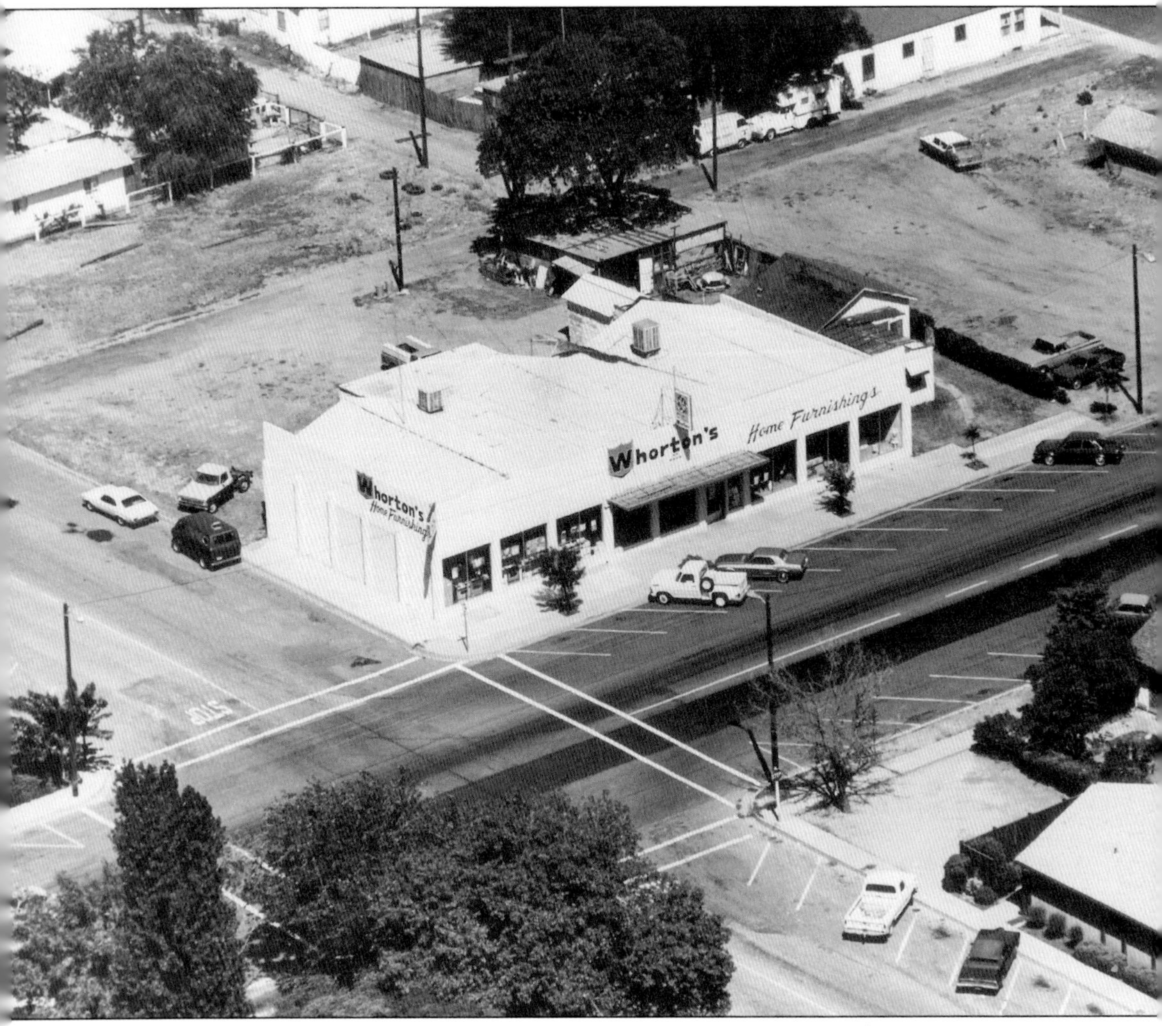

Whorton's Home Furnishings was another very well-known business in the 1940s.

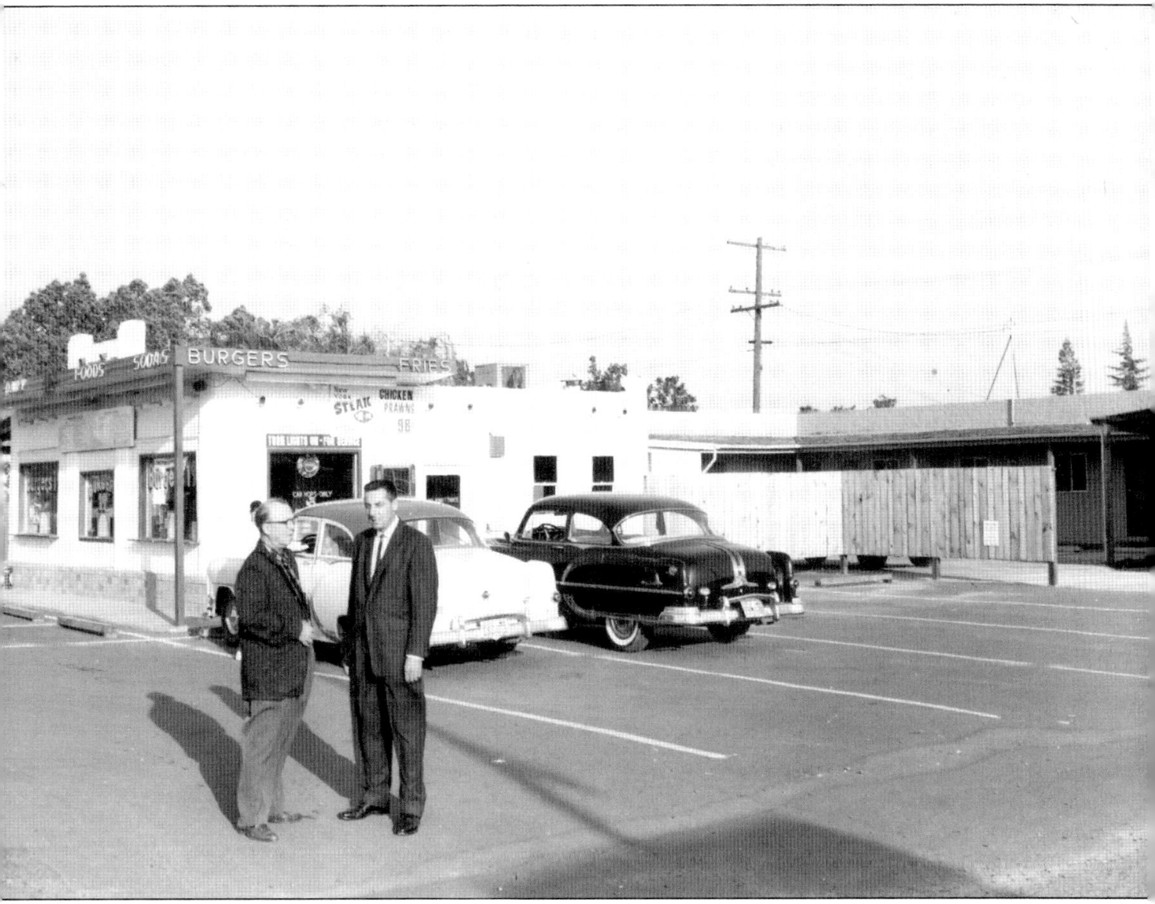

The Snow White Drive In also had its start in the 1940s and is still around today, providing good food to travelers on Highway 108.

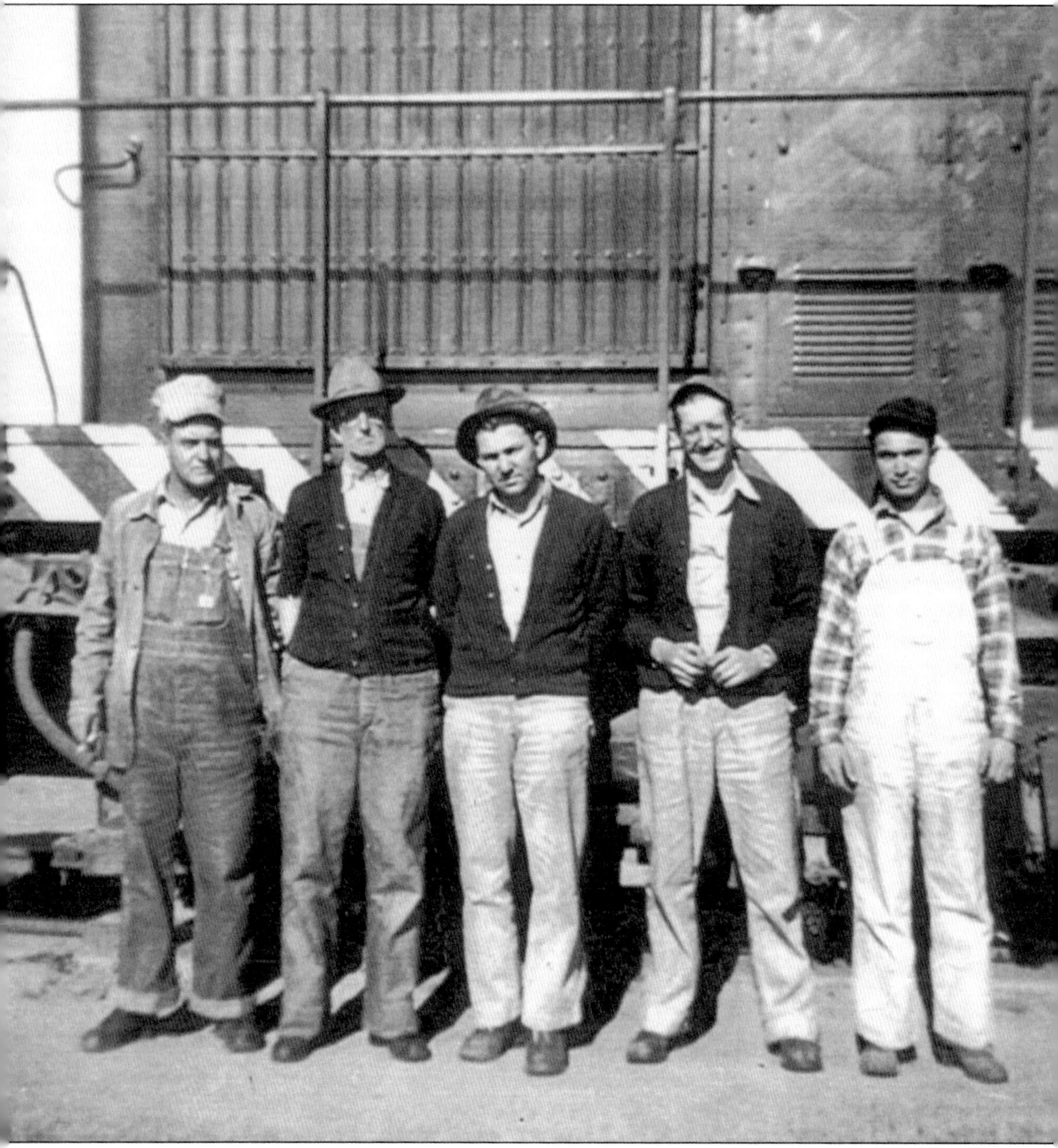

By the end of the 1940s, Riverbank had lost its status as a terminal stop. Over the years, faster streamlined freight and passenger trains had replaced the old steam engines that had to refuel on a regular basis. Even jobs within the Riverbank's switching yard were beginning to fade away. This image, captured around 1950, shows the last five-man switch engine crew. The men are, from left to right, Bob Harper (engineer), Mickey O'Connell (foreman), Mervin Powers (foreman), Karl Branning (fireman), and Tommy Williams (helper).

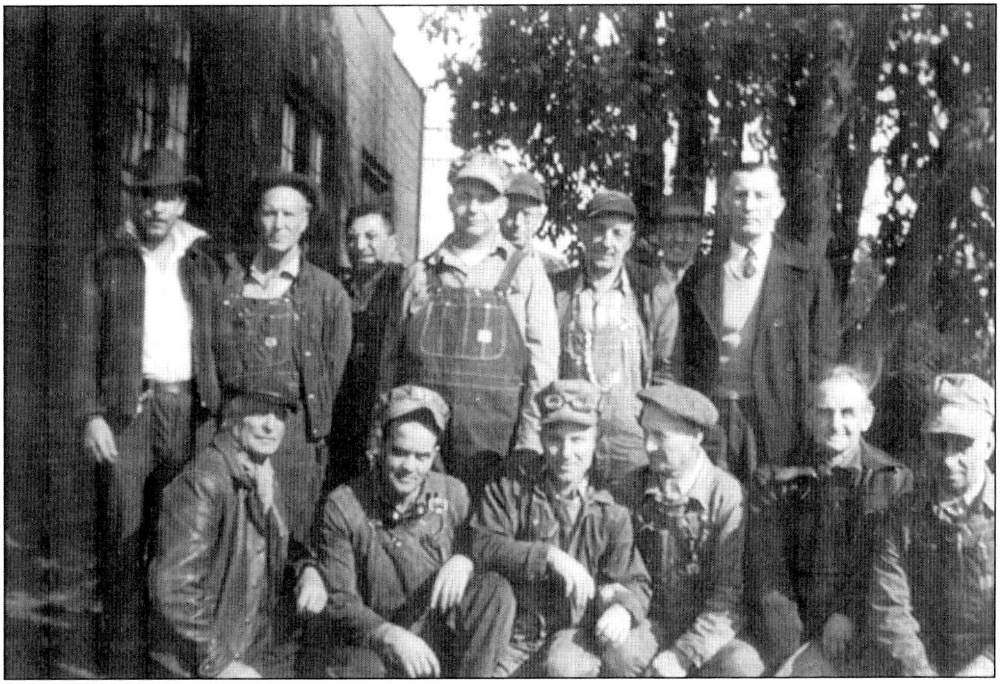

This is a picture of the last mechanical department crew taken around 1950.

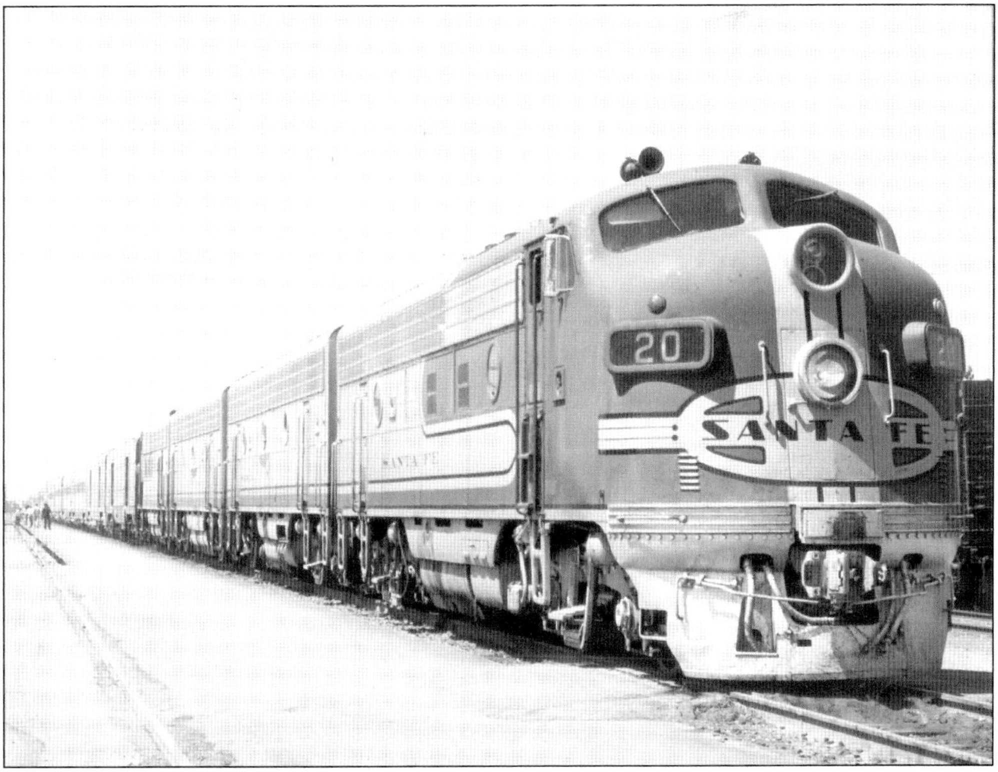

By the 1950s, the railroad had completely switched to diesel power for both its passenger and freight trains. The yard buildings in Riverbank were no longer needed and were abandoned.

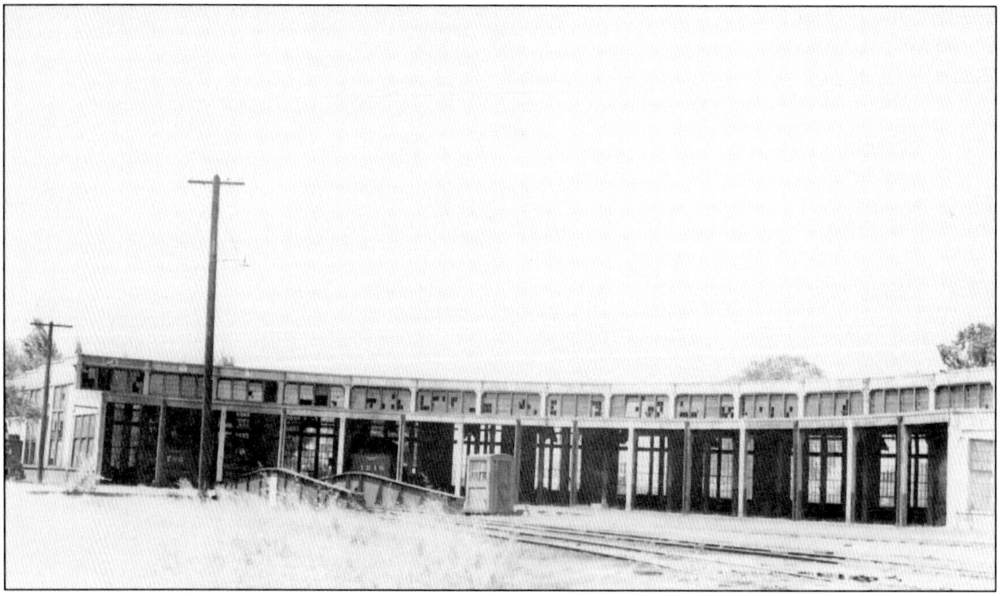

As the railroad era continued to decline, the once-thriving roundhouse and engine shops fell into disrepair and ruin. Even the depot itself would not last forever, as many of the ruins have been bulldozed in the name of progress. Only the remnants of an icehouse standing beside the tracks on Terminal Avenue give testimony to the railroad's glory days.

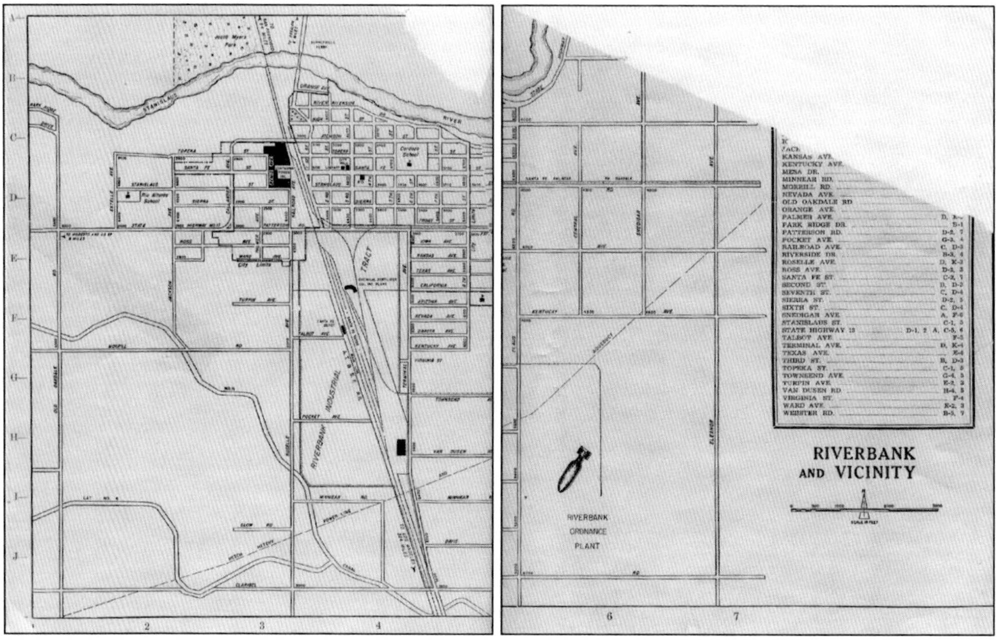

The left side of the 1940s townsite map above shows the location of some of the major buildings in town, including the cannery, terminal, roundhouse, and the major schools. The right side of the map shows the location of the ammunitions plant off Claus Road. Although the upper legend of the map is torn, some of the major street locations can still be seen.

Five

EDUCATION AND YOUTH

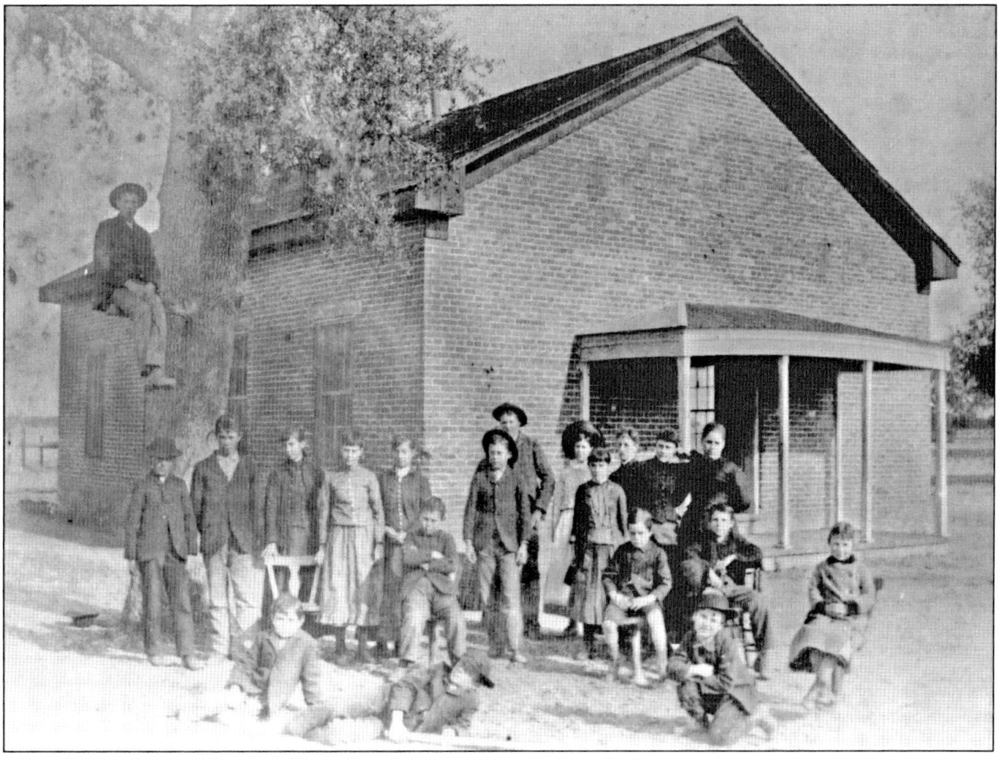

During the days of Burneyille, after Riverbank was founded, and up into the 1920s, the main school in the area was the Langworth School, which was established in the late 1800s. Even after the town of Burneyville had faded away, the school still remained. Today, there is nothing left but the photograph.

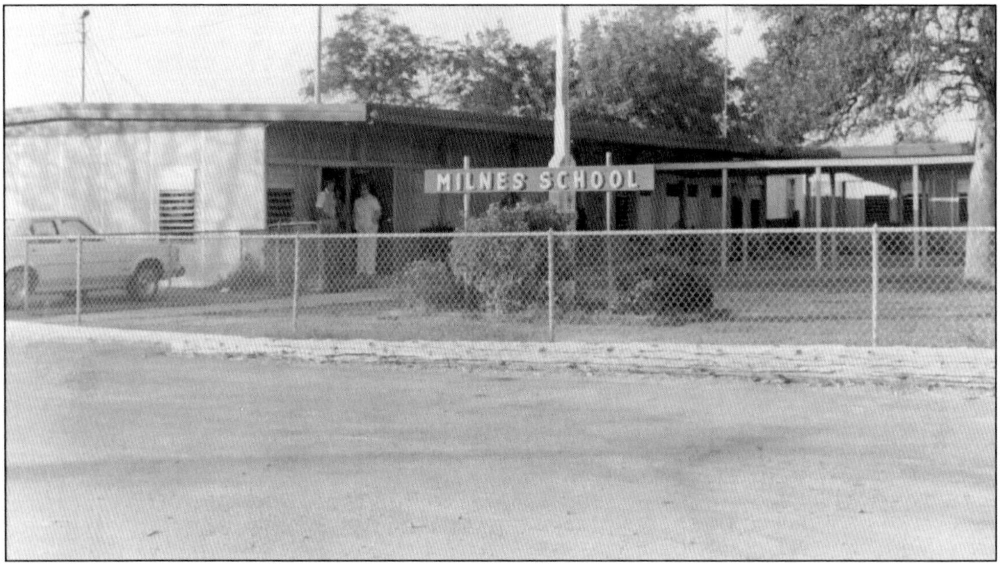

Another school that Riverbank children attended was the Milnes School, founded in 1881 on land of John L. Milnes. Originally, it was a one-room school, and it was expanded twice during the first half of the 20th century. It joined the Riverbank School District in the 1960s.

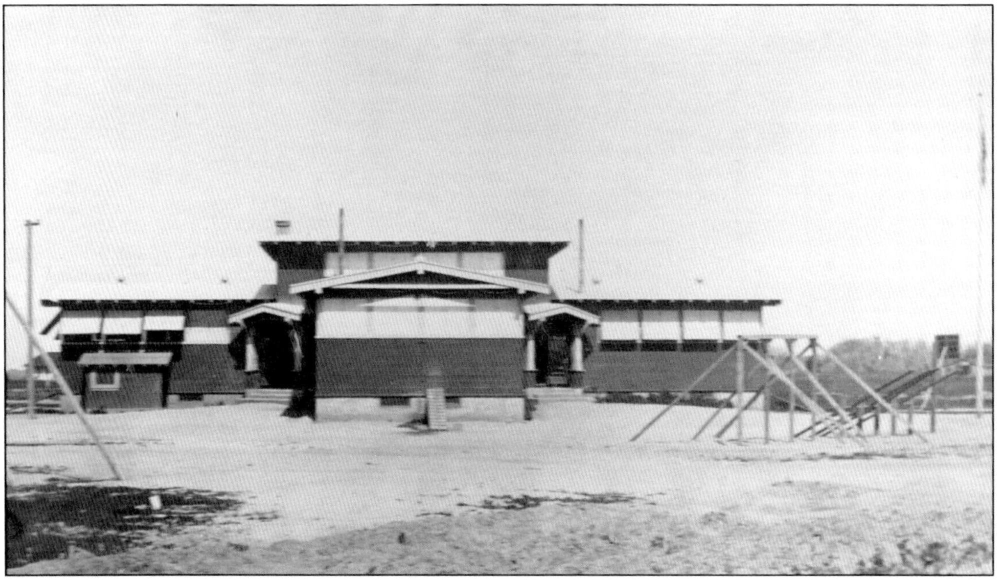

The very first school in Riverbank was held inside the fellowship hall of the Methodist church. As the town grew and acquired more students, a new open-air school was designed and featured at the 1915 World's Fair in San Francisco. World War I delayed its construction, so it was built in 1922 on the east side of town. The school did not have windows, but canvas was pulled down over the openings, and the only glass was in the doors. In the wintertime, students often became sick from rain pouring in, and on sunny days, the chalkboards were difficult to see due to the glare of the sun.

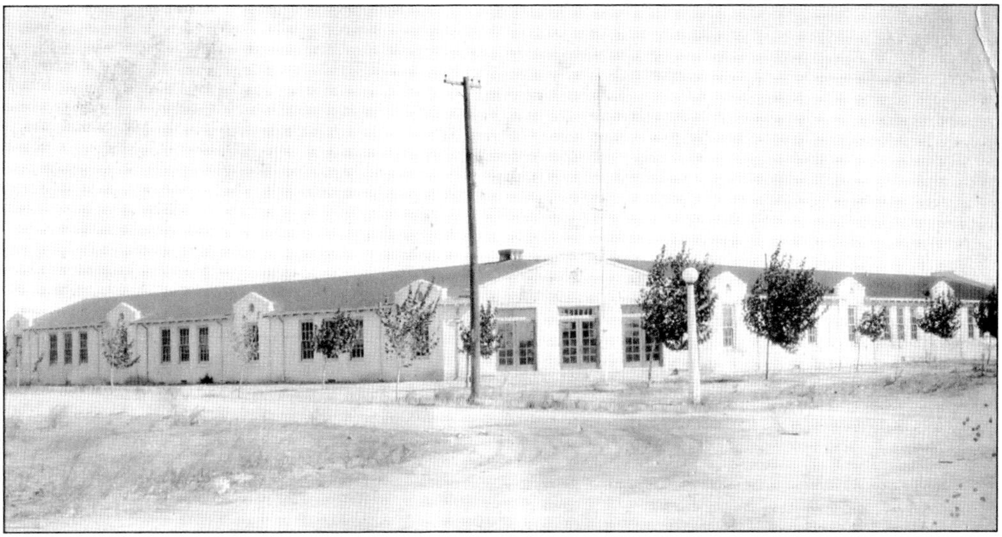

Riverbank Grammar School was the next school built in the mid-1920s. Truman V. Cardozo was the principal. It originally stood on Fifth Street where Cardozo Junior High School now stands.

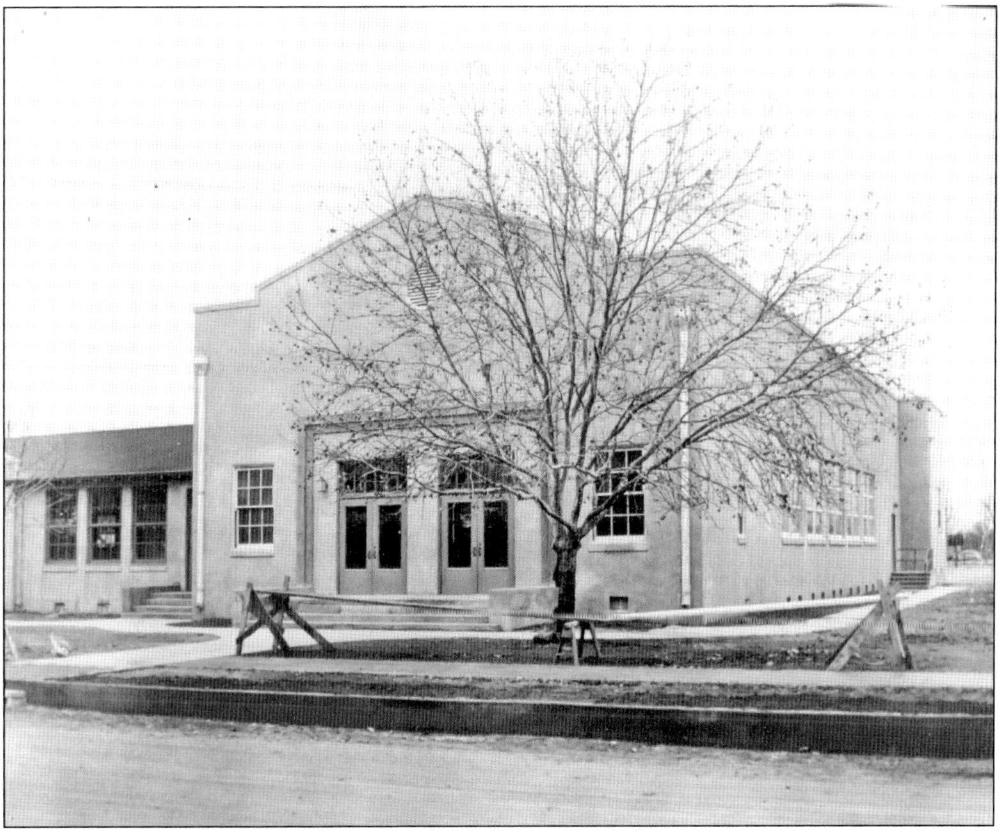

The Cardozo School, seen here, was constructed in the 1940s. It was named for Truman Cardozo, who was the principal of Riverbank Grammar School.

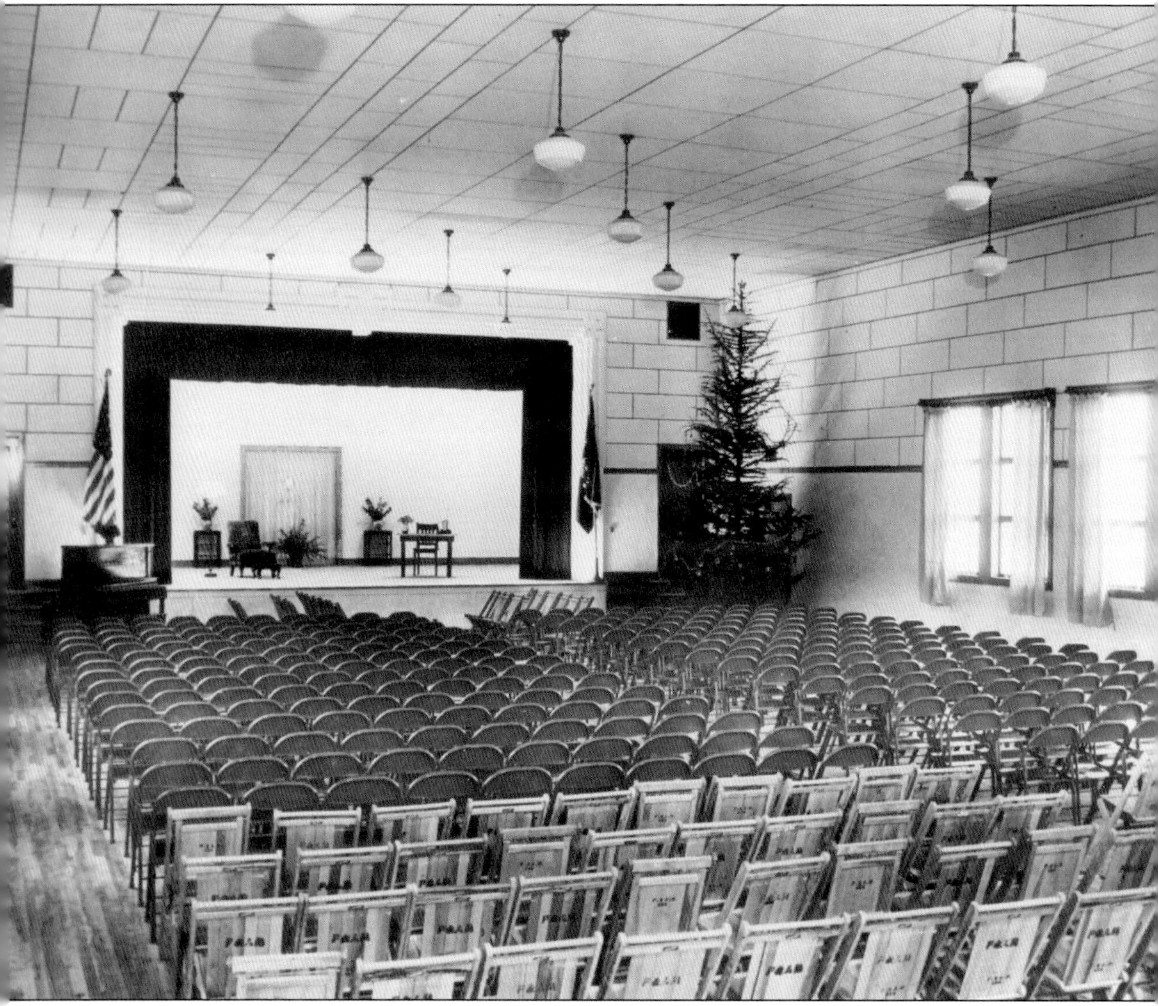

The Cardozo School auditorium was not only used for school activities but also for community events. It has also been used as a gymnasium and cafeteria.

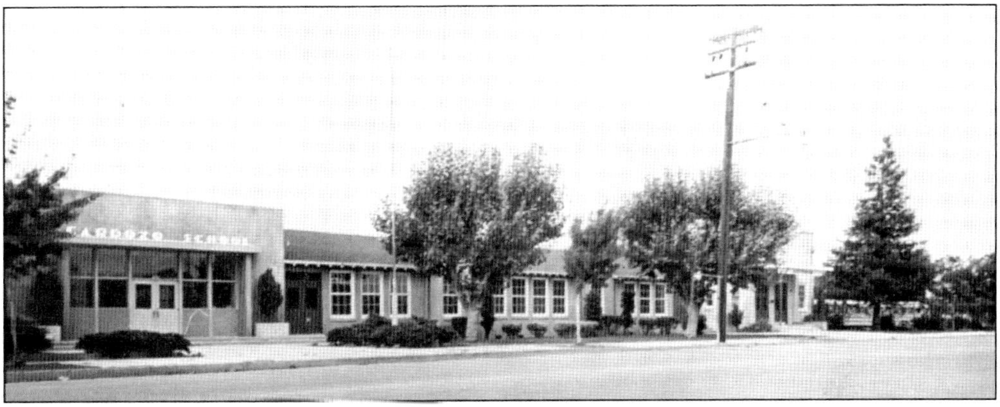

The Cardozo School was expanded during the Korean War, adding wings to either side. Today, the school serves the community as its junior high school.

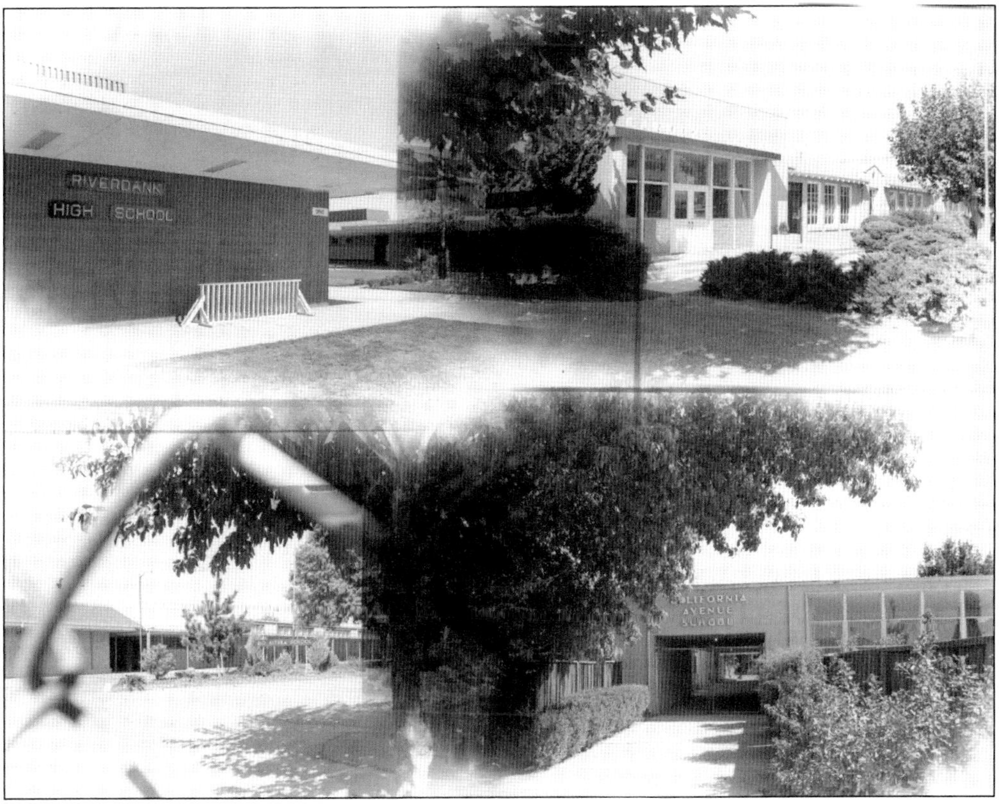

Here is a collage of some of Riverbank's major schools. Clockwise from the upper left are the Riverbank High School, Cardozo Middle School, California Avenue Elementary School, and the Rio Altura School.

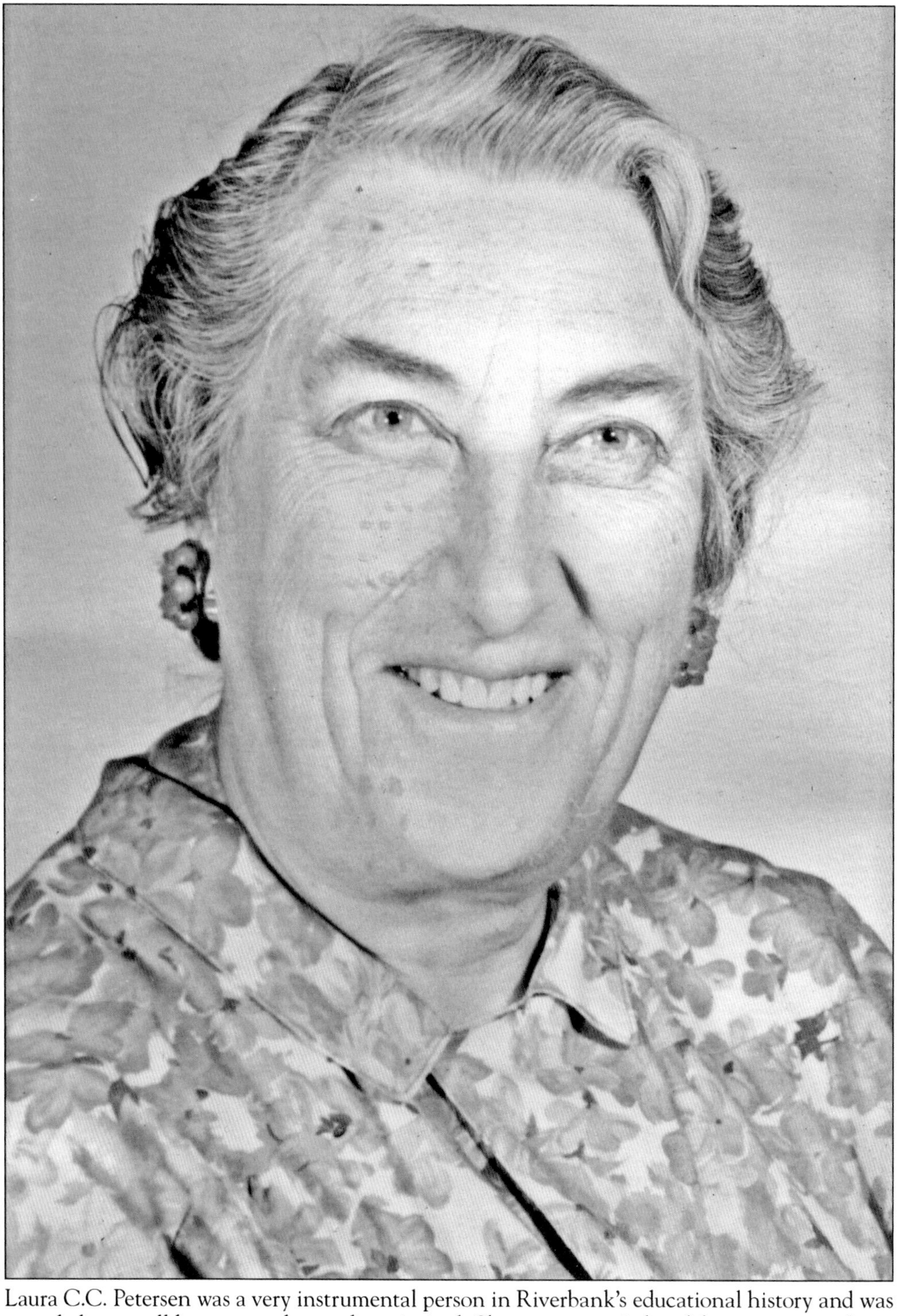

Laura C.C. Petersen was a very instrumental person in Riverbank's educational history and was regarded as a well-known teacher and a principal. She never married and for many years drove a Ford Model A sedan that was kept up so well it is now on display in an automobile museum back east.

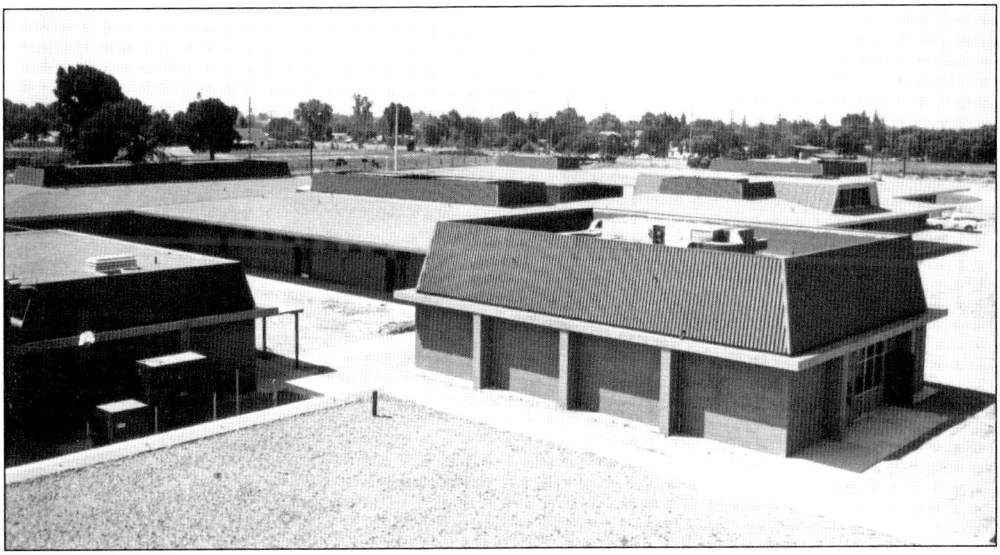

Riverbank High School was constructed in the 1970s. Prior to this high school, students in Riverbank attended Oakdale High School.

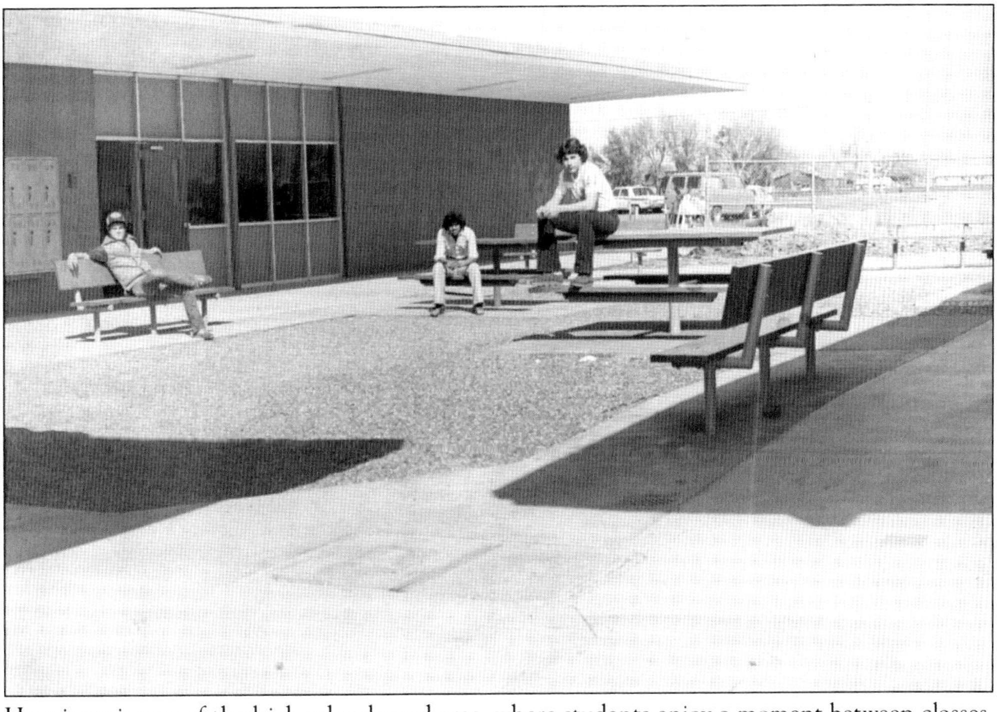

Here is an image of the high school quad area, where students enjoy a moment between classes.

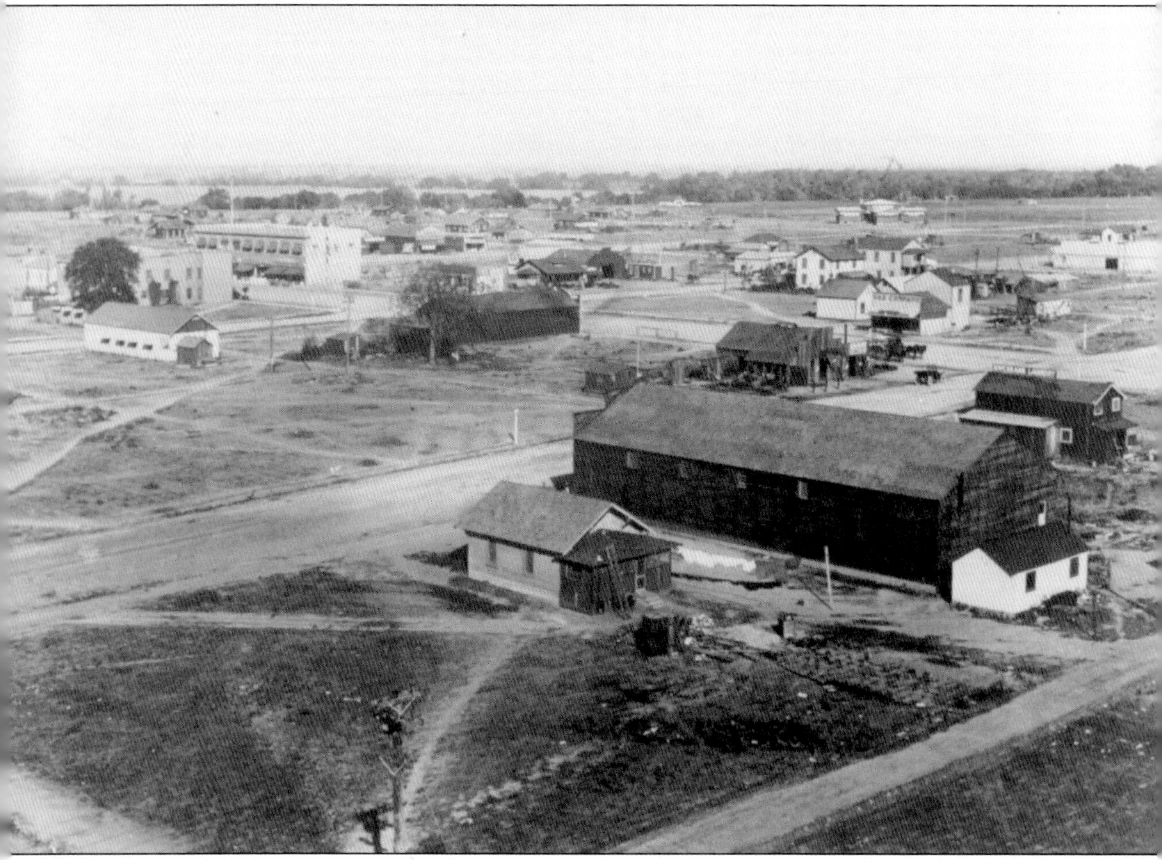

Many buildings from the early 20th century can be seen in this photograph. Running at an angle through the middle of the picture from left to right is Sierra Street. The cross street is Third Street. On the southwest corner of Third and Sierra Streets is the first laundry. Immediately to the west of this is the Legion Theater, and to the north of the laundry is Pete Paglia's blacksmith shop. Almost on the northeast corner is the gas company. On the opposite side of Third Street can be seen the Dreamland Theater. Toward the left-hand side of the picture on the corner of Third Street and Santa Fe Avenue can be seen the bank building, and in the distance below the trees on the right is the open air school.

In 1921, the citizens of Riverbank came together in order to purchase land on which to construct a library. The area behind a large oak tree on Santa Fe Avenue was selected, and the library was built. Citizens contributed books, plants, and time to see that the library was well stocked and a pleasant place to be.

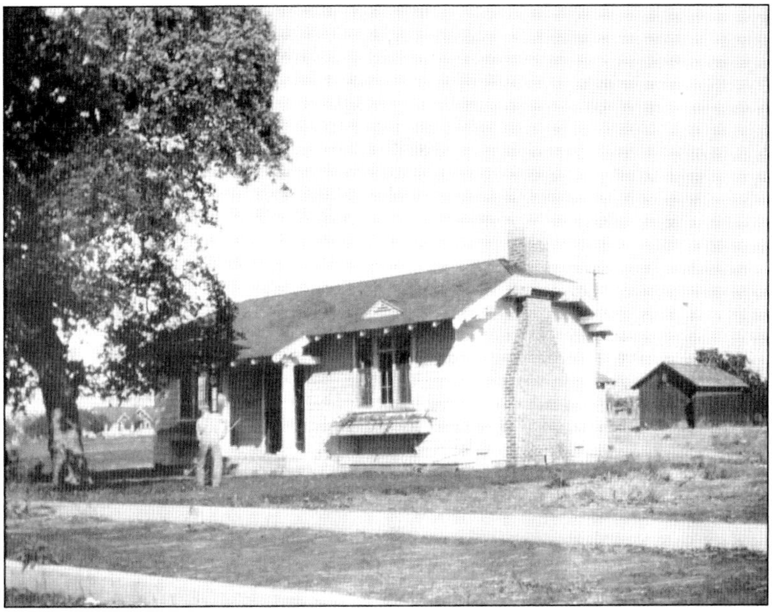

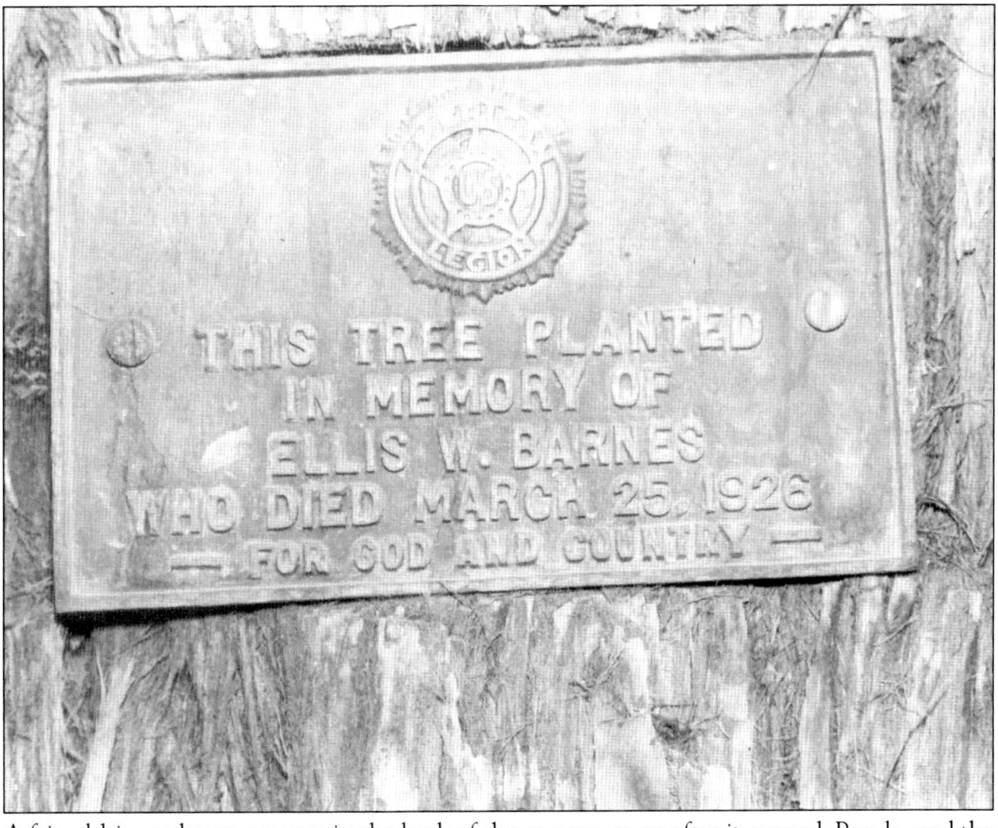

A friendship garden was grown in the back of the museum soon after it opened. People used the flowers to cheer up the sick, create funeral arrangements, and decorate the library. A redwood tree was planted in one corner of the garden and dedicated to a World War I veteran. Since that time the plaque has been removed, but the tree still stands to this day.

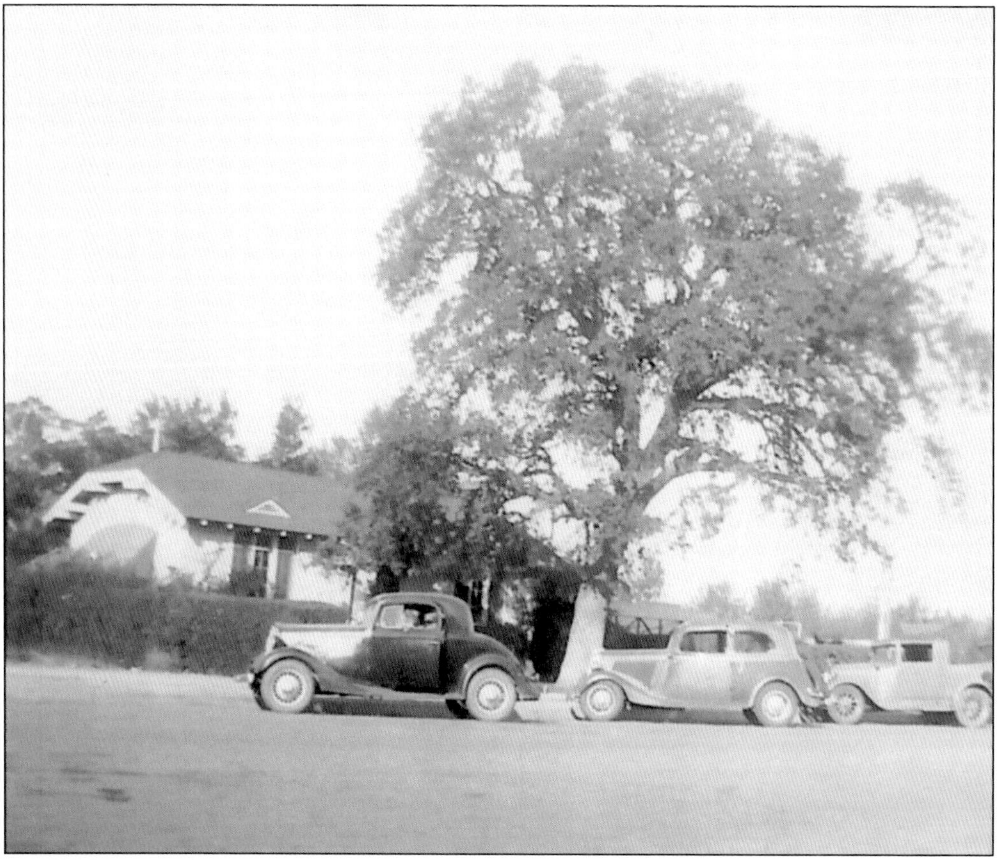

Here is a 1930s image of the library. To the right of the oak tree, a stage area that was used for plays and community events can be seen. This was torn down in the 1950s to make way for a city hall that contained a police station and jail in the rear of the building.

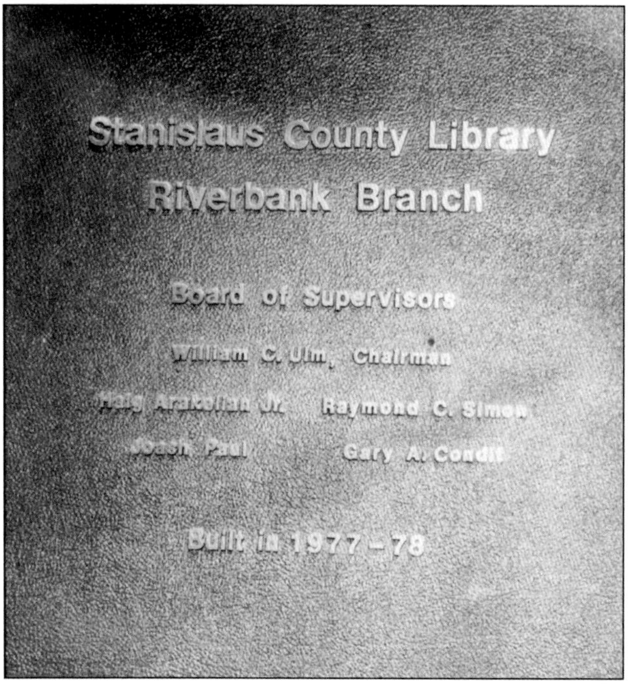

In 1977, the Bessac Library was built on Santa Fe Avenue and Eighth Street. The old library building served as the chamber of commerce up into the 1990s, when a new chamber of commerce building was constructed on Third and Topeka Streets.

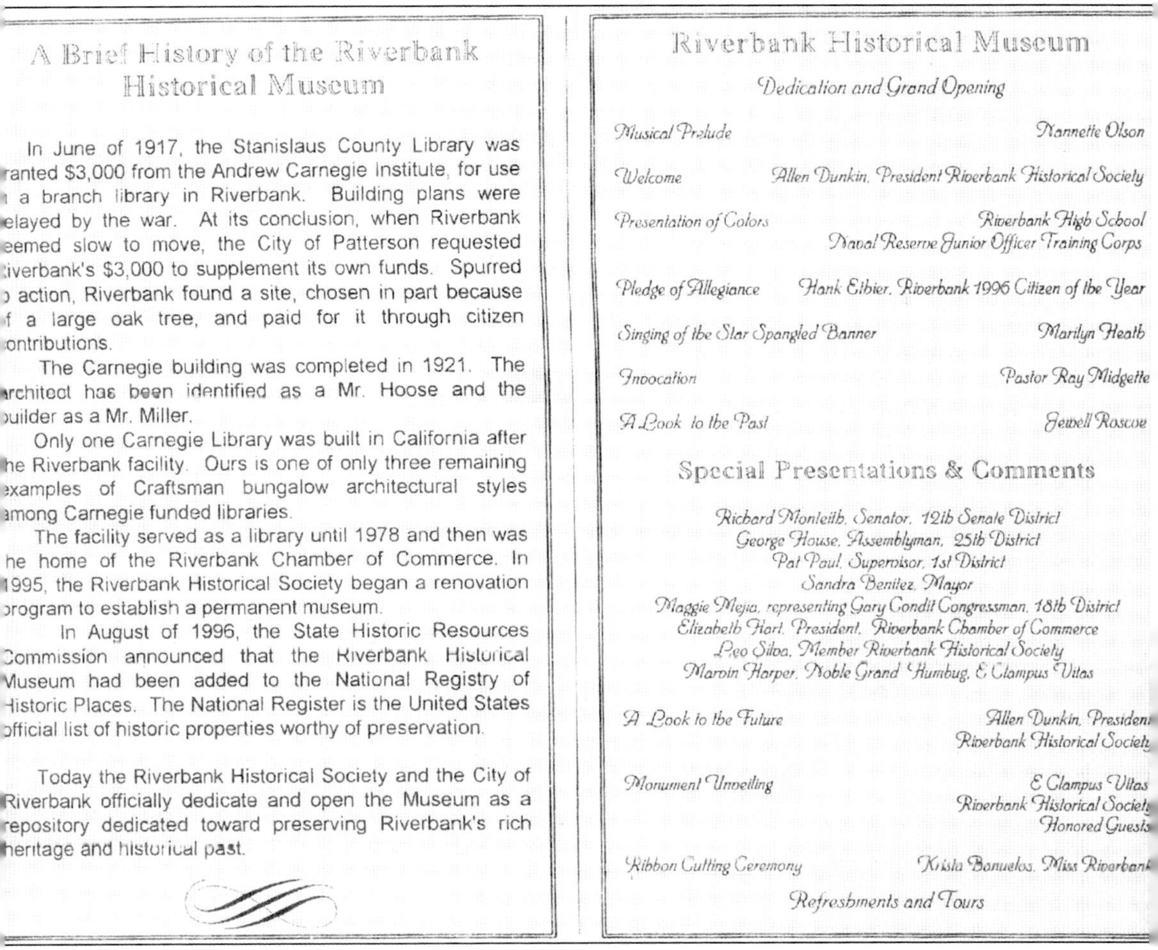

A Brief History of the Riverbank Historical Museum

In June of 1917, the Stanislaus County Library was ranted $3,000 from the Andrew Carnegie Institute, for use a branch library in Riverbank. Building plans were elayed by the war. At its conclusion, when Riverbank eemed slow to move, the City of Patterson requested iverbank's $3,000 to supplement its own funds. Spurred action, Riverbank found a site, chosen in part because f a large oak tree, and paid for it through citizen ontributions.

The Carnegie building was completed in 1921. The rchitect has been identified as a Mr. Hoose and the uilder as a Mr. Miller.

Only one Carnegie Library was built in California after he Riverbank facility. Ours is one of only three remaining xamples of Craftsman bungalow architectural styles among Carnegie funded libraries.

The facility served as a library until 1978 and then was he home of the Riverbank Chamber of Commerce. In 1995, the Riverbank Historical Society began a renovation program to establish a permanent museum.

In August of 1996, the State Historic Resources Commission announced that the Riverbank Historical Museum had been added to the National Registry of Historic Places. The National Register is the United States official list of historic properties worthy of preservation.

Today the Riverbank Historical Society and the City of Riverbank officially dedicate and open the Museum as a repository dedicated toward preserving Riverbank's rich heritage and historical past.

Riverbank Historical Museum

Dedication and Grand Opening

Musical Prelude — *Nannette Olson*

Welcome — *Allen Dunkin, President Riverbank Historical Society*

Presentation of Colors — *Riverbank High School Naval Reserve Junior Officer Training Corps*

Pledge of Allegiance — *Hank Ethier, Riverbank 1996 Citizen of the Year*

Singing of the Star Spangled Banner — *Marilyn Heath*

Invocation — *Pastor Ray Midgette*

A Look to the Past — *Jewell Roscoe*

Special Presentations & Comments

Richard Monteith, Senator, 12th Senate District
George House, Assemblyman, 25th District
Pat Paul, Supervisor, 1st District
Sandra Benitez, Mayor
Maggie Mejia, representing Gary Condit Congressman, 18th District
Elizabeth Hart, President, Riverbank Chamber of Commerce
Leo Silva, Member Riverbank Historical Society
Marvin Harper, Noble Grand Humbug, E Clampus Vitas

A Look to the Future — *Allen Dunkin, President Riverbank Historical Society*

Monument Unveiling — *E Clampus Vitas, Riverbank Historical Society, Honored Guests*

Ribbon Cutting Ceremony — *Krista Banuelos, Miss Riverbank*

Refreshments and Tours

In 1995, an effort was made to preserve the library building as the Riverbank Historical Society and Museum. Displays and photographs continue to expand as new information is brought in to expand the knowledge of the town's history.

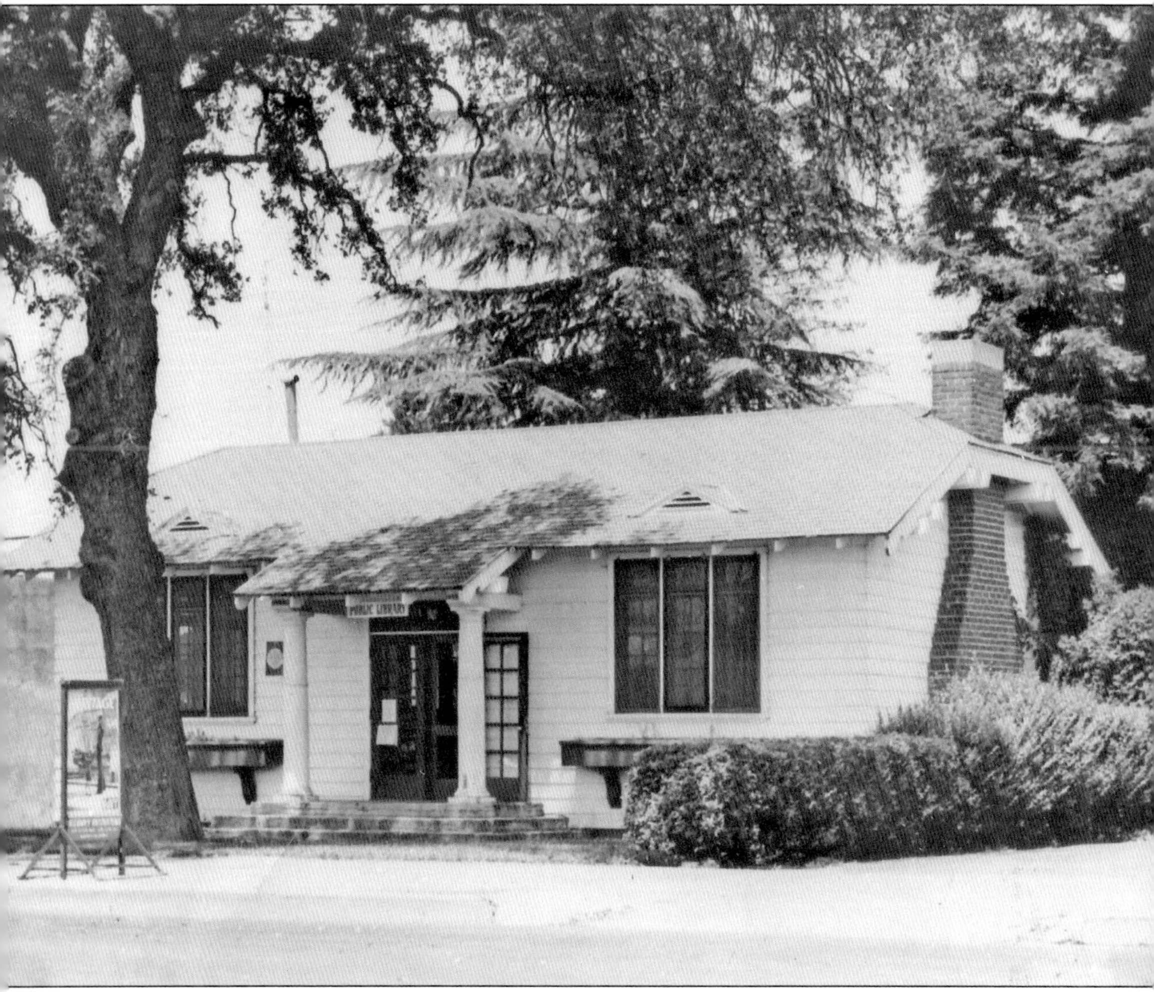

Here is the old library building, preserved today as the Riverbank Historical Society and Museum.

Six

Fire Department

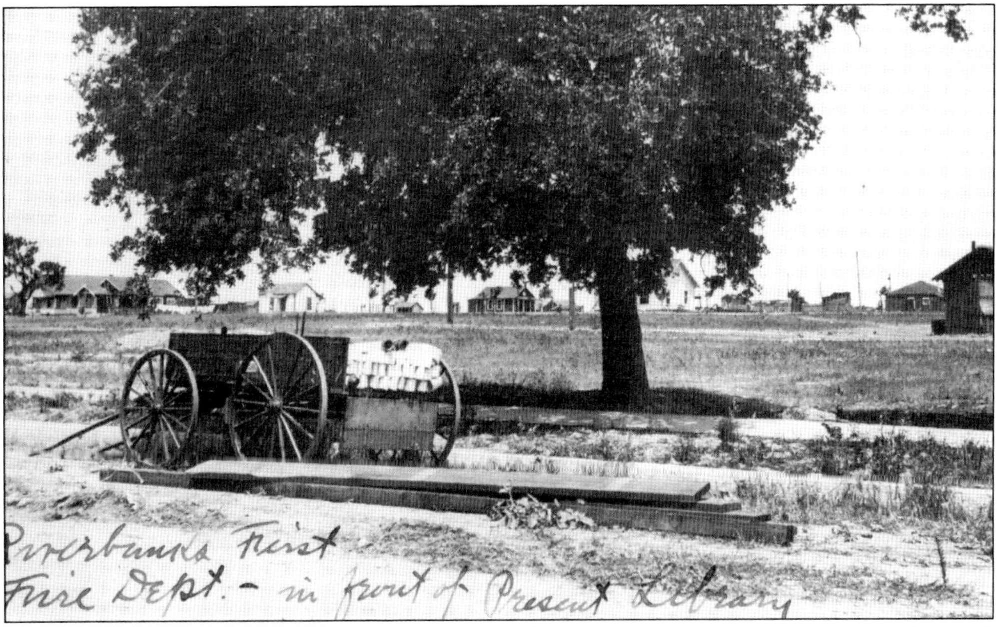

Riverbank's first fire department was completely voluntary. The City of Modesto donated a small fire hose cart and a saw blade to the new town. The blade was used in place of an alarm to alert volunteers to the event of a fire. The hose was towed by a Ford Model A. The first person to the station wrote down the location of the fire so other volunteers could find their way.

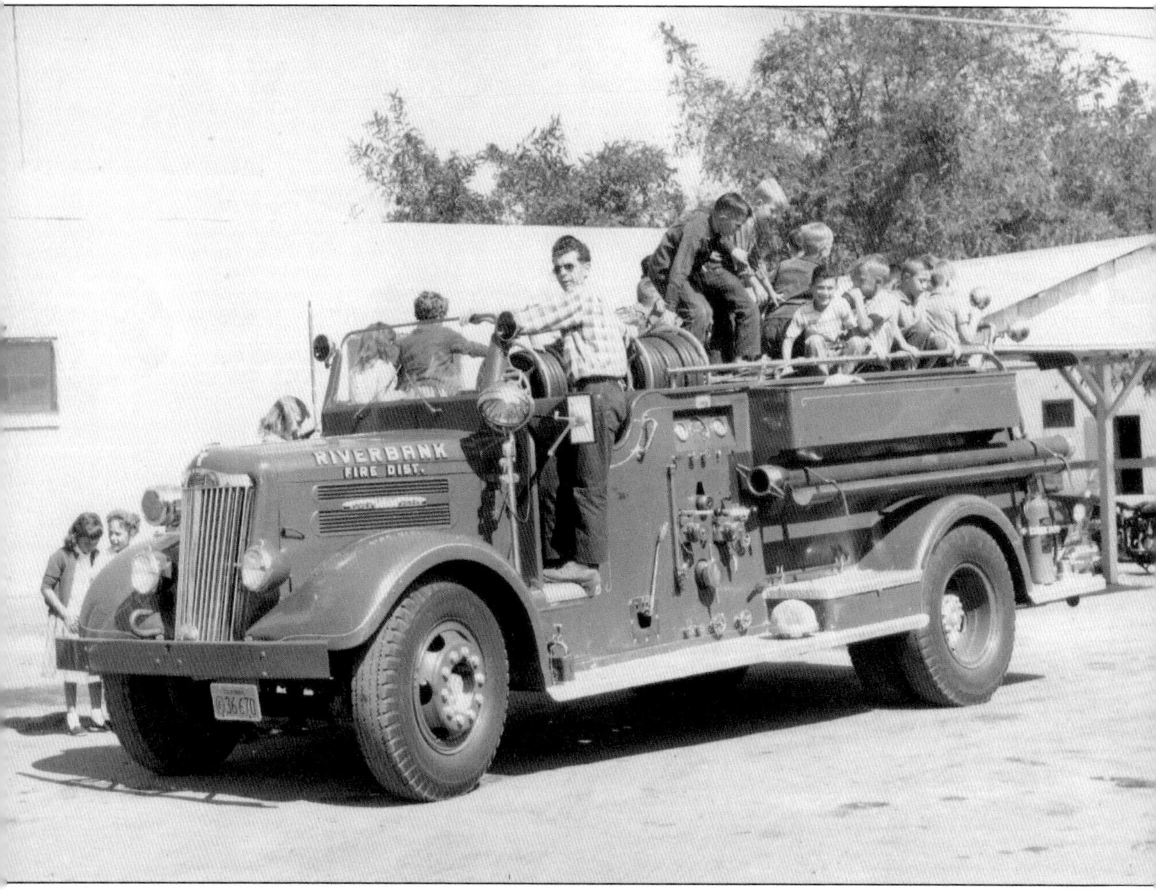

By the 1940s, the fire department had acquired more reliable vehicles, including the truck shown here.

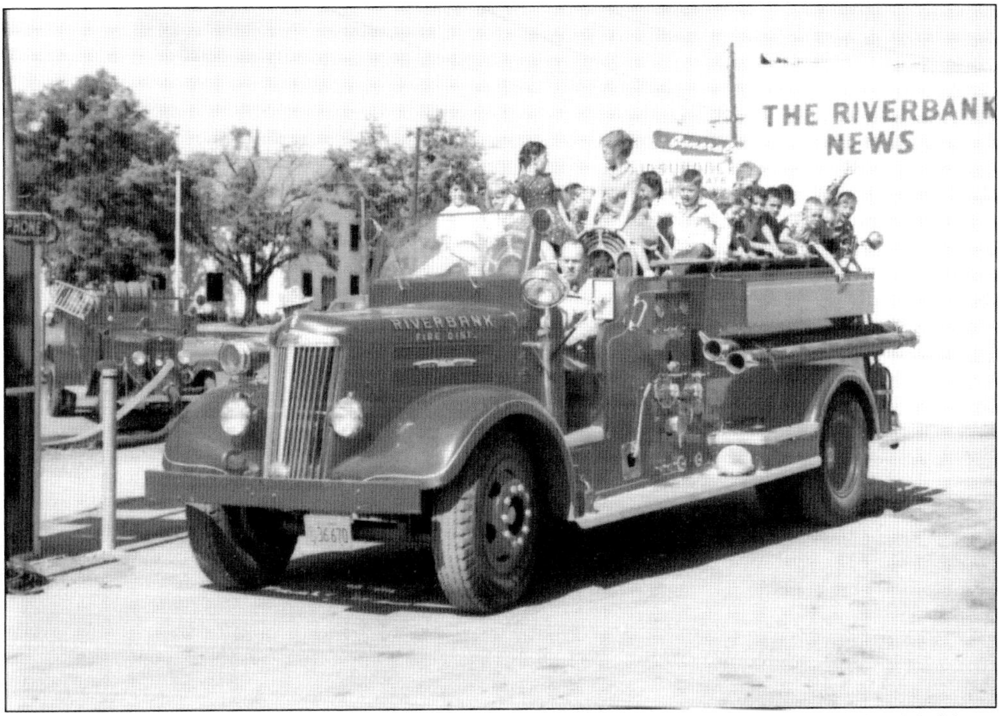

In the 1950s, visiting the town fire station was an important and memorable event for schoolchildren. Class pictures were often taken in front of the truck by the Harris Photo Studio.

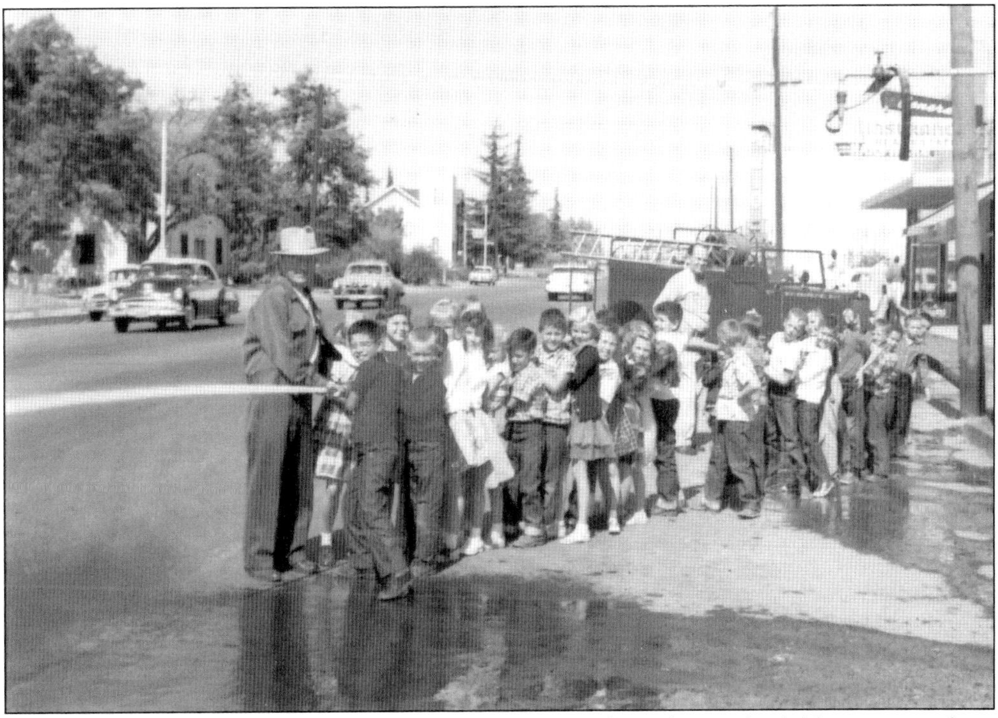

Of course, one of the most memorable events for many students during the field trip was working the fire hose.

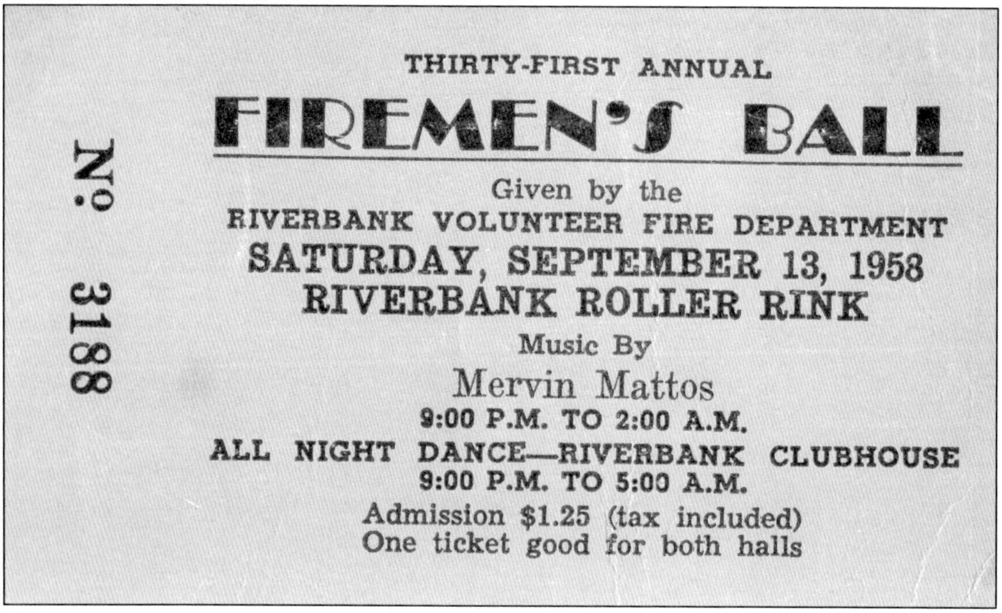

THIRTY-FIRST ANNUAL

FIREMEN'S BALL

Given by the

RIVERBANK VOLUNTEER FIRE DEPARTMENT

SATURDAY, SEPTEMBER 13, 1958

RIVERBANK ROLLER RINK

Music By

Mervin Mattos

9:00 P.M. TO 2:00 A.M.

ALL NIGHT DANCE—RIVERBANK CLUBHOUSE

9:00 P.M. TO 5:00 A.M.

Admission $1.25 (tax included)

One ticket good for both halls

No 3188

One of the popular ways to raise money for the department was the anticipated event of the Fireman's Ball.

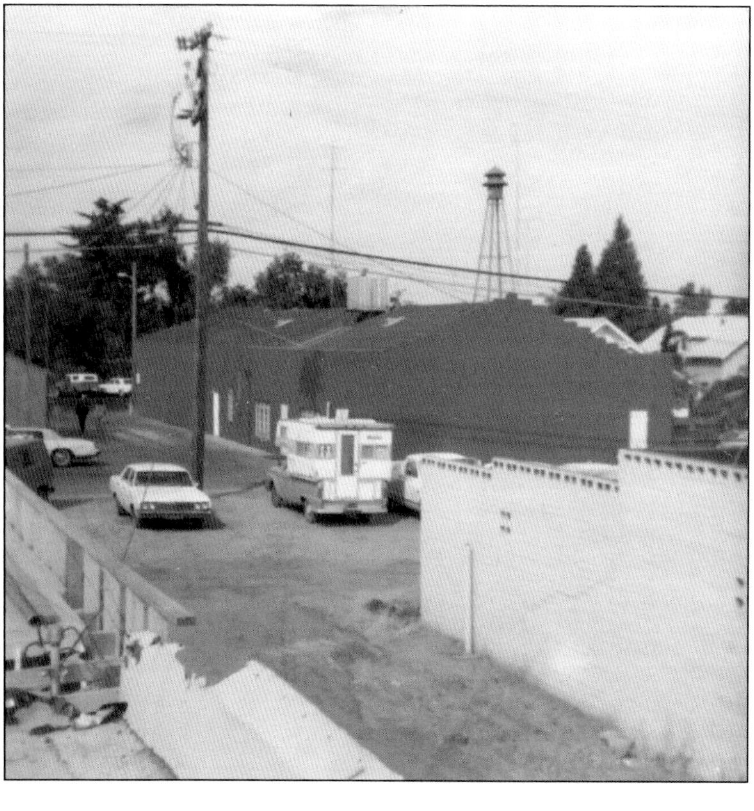

Vehicles were stored in a red fire shed barn on the corner of Topeka and Third Streets. In the latter part of the 20th century, the fire department was taken over by Stanislaus County, and the old fire shed was torn down to make way for new city buildings.

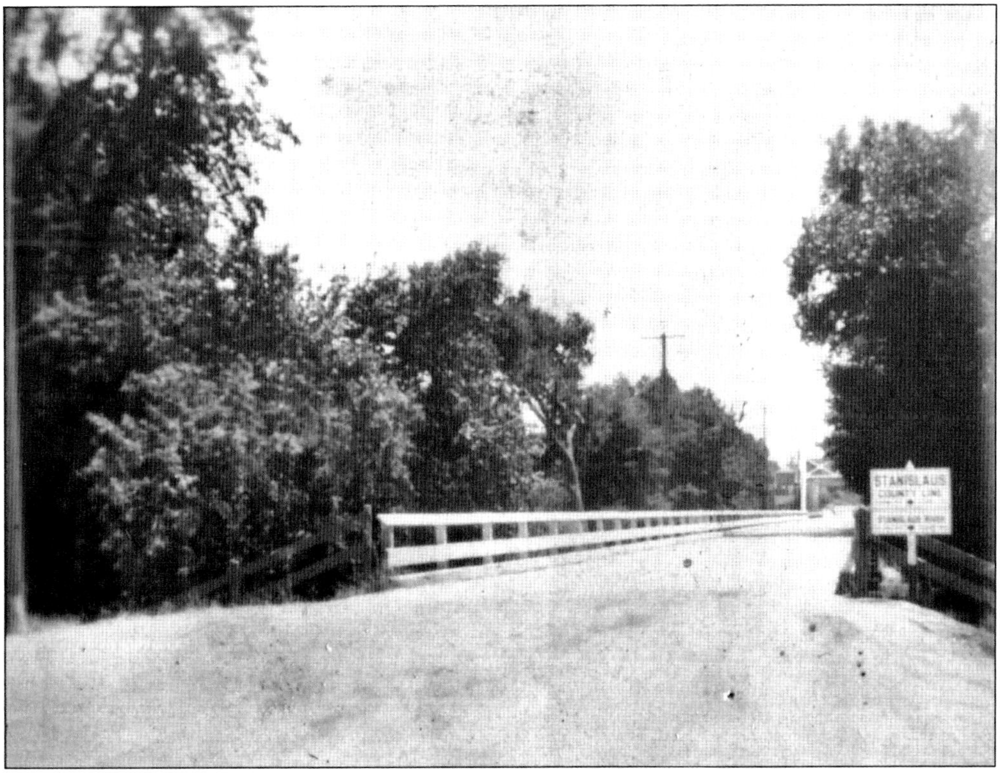

The original Burneyville Bridge was a simple wooden structure across the river. In 1928, a stronger steel structure was built. Many people remember measuring the severity of the flooding river in wintertime by seeing where the waters came up to on the bridge structure.

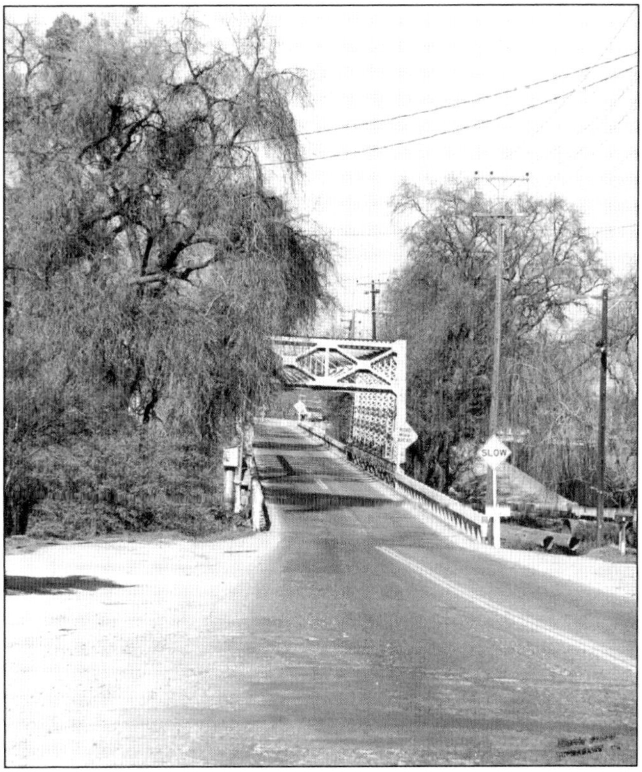

This 1960s picture shows the steel bridge slightly before a new concrete bridge was constructed.

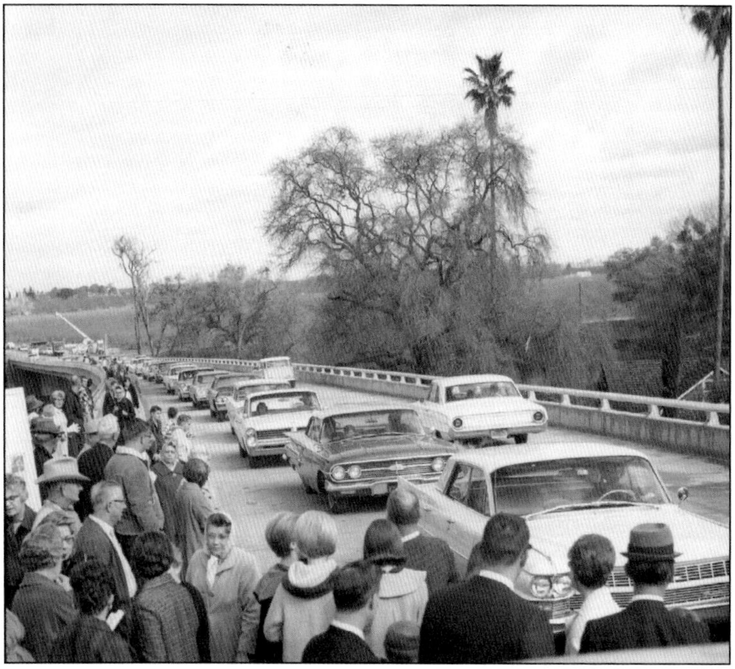

The Burneyville Road Bridge has seen many incarnations, from a simple wooden bridge spanning the river to a truss bridge in the 1920s to the current concrete bridge that was constructed in the 1960s. This scene shows the celebration during the opening of the newest bridge.

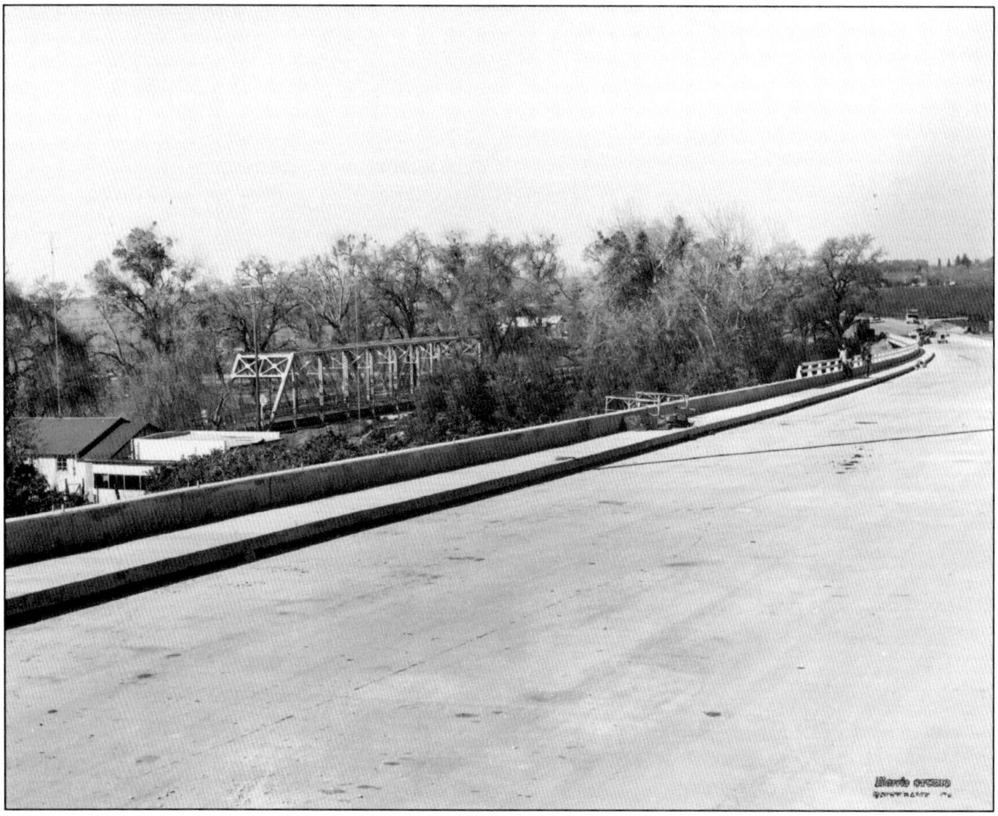

Here is a view of the steel and concrete bridges side by side before the old steel structure was removed.

Seven

ENTERTAINMENT AND RECREATION

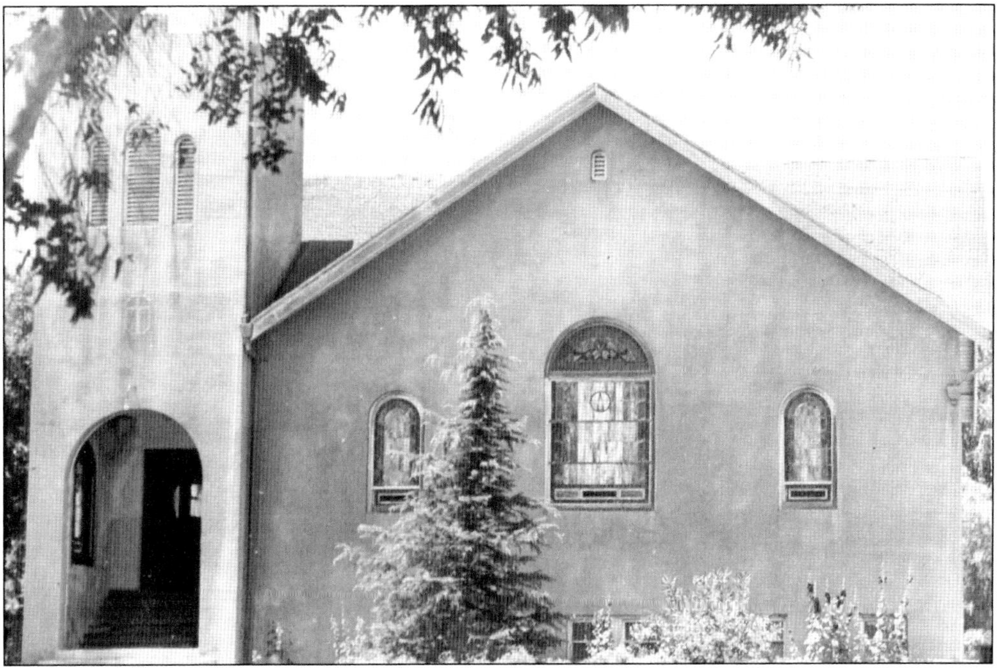

The Methodist Episcopal church began in 1865 in Burneyville. In 1874, the Methodist and Brethren churches combined and shared a building, alternating Sunday services. The Methodist church moved away from its old location in Burneyville to its present location on Third and Atchison Streets on December 11, 1911. Construction of the actual building was not completed until February 28, 1912, and the first service was held on March 3. In 1923, a new building was constructed that became known as the "Highway Church." The building to the west of the church was the original location of Riverbank's first school.

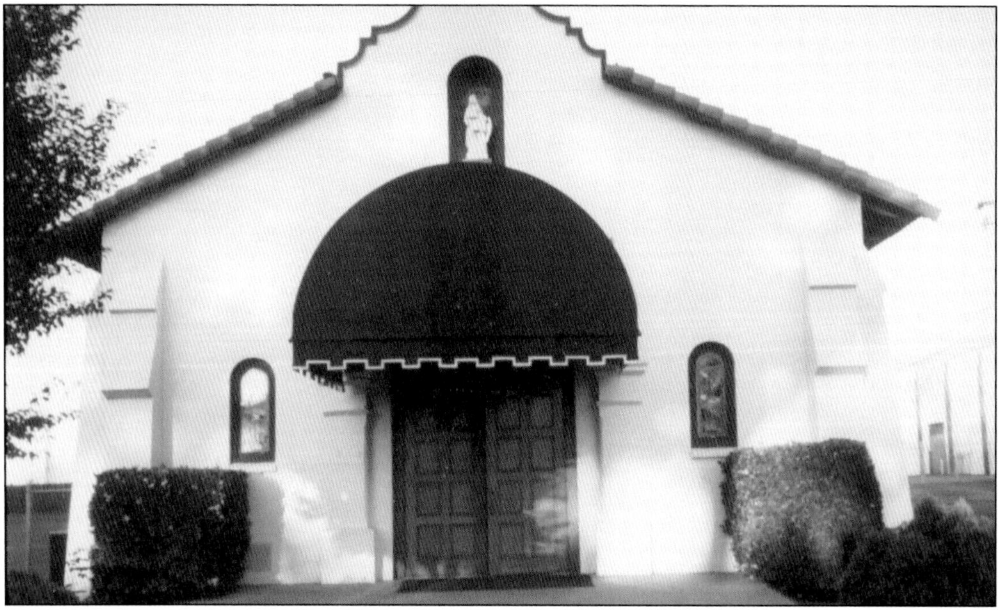

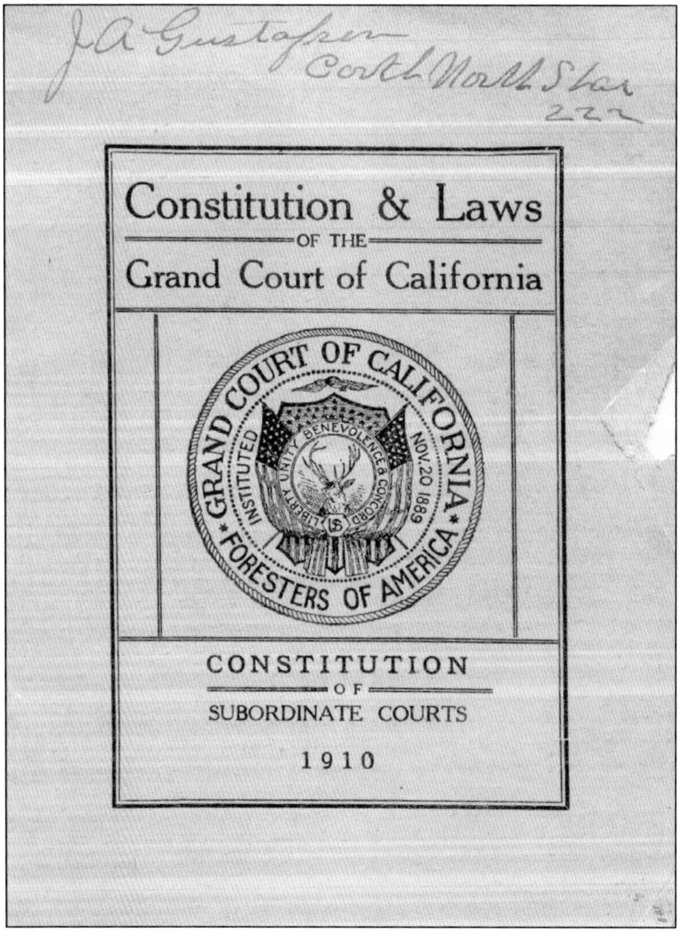

Constitution & Laws

OF THE

Grand Court of California

GRAND COURT OF CALIFORNIA

FORESTERS OF AMERICA

INSTITUTED NOV. 20 1889

LIBERTY UNITY BENEVOLENCE & CONCORD

CONSTITUTION

OF

SUBORDINATE COURTS

1910

St. Frances Catholic Church is named for the wife of Lorenzo Zerillo, a former opera singer, and was constructed in the 1920s. Frances often sang in the choir. A pathway led from the church right up to the Zerillos' back door.

Riverbank had many fraternal orders in town. The Forester's Union is a fraternal order that has been around since Riverbank's earliest days.

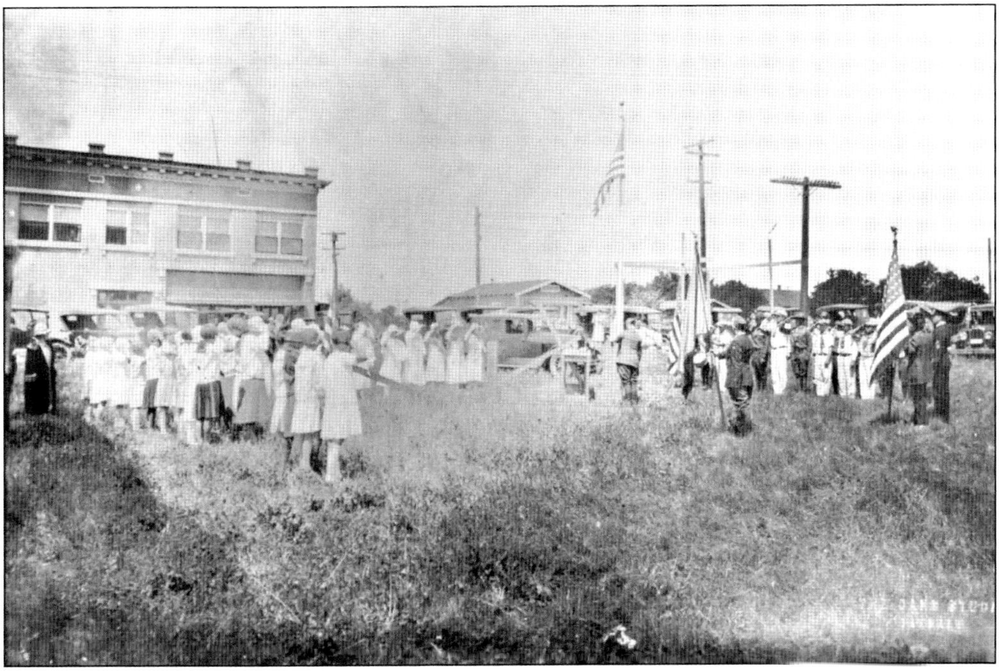

The Boy and Girl Scouts have been active in Riverbank since its earliest days. This scene is from a May Day celebration that took place on the corner of Second and Santa Fe Streets across from the Callander Building in the 1920s.

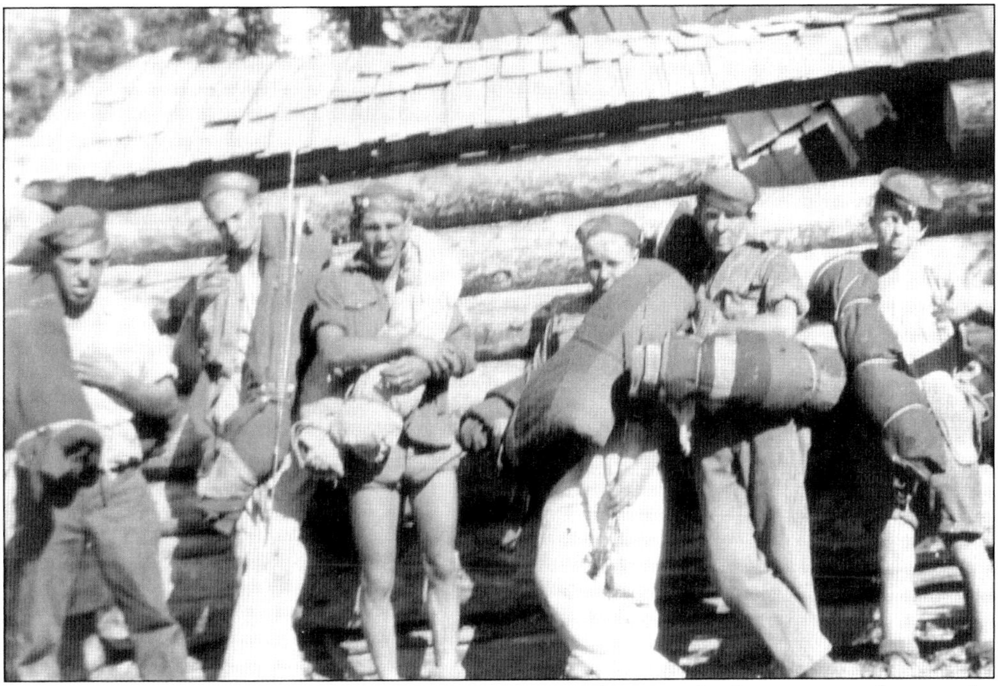

Camping was a very important part of being a Boy or Girl Scout, whether it was outdoors in the elements or inside a cabin, such as the one behind this Boy Scout troop.

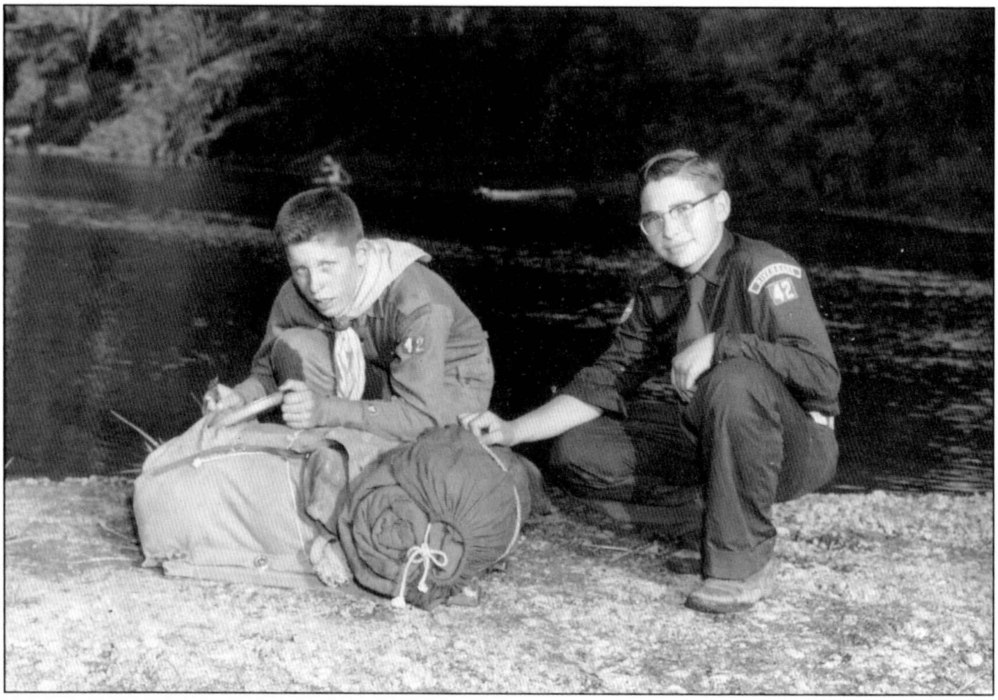

At the time this image was captured, these two young men have earned merit badges and are considered accomplished Scouts.

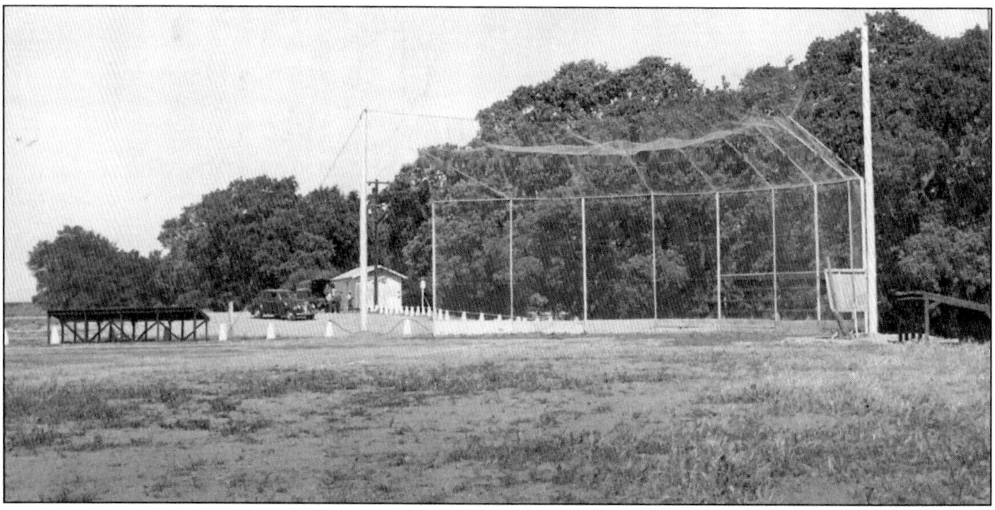

Jacob Myers Park was created from land once owned by the Myers family on the northern side of the Stanislaus River. This picture shows the main ball field in the park around the 1940s.

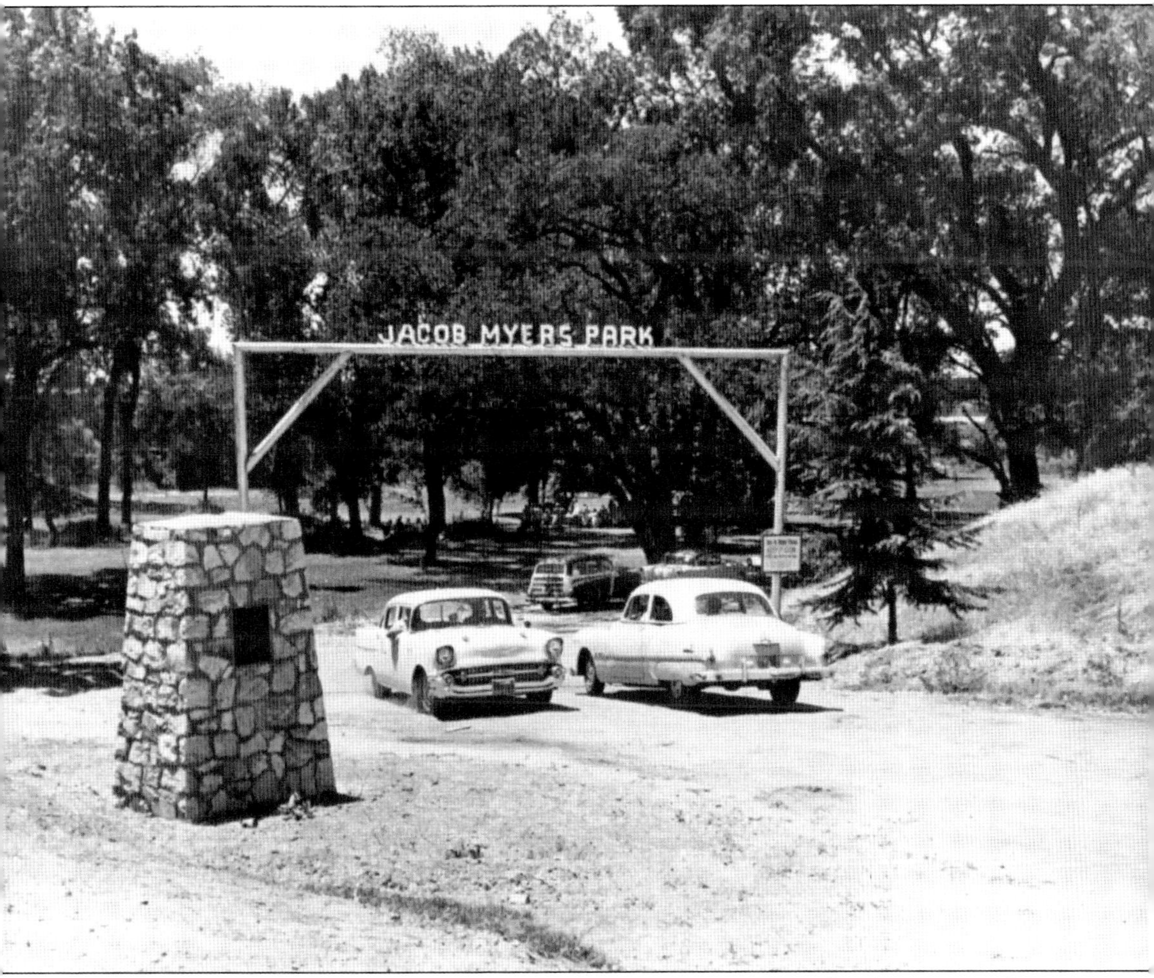

Jacob Myers Park, seen here in the 1950s, has been the site of numerous family picnics and city activities such as rodeos, baseball games, and other community events. Swimming and fishing are also enjoyed along the riverside.

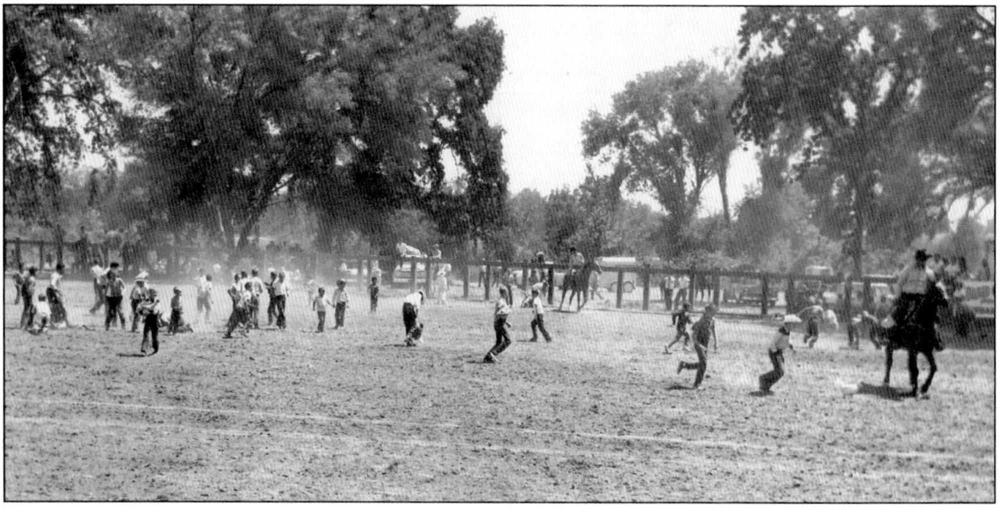

The park also features rodeo grounds where events take place annually. The rodeos are fun for parents and children alike.

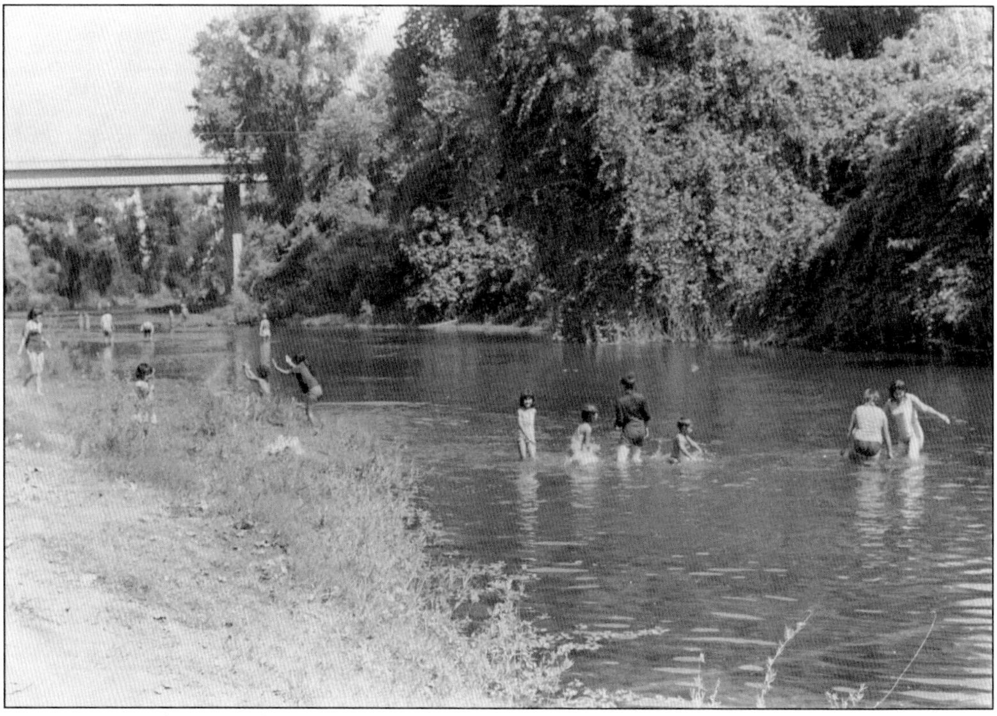

Swimming in the Stanislaus River has always been a popular activity in Riverbank and is still enjoyed in Jacob Myers Park today.

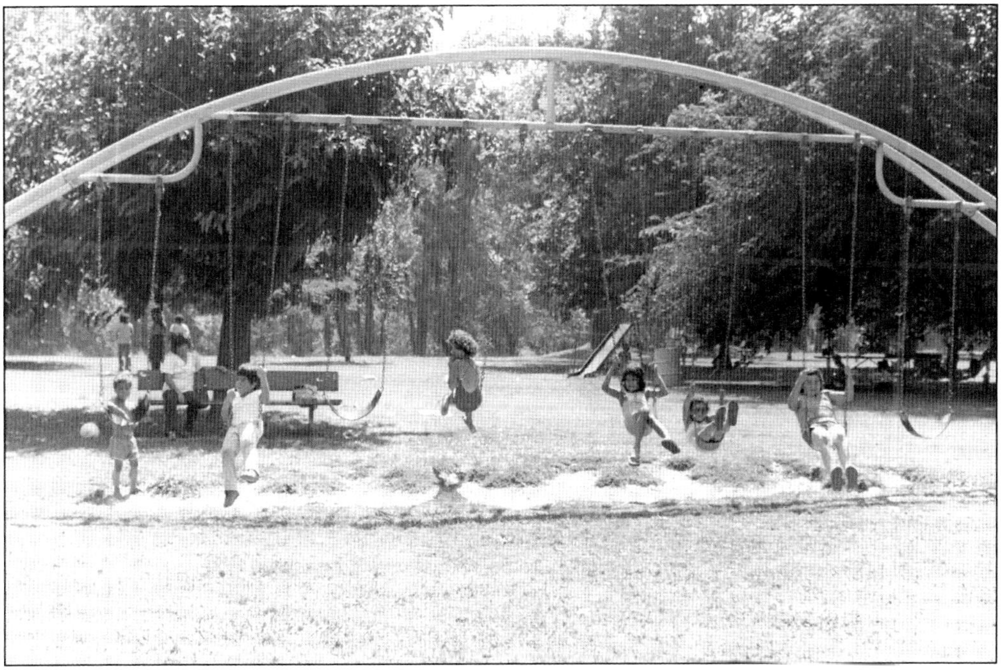

The park also has a large playground area with swings, monkey bars, and other equipment.

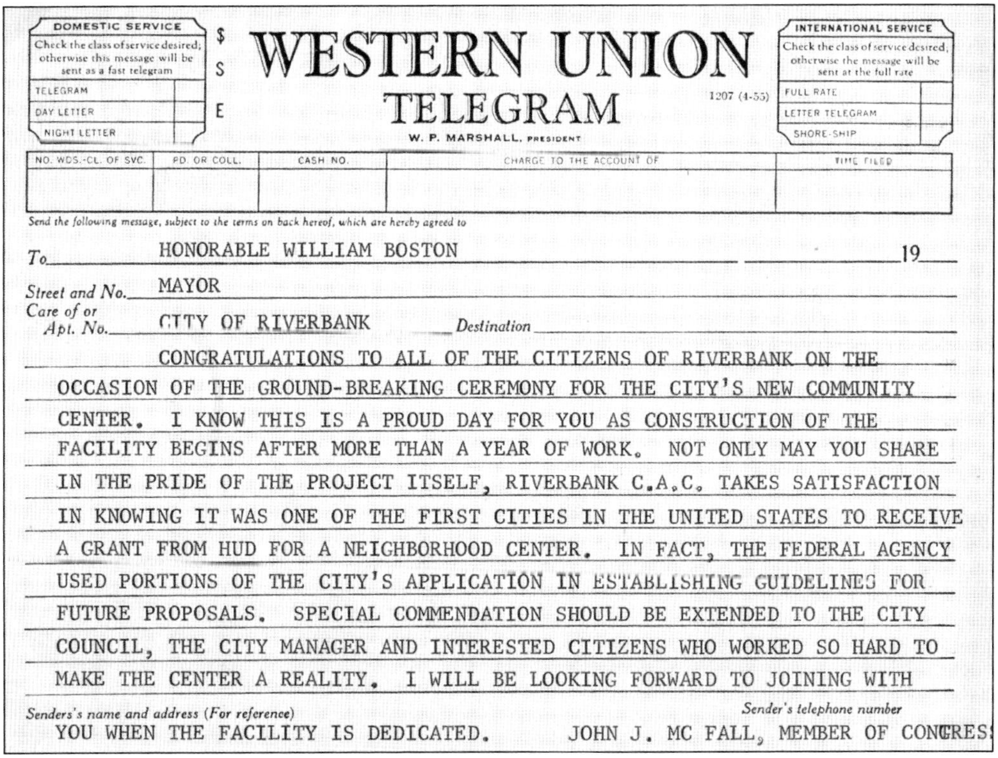

DOMESTIC SERVICE
Check the class of service desired; otherwise this message will be sent as a fast telegram
TELEGRAM
DAY LETTER
NIGHT LETTER

$
S
E

WESTERN UNION
TELEGRAM
W. P. MARSHALL, PRESIDENT

1207 (4-55)

INTERNATIONAL SERVICE
Check the class of service desired; otherwise the message will be sent at the full rate
FULL RATE
LETTER TELEGRAM
SHORE-SHIP

NO. WDS.-CL. OF SVC.	PD. OR COLL.	CASH NO.	CHARGE TO THE ACCOUNT OF	TIME FILED

Send the following message, subject to the terms on back hereof, which are hereby agreed to

To HONORABLE WILLIAM BOSTON 19

Street and No. MAYOR

Care of or Apt. No. CITY OF RIVERBANK Destination

CONGRATULATIONS TO ALL OF THE CITIZENS OF RIVERBANK ON THE OCCASION OF THE GROUND-BREAKING CEREMONY FOR THE CITY'S NEW COMMUNITY CENTER. I KNOW THIS IS A PROUD DAY FOR YOU AS CONSTRUCTION OF THE FACILITY BEGINS AFTER MORE THAN A YEAR OF WORK. NOT ONLY MAY YOU SHARE IN THE PRIDE OF THE PROJECT ITSELF, RIVERBANK C.A.C. TAKES SATISFACTION IN KNOWING IT WAS ONE OF THE FIRST CITIES IN THE UNITED STATES TO RECEIVE A GRANT FROM HUD FOR A NEIGHBORHOOD CENTER. IN FACT, THE FEDERAL AGENCY USED PORTIONS OF THE CITY'S APPLICATION IN ESTABLISHING GUIDELINES FOR FUTURE PROPOSALS. SPECIAL COMMENDATION SHOULD BE EXTENDED TO THE CITY COUNCIL, THE CITY MANAGER AND INTERESTED CITIZENS WHO WORKED SO HARD TO MAKE THE CENTER A REALITY. I WILL BE LOOKING FORWARD TO JOINING WITH

Senders's name and address (For reference) Sender's telephone number

YOU WHEN THE FACILITY IS DEDICATED. JOHN J. MC FALL, MEMBER OF CONGRES

This telegram arrived in Riverbank to congratulate the community on the completion of its new community center. The design is slightly different than what the architect envisioned, but most of the elements of the design were unchanged.

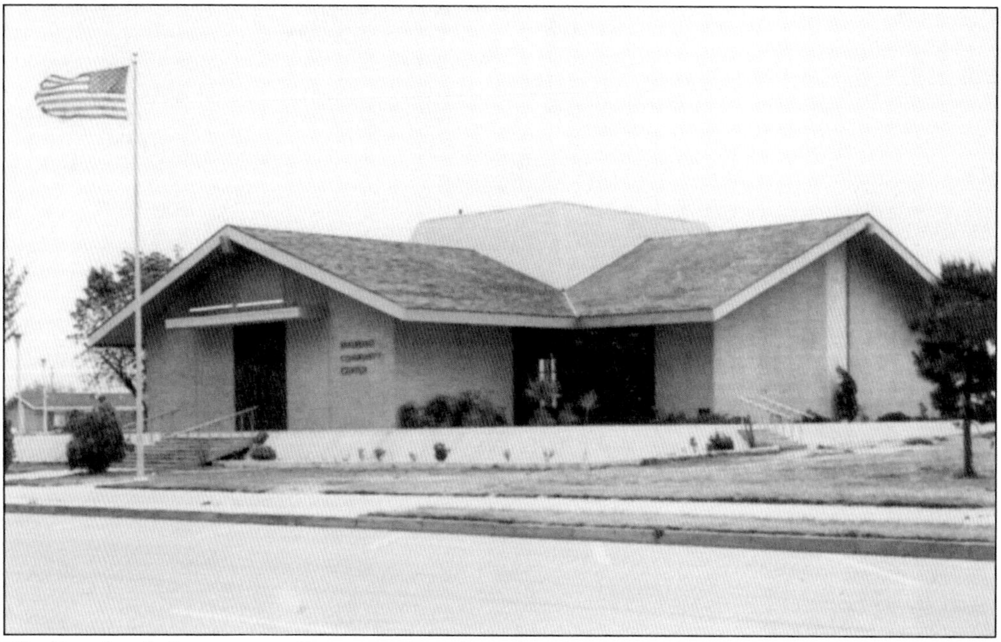

The Riverbank Community Center, built in the 1970s, has been a busy place for many community events sponsored by different clubs, activities, and groups.

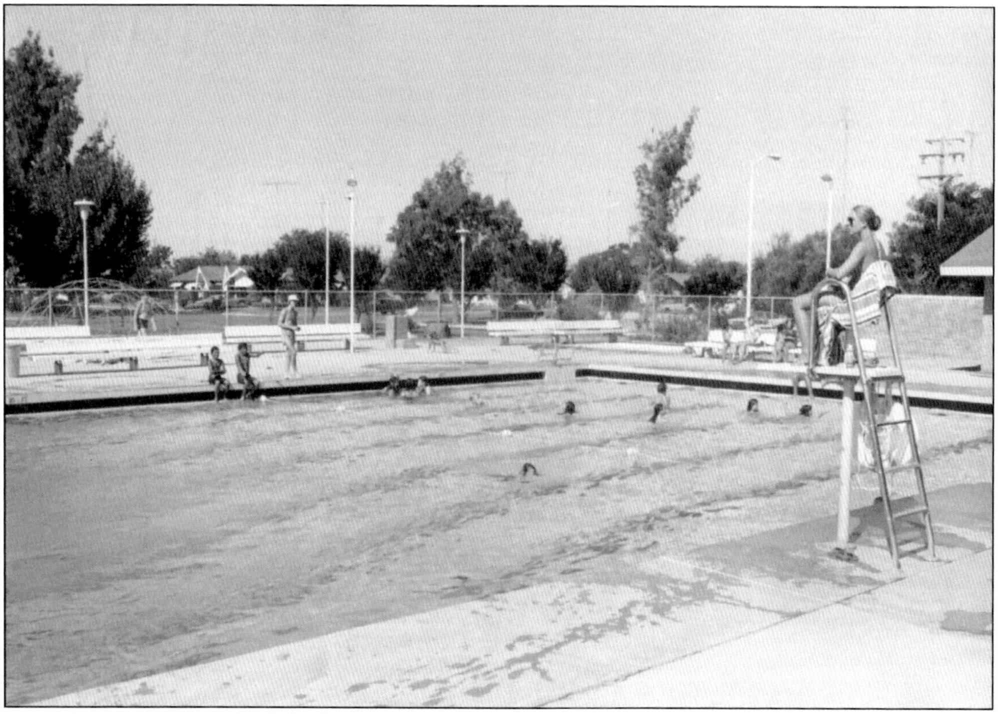

As early as 1916, Riverbank had a community pool known as the Riverbank Plunge, which stood by the river and was the center of dances, contests, and beauty pageants. In the 1970s, a new pool was constructed, and "the Plunge" was covered over.

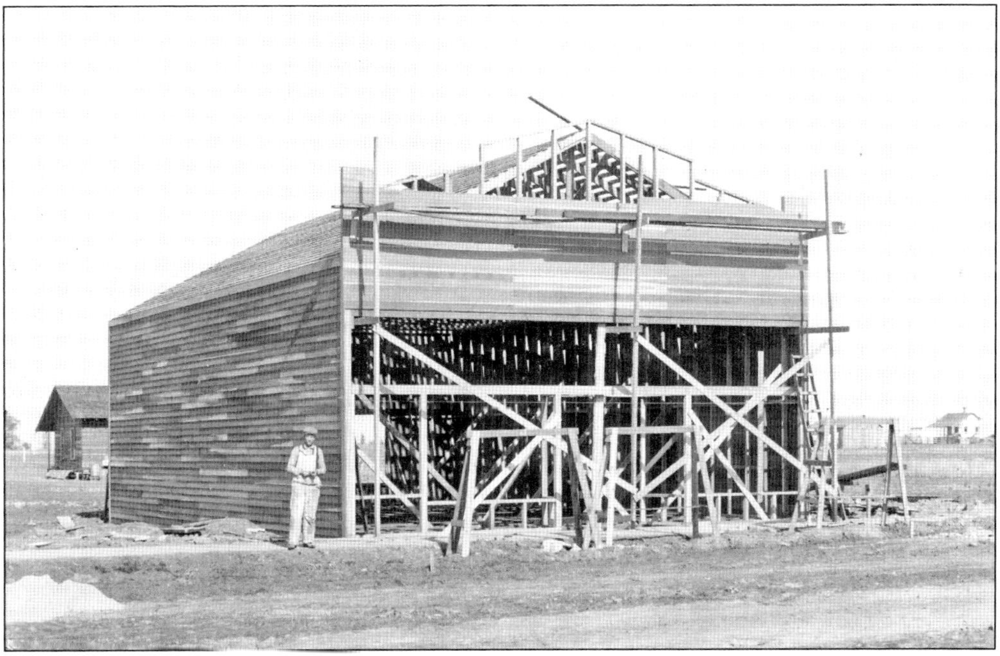

The Dreamland Theater was one of Riverbank's earliest of its kind. Established by the Reichmann brothers, it was a vaudeville theater that also hosted live performances; movies were also shown.

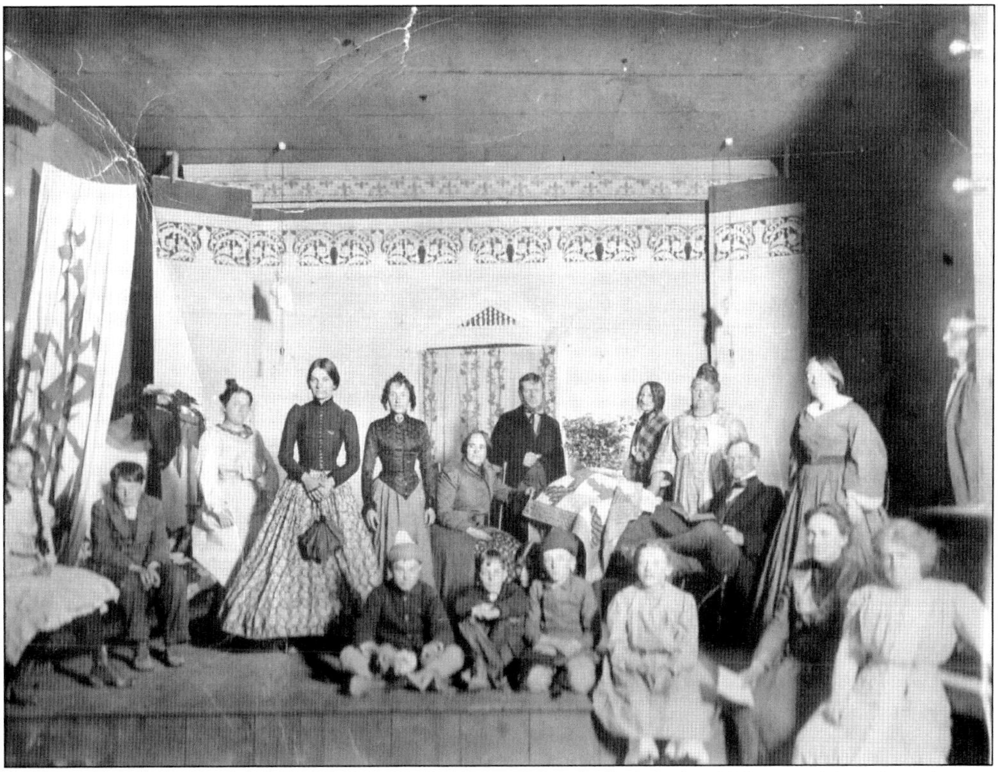

This image shows one of the early live performances in the Dreamland Theater. Traveling theater groups such as the one seen here were welcome to perform and entertain the growing town.

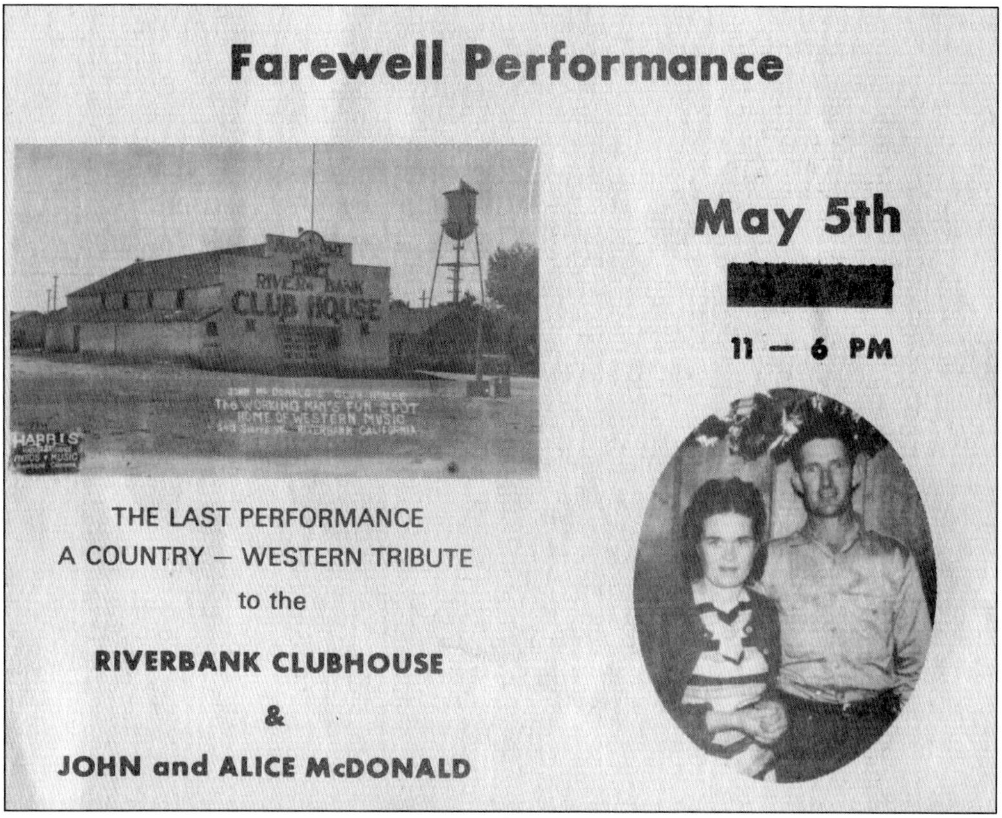

The Legion Theater was constructed in the early 1900s as a movie house. In the 1940s, John and Alice McDonald turned it into the Riverbank Clubhouse, which played host to country western singers that came from miles around. It may be here that Riverbank obtained its nickname as the "City of Action."

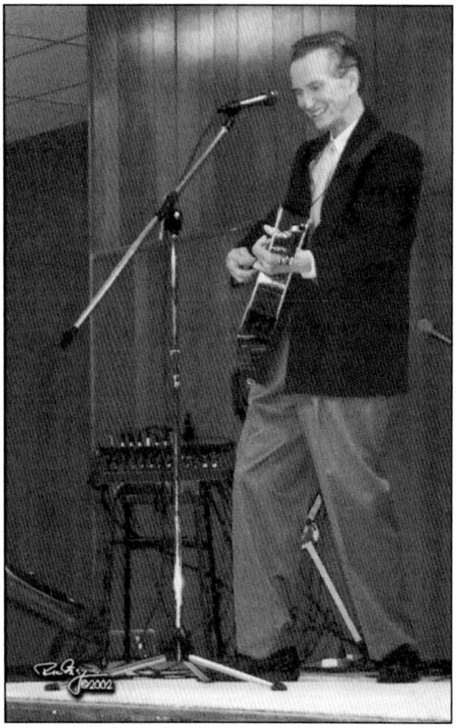

Chester Snyder was one of many country western singers who appeared at the clubhouse. The venue was one of only a handful of places to dance on the weekends; in other parts of the county, dancing was banned.

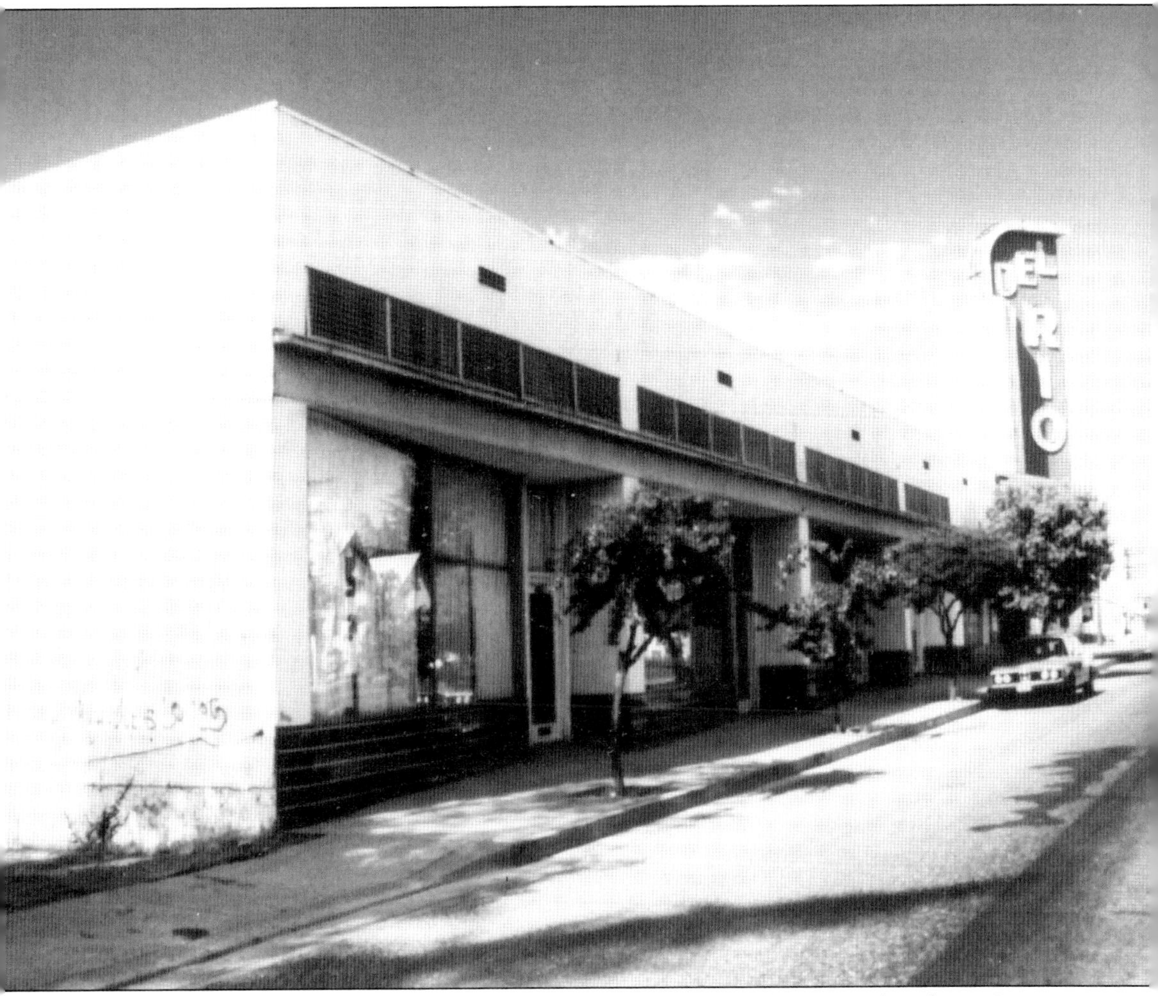

The Del Rio Movie Theater, which still stands on the corner of Third Street and Atchison Street, was constructed in 1936 by William Peters. The theater opened for business in 1937. The movie theater closed in 1971, as it could not compete with the popularity of television. Six years after the theater closed its doors, Allen Seaman, the leader of the Riverbank Community Theater, wanted to use the building for movies, live performances, and music concerts, but the city turned down the idea. The Del Rio Restaurant opened in 1994 and closed in the early 2000s. The city bought the building, planning to restore it, but due to a lack of funds, the building currently sits empty.

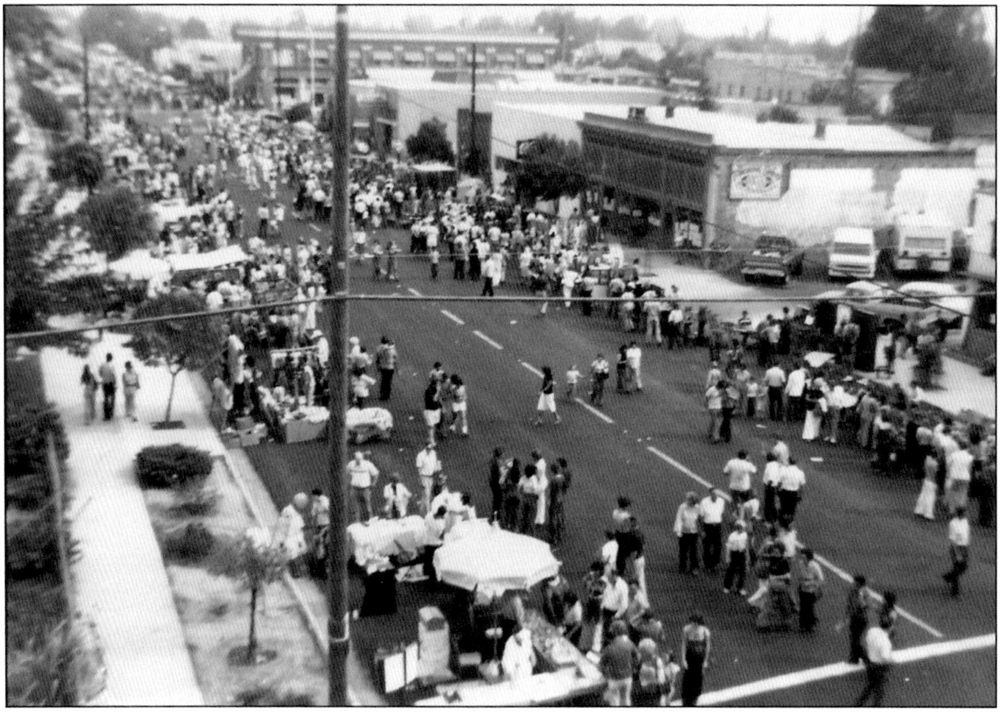

In the 1970s, there were two cheese companies in Riverbank, both located on Second Street: the Riverbank Cheese Company, owned by the Costalupes family, and the StanCo Cheese Company, owned by Stan Tshoubinudous. Both owners were of Greek heritage. The town was the self-proclaimed cheese capital of the world. Both families remembered street fairs in Greece and decided to carry the idea to their own town, thus creating the Riverbank Cheese and Wine Festival. The first of these festivals began in October 1977. The festival has become an exhibition of all that Riverbank has to offer by way of food, wine, artwork, antiques, entertainment, and fun.

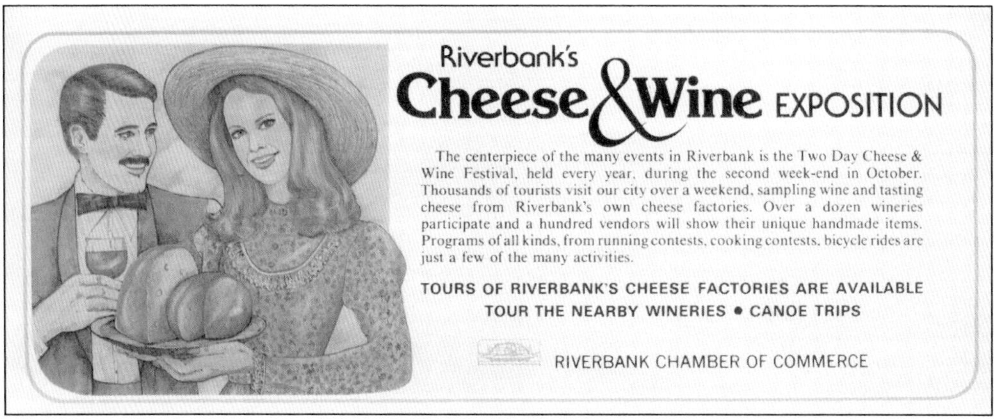

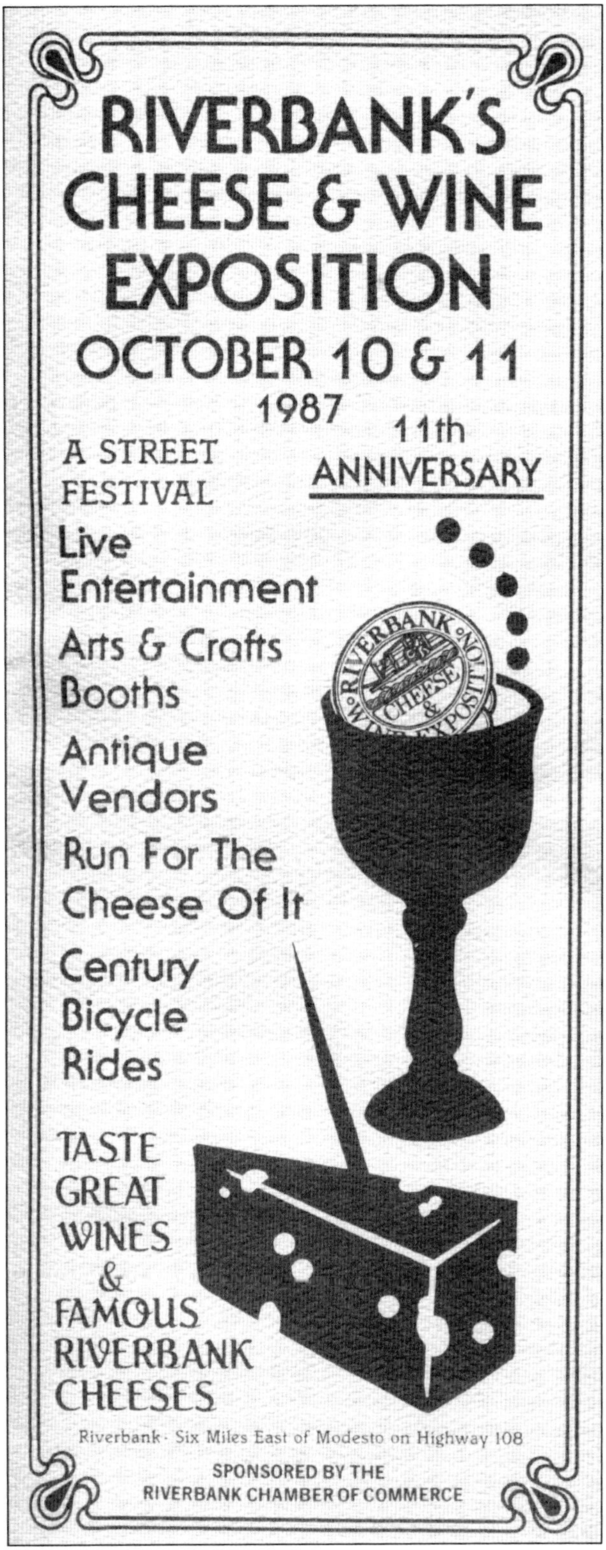

The program of the Riverbank Wine and Cheese Festival did not change much in 1987, as evidenced by this published program. There are still arts and crafts, antiques, and wine tasting to be found, along with the traditional bike race and run.

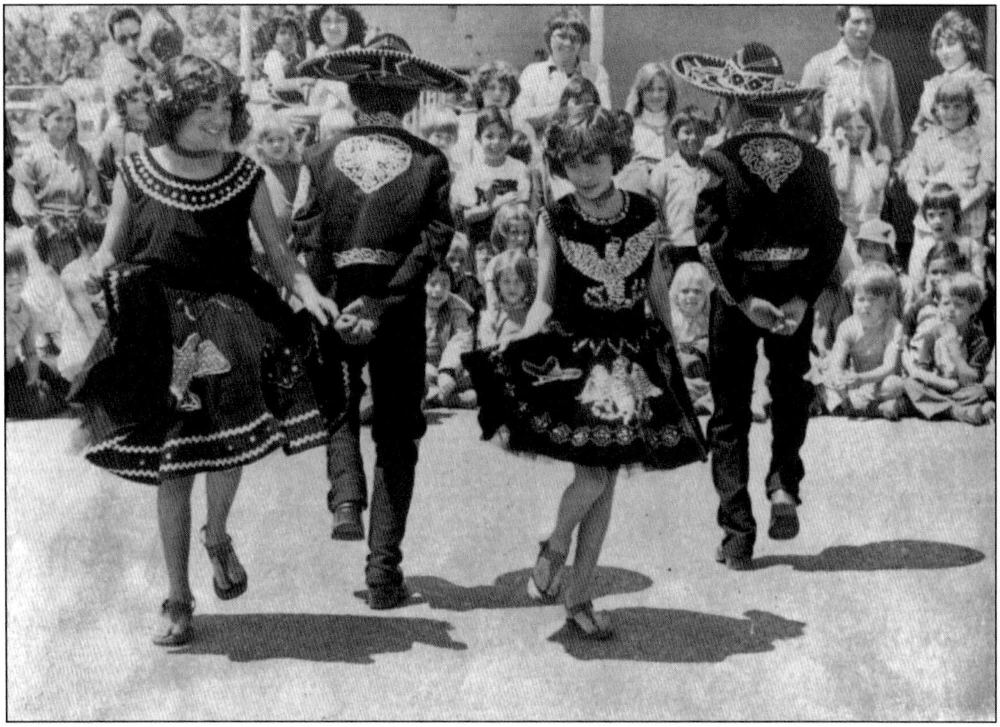

Another popular festival in Riverbank is its fiesta, which is attended by many celebrating traditions from Mexico, Chile, Brazil, and other Central and South American countries.

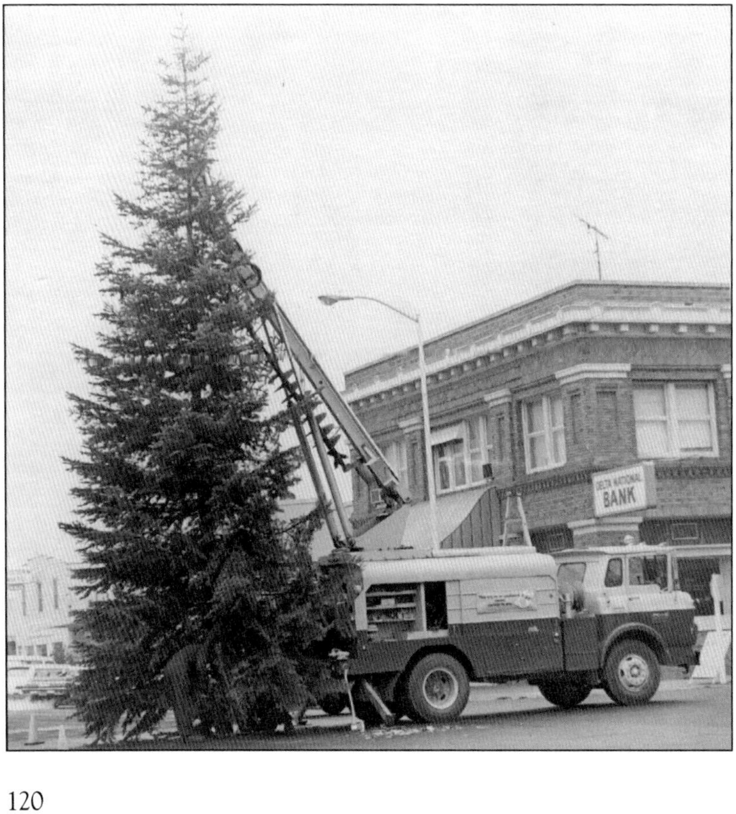

Riverbank also celebrates other festivals during the course of the year. One special occasion is the raising of the town Christmas tree and its Christmas parade.

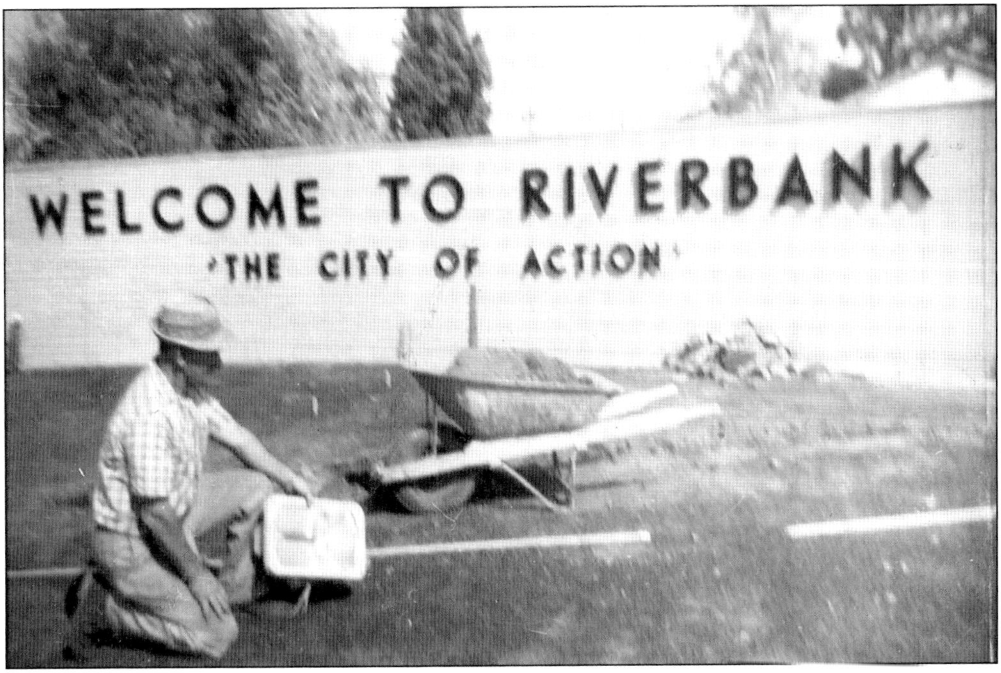

The Riverbank sign has stood for years at the intersection of Patterson Road and Highway 108. At Christmastimes in the past, it has been decorated with a nativity scene.

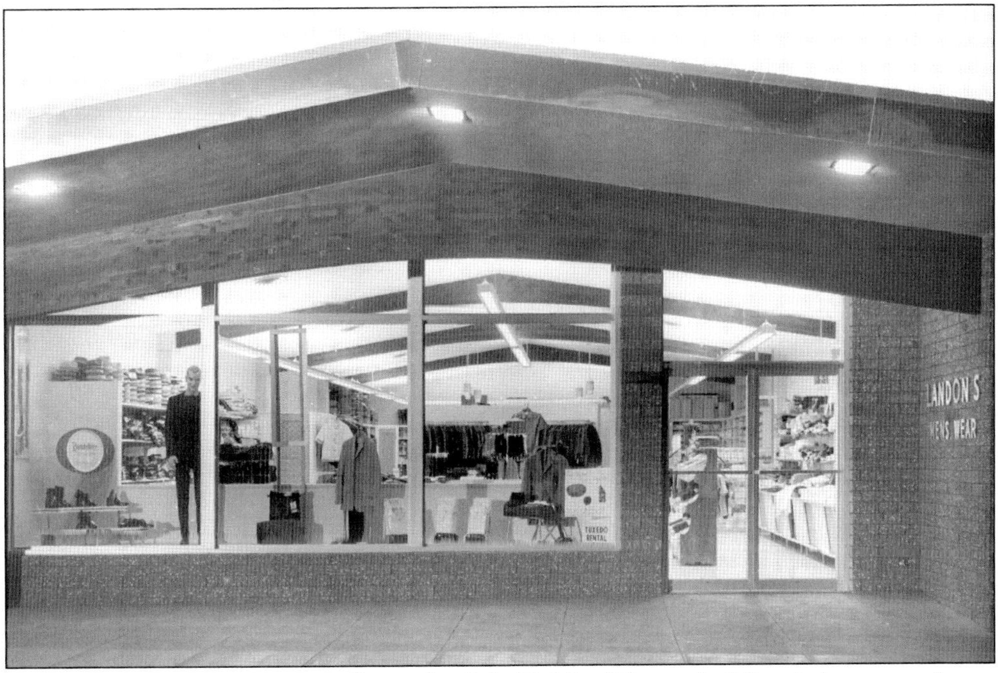

Landon's Men's Store was originally inside of the Del Rio Theater building. It later moved onto Santa Fe Avenue. Many people in town remember the Landons extending credit to customers in need of a much-needed prom suit, tuxedo for an upcoming wedding, or a business suit for an interview or work. Landon's has an excellent selection of men's clothing and accessories to meet Riverbank's needs.

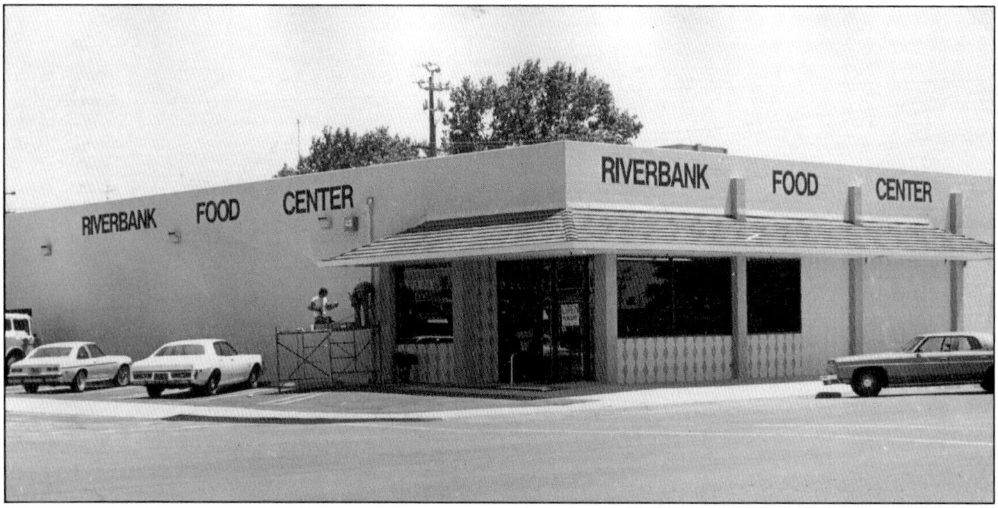

The Riverbank Food Center was a popular supermarket in the 1980s. It is now Garcia's, which is a Mexican market.

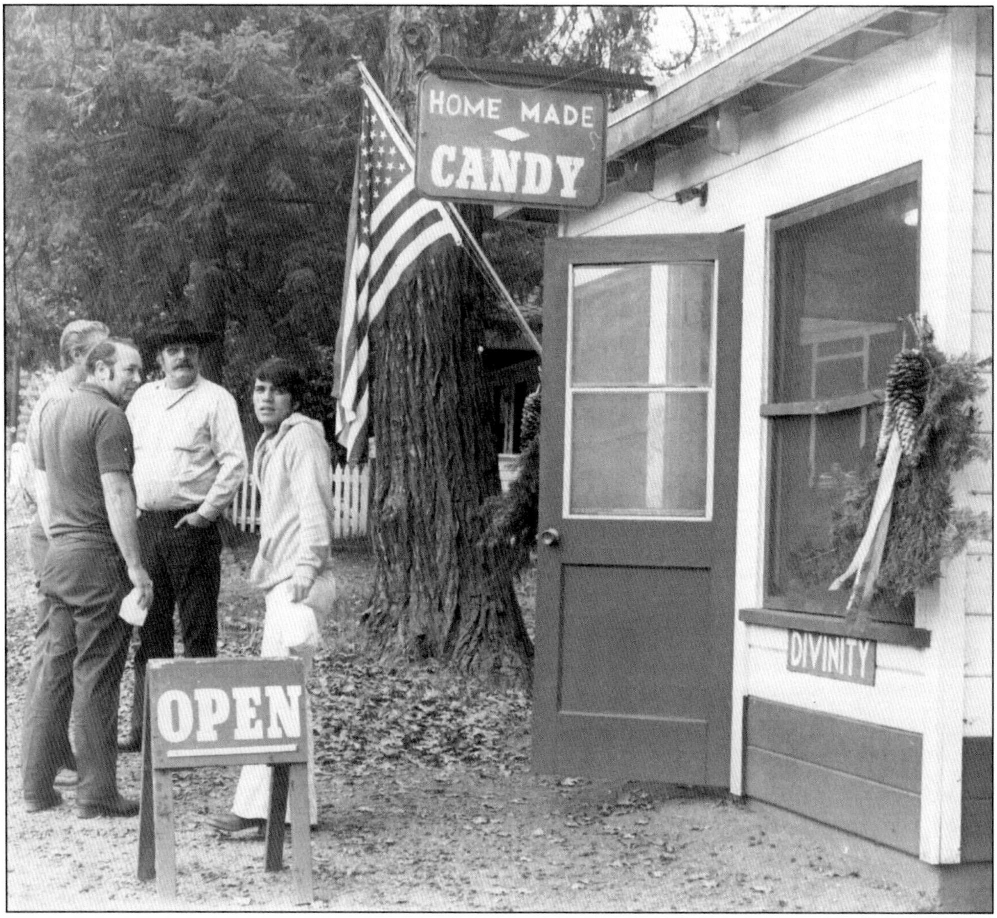

This candy store harkens back to that owned by the Jackson family in the early part of the last century.

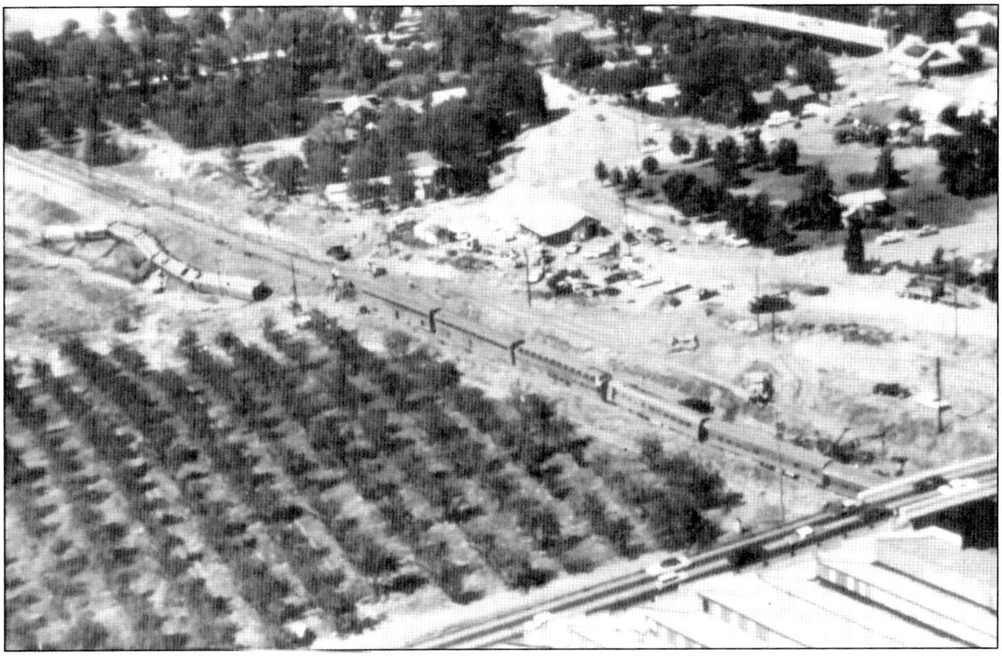

On Mother's Day, 1970, Riverbank saw one of the worst railroad accidents in its history. The northbound *Super Chief* train crashed into a construction crane that was doing work outside of the cannery in Riverbank. The crane operator literally had to leap for his life, and the train slammed onto its side after the collision. Fortunately, there were no severe injuries from the crash and no fatalities.

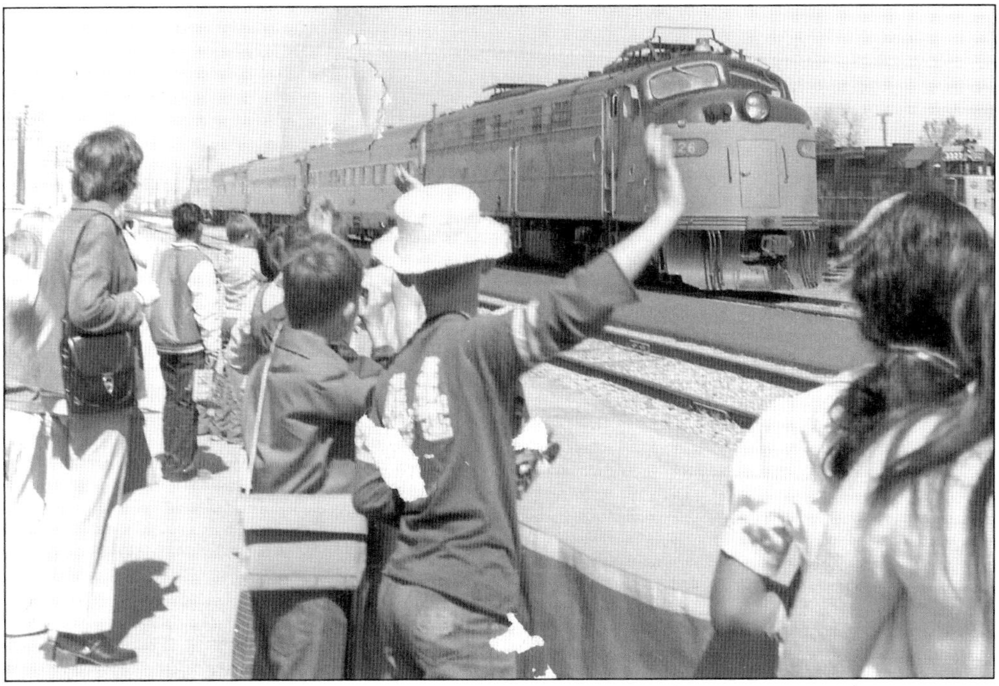

In 1972, Amtrak took over the old Santa Fe Railroad route, bringing renewed attention to Riverbank as a stop along the course.

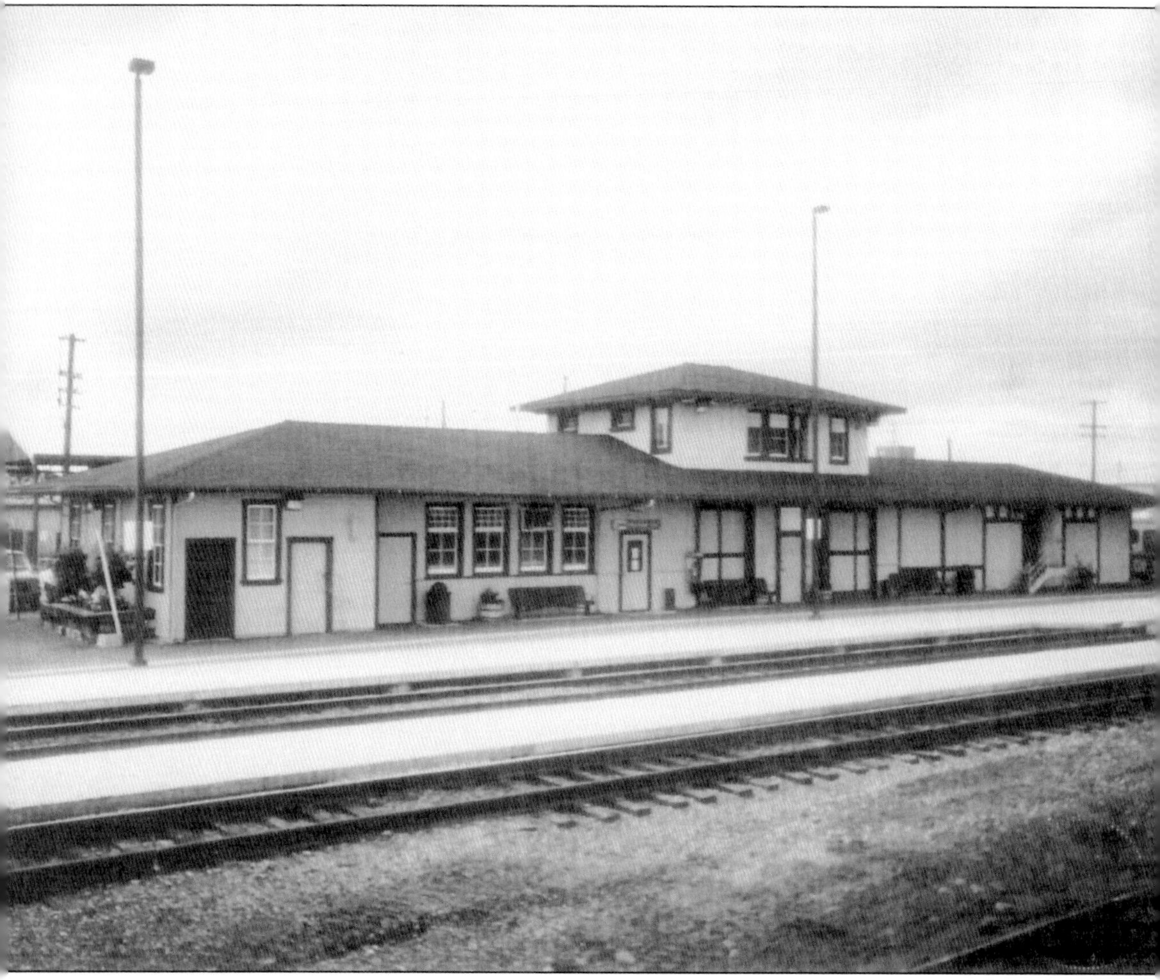

Here is one of the last pictures taken of the Riverbank Station in the 1990s. The depot was destroyed by fire in the early part of the 21st century. A new depot was built in the city of Modesto, located south of Riverbank, making Riverbank's days as a busy stop along the Santa Fe Railroad a receding memory.

This statue of children fishing stands at Riverbank's southern entrance by one of its newest shopping centers, which includes Best Buy, Kohl's, Staples, Red Robin, and other modern stores and restaurants. (Courtesy of Rick McGinnis.)

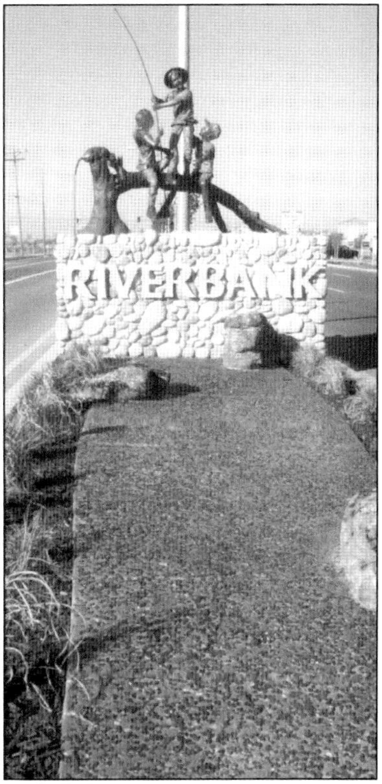

The ferryman statue stands in Plaza Del Rio Park at Third Street and Santa Fe Avenue. It is a reminder of early Burneyville and its ferry across the river. (Courtesy of Rick McGinnis.)

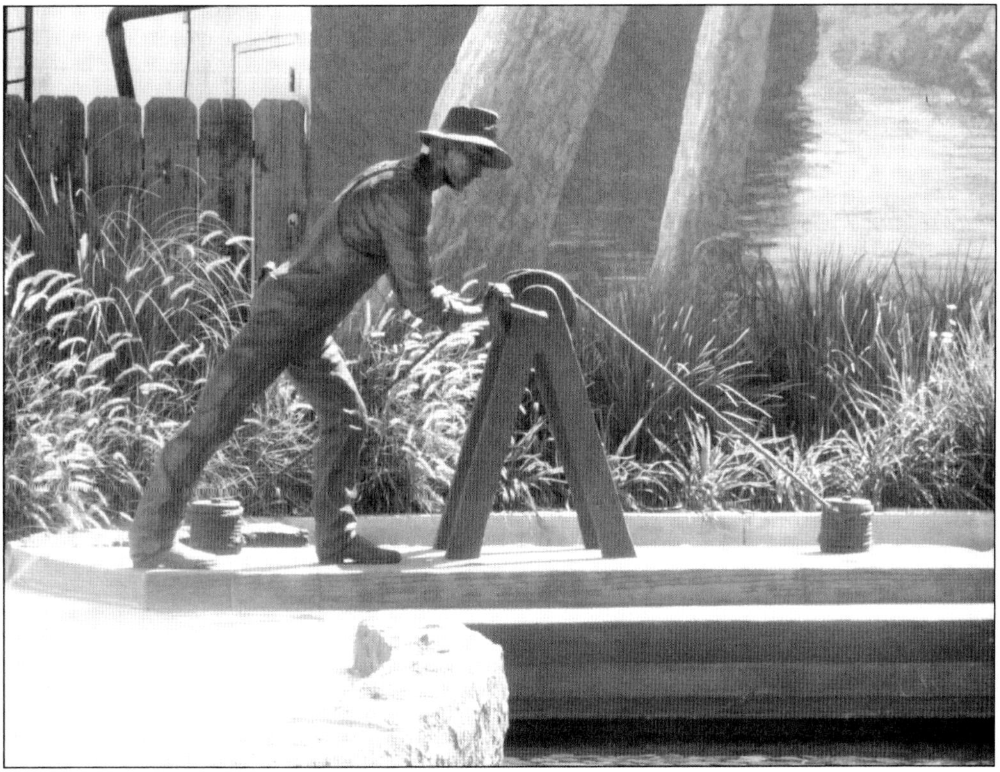

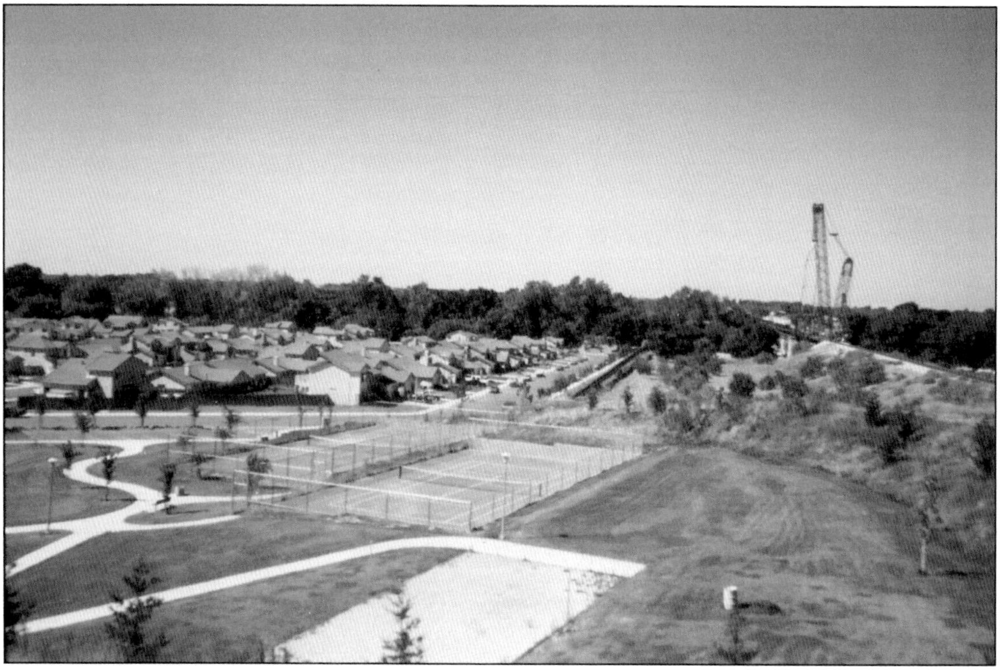

In the new millennium, Riverbank has continued to expand, revitalize, and regrow. A new community known as Riverglen was constructed along the river south of the railroad bridge. Riverbank has also acquired more than one shopping center to the southwestern side of town.

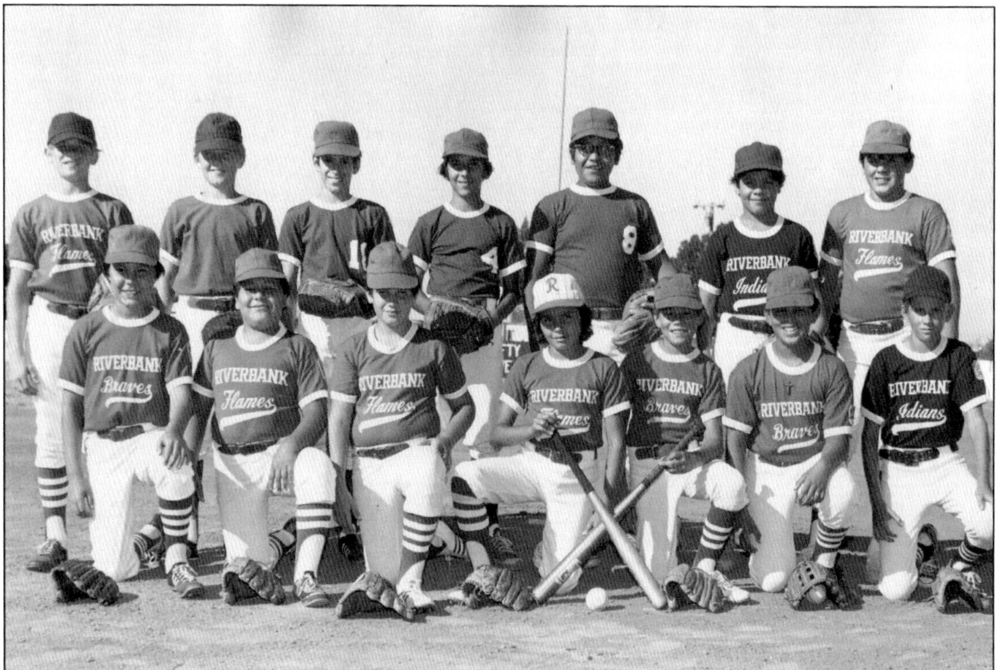

Compare the young baseball players to those pictured on page two. Much has changed in Riverbank, but the game remains more or less the same.

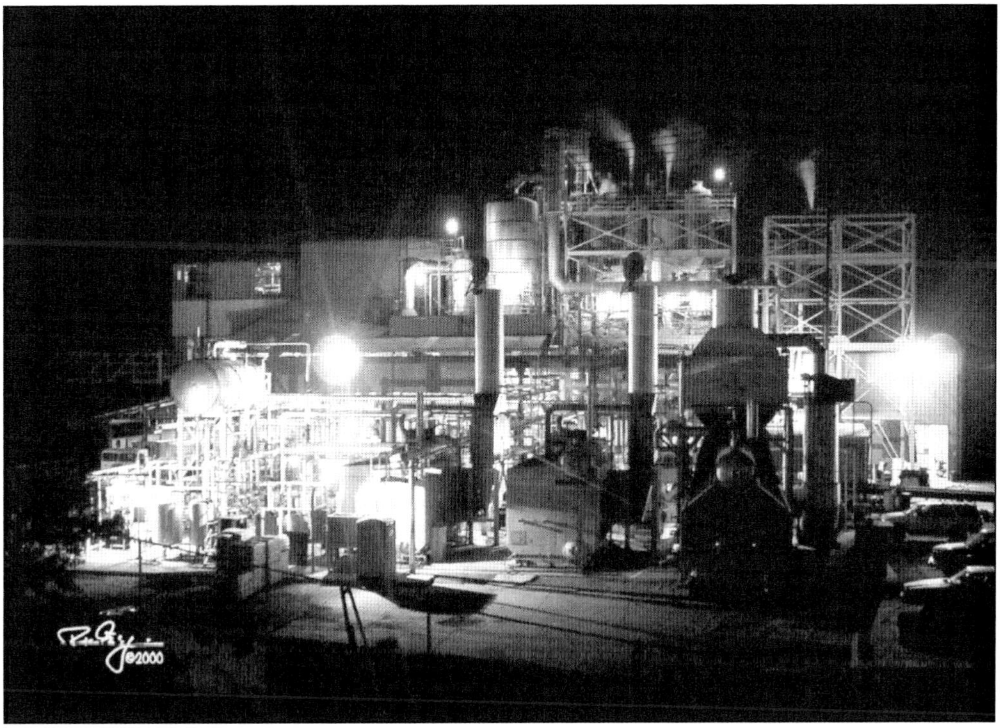

Rick McGinnis took this photograph in 2002 just before the demolishment of the cannery that stood in Riverbank for so many years. Some of the cannery's buildings still remain in the form of storage buildings, but the large structure that dominated the skyline is now gone. (Courtesy of Rick McGinnis.)

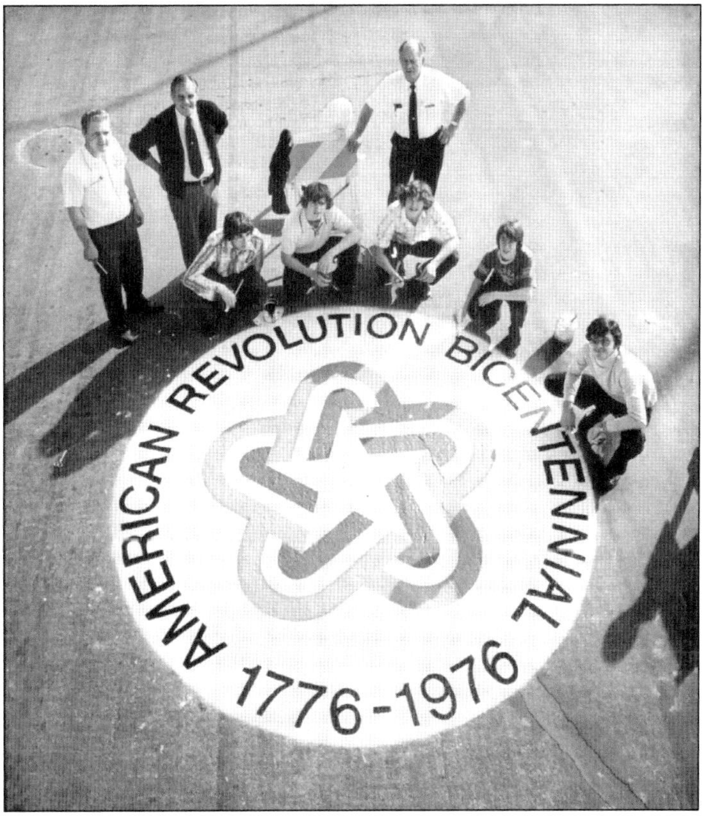

Riverbank celebrated the 1976 Bicentennial with storefront decor and a central logo displayed at the intersection of Third Street and Santa Fe Avenue, surrounded here by local civic leaders, including Alan Trowick (left), Karl Hutchison (standing at right), and Hank Ethier (second from left) with various local students.

Discover Thousands of Local History Books Featuring Millions of Vintage Images

Arcadia Publishing, the leading local history publisher in the United States, is committed to making history accessible and meaningful through publishing books that celebrate and preserve the heritage of America's people and places.

Find more books like this at
www.arcadiapublishing.com

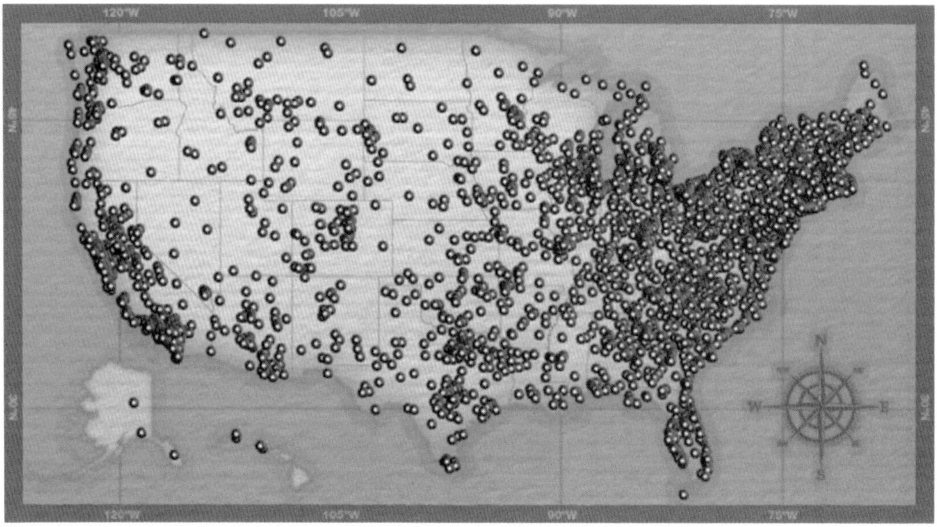

Search for your hometown history, your old stomping grounds, and even your favorite sports team.

Consistent with our mission to preserve history on a local level, this book was printed in South Carolina on American-made paper and manufactured entirely in the United States. Products carrying the accredited Forest Stewardship Council (FSC) label are printed on 100 percent FSC-certified paper.

MADE IN THE USA